Karate Masters

Volume 5

Karate Masters
Volume 5

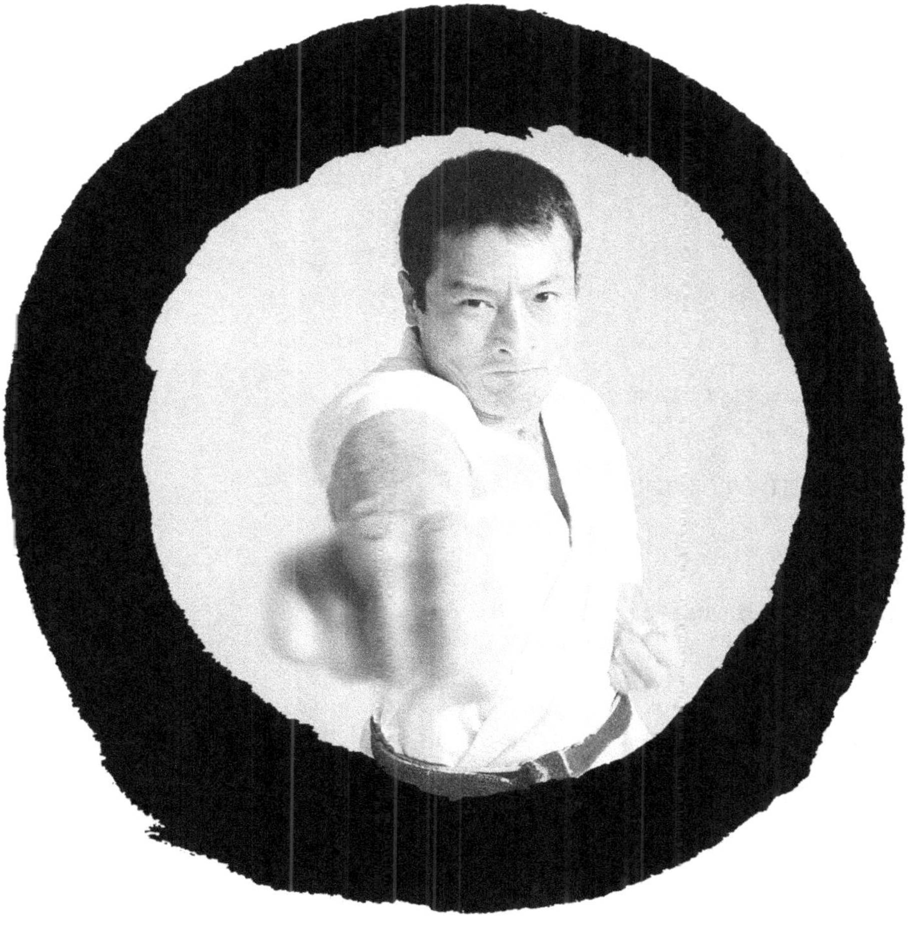

Jose M. Fraguas

P.O. Box 491788, Los Angeles, CA 90049

Disclaimer
Please note that the author and publisher of this book are NOT RESPONSIBLE in any manner whatsoever for any injury that may result from practicing the techniques and/or following the instructions given within. Since the physical activities described herein may be too strenuous in nature for some readers to engage in safely, it is essential that a physician be consulted prior to training.

First publish in 2014 by AWP LLC/Empire Books.
Copyright (c) 2014 by Jose M. Fraguas.

All rights reserved. No part of this publication may be reproduced or utilized in any form or by any means, electronic or mechanical, including photocopying, recording, or by any information storage and retrieval system, without prior written permission from AWP LLC/Empire Books.

EMPIRE BOOKS
P.O. Box 491788
Los Angeles, CA 90049

First edition
Library of Congress Catalog Number:
ISBN-13: 978-1-933901-53-4

14 13 12 11 10 09 08 07 06 05 04 03 02 01 00

Library of Congress Cataloging-in-Publication Data
Fraguas, Jose M.
Karate masters / by Jose M. Fraguas. -- 1st ed.
p. cm.
Includes index.
ISBN 1-933901-53-4 (pbk. : alk. paper)
1. Karate. 5. Martial artists--Interviews. 3. Large type books. I. Title.
GV1114.3.F715 2014
796.815'3--dc22

2006012534.
Printed in the United States of America.

*"Even a life-long prosperity is but one cup of sake;
A life of fifty-one years is passed in a dream;
I know not what life is, nor death.
Year in year out-all but a dream.
Both Heaven and Hell are left behind;
I stand in the moonlit dawn,
Free from clouds of attachment."*

- **Uesugi Kenshin (1530-1578)**

Dedication

I dedicate this book to the memory of Shihan Ted Tabura, who passed away on August 12th, 2013. His name stands preeminent in the world of Karate-do and Martial Arts.

Acknowledgments

I gratefully acknowledge the help of a wide range of people who assisted me with great will and generosity.

Special thanks go to designer Mario M. Rodriguez; France's Thierry Plée, long-time friend and president of Sedirep and Budo Editions; Germany's leading martial Arts publisher, Mr. Schlatt (director of Schlatt-Books) for his endless and friendly support to the "Karate Masters" series; Shorin Ryu stylist and writer Jerry Figgiani, who provided additional material to be included in this book; Shaun Banfield and Holly Forsyth (theshotokanway.com) for their friendship and kindness for supplying excellent interviews for this work; Okinawa karate great and master calligrapher Tetsuhiro Hokama; Harold E. Sharp, a true legend in the world of martial arts and who kindly supplied great photos from his personal archives; Bill Bly, dear friend and leading force of "American Samuri". Robert Chu for providing additional material, Larry Wicklund, and Oleg Larionov of Moscow, Russia...your amazing talent and heart as karate-ka is only surpassed by your kindness as a friend.

I would foremost like to give my most heartfelt gratitude to all the masters appearing in this book. Not only did they generously give me an enormous amount of personal time for the long interviews, but they also provided me with great pictures to illustrate the work.

And last but not least, to all my instructors, past and present, for giving me the understanding and knowledge to undertake all the Karate projects I've done during my life. My understanding of the art has grown over the years, thanks, in great part, to the questions they made me ask myself. These questions - both perceptive and practical - have sent me further and deeper in search for answers.

—Jose M. Fraguas

About the Author

Born and raised in Madrid, Spain, Jose "Chema" Fraguas began his martial arts studies with judo, in grade school, at age 9. From there he moved to taekwondo and then to kenpo karate, earning black belts in both styles. During this same period, he also studied shito-ryu karate under Japanese Masters Masahiro Okada and Yashunari Ishimi and eventually received the *Shihan* title from Soke K. Mabuni. He began his career as a writer at age 16 as a regular contributor to martial arts magazines in Great Britain, France, Spain, Italy, Germany, Portugal, Holland and Australia. Having black belts in three different styles allowed him to better reflect the physical side of the martial arts in his writing: "Feeling before writing," Fraguas says.

In 1980, he moved to Los Angeles, California, where his open-minded mentality helped him to develop a realistic approach to the martial arts. Seeking to supplement his previous training, he researched other disciplines such as jiu-jitsu, escrima and muay Thai.

In 1986, Fraguas founded his own publishing company in Europe, authoring dozens of books and distributing his magazines to 35 countries in three different languages. His reputation and credibility as a martial artist and publisher became well known to the top masters around the world. Considering himself a martial artist first and a writer and publisher second, Fraguas feels fortunate to have had the opportunity to interview many legendary martial artists. He recognizes that much of the information given in the interviews helped him to discover new dimensions in the martial arts. "I was constantly absorbing knowledge from the great masters," he recalls. "I only trained with a few of them, but intellectually and spiritually all of them have made very important contributions to my growth as a complete martial artist."

However, there were some drawbacks to his position as a publisher, Fraguas acknowledges, that directly affected his personal martial arts development. "Of course, some people taught me because of my position as a publisher and not because who I was as a person. Even though I recognize that, I'm still grateful for the knowledge they shared with me."

Steeped in tradition yet looking to the future, Fraguas understands and appreciates martial arts history and philosophy and feels this rich heritage is a necessary steppingstone to personal growth and spiritual evolution. His desire to promote both ancient philosophy and modern thinking provided the motivation for writing this book. "If the motivation is just money, a book cannot be of good quality," Fraguas says. "If the book is written to just make people happy, it cannot be deep. I want to write books so I can learn as well as teach. Karate-do, like human life itself, is filled with experiences that seem quite ordinary at the time and assume a fabled stature only with the passage of the years. I hope this work will be appreciated by future practitioners of the art of the empty-hand."

"Regardless of what level the practitioners find themselves in, there really is only one teacher: experience itself. The true karate-ka follows one abiding principle: to pay attention to what is happening in one's immediate experience. And, this is something that cannot be expressed in words. Words and science are one part of the complete process of understanding the art of Karate, but neither one of them can replace what can be discovered by personal physical experience. Only physical experience can fully transmit the true essence of Karate-do from one generation to another."

As the famous Japanese writer Yukio Mishima, practitioner of Martial Arts, personal friend of Karate master, Masatoshi Nakayama and fifth dan in the art of kendo said: "Words are a medium that reduces reality to abstraction for transmission to our reason. In their power, they corrode reality. Inevitably, danger lurks that the words themselves will be corroded, too."

Originally from Madrid, Spain, he is currently living in Los Angeles, California.

Introduction

Some of my best days were spent interviewing and meeting the masters in this book. There is little I enjoy more than reading a great interview while time slows and sometimes even seems to stop. Having the opportunity to meet and interview the most prestigious martial artists of the past four decades is something that every martial artist doesn't have the chance to do. Hopefully, in some small way, this will help make up for that.

Meeting the masters and having long conversations with them allowed me to do more than simply scratch the surface of the technical aspects of their respective styles; it also allowed me to understand the human beings behind the teachers. Some of the dialogues and interviews began by simply commenting about the superficial techniques of fighting, and ended up turning into a spiritual conversation about the philosophical aspects of the martial arts. Although these masters are all very different, they share a common thread of traditional values such as discipline, respect, positive attitude, dedication and etiquette.

For more than 35 years I've interviewed these martial arts masters, one-on-one, face-to-face, with no place to run if I asked a stupid question. Many times it was a real challenge to not just talk to them, but to make the questions interesting enough to bring out their deepest knowledge. I tried to absorb as much knowledge as I could, ranging from their training methods, to their fighting methods, to their philosophies about life itself. Their different cultural backgrounds never prevented them from analyzing, researching or modifying anything they considered important. They always kept their minds open to improving their arts and themselves. From a formal philosophical point of view, many of them followed classical philosophies and religions—but they all tempered that with vast amounts of common sense.

They devoted themselves to their arts, often in solitude, to the exclusion of other "normal" pursuits. They worked themselves into extraordinary physical condition. They ignored distractions and diversions and concentrated on their mental and physical training. They got as good as they could possibly get at performing and teaching their chosen art while the rest of us watched them, leading our "balanced lives," and wondering how good we might have gotten at something had we devoted ourselves to it as ferociously as these masters embraced their arts. In that respect, they bear our dreams.

If you read carefully between the lines, you'll see that none of these men were trying to become a fighting machine, or create the most devastating martial arts system known to man. They focused, rather, on how to use martial arts to become a better person. There are many principles that once discovered open a wide spectrum of possibilities, not only to martial arts, but to a better existence as individuals.

The interviews often lasted as long as three or four hours. I would begin at their school and finish the conversation at a restaurant or coffee shop. Much of this information had never been published before and some had to be trimmed either at the master's request or edited to avoid misunderstandings. It is not the questions that make an interview. An interview is either good or bad depending on the answers. Considering the masters in this book, I had an easy job. My goal was to make them comfortable talking about life and training—especially those who trained under the founders of original systems. In modern times, there are not many who have had the privilege of living and learning under these legendary founders.

"The masters are gone," many like to say. But as long as we keep their teachings in our heart, they will live forever. To understand martial arts properly, it is necessary to take into account their philosophical methods as well as their physical techniques. There is a deep distinction between a fighting system and a martial arts. Unfortunately, the roots of the martial arts have been de-emphasized, neglected or totally abandoned today. Martial arts are not a sport. Someone who chooses to devote himself to a sport such as basketball, tennis, soccer or football—which is based on youth, strength, and speed—chooses to die twice. When you can no longer do that sport, due to the lack of their required attributes, waking up in the morning without the activity that has been the center of your life for 25 years is troubling and unsettling. In contrast, the martial arts can and should be practiced for life—they never leave you.

A true martial artist is like a musician, painter, writer or actor—their art is an expression of themselves. The need to discover who they are becomes the reason for an endless search for the perfect technique, great melody, inspiring poetry, amazing painting or Academy Award performance. It is this motivation to reach that impossible dream that allows a simple individual to become an exceptional artist and master of his craft.

Many of the greatest teachers share a commonly misunderstood teaching methodology. They know the words they could use to teach their students have little or no meaning. They know that to try "self-discovery" in quantitative or empirical terms is a useless task. A great deal of knowledge and wisdom comes from oral traditions, which martial arts, like every other cultural expression, has. These oral traditions have always been reserved for a certain kind of student and considered "secrets," given only to a special few who have the minds and attitudes to fully grasp them.

Alexandra David-Neel wrote: "It is not on the master that the secret depends but on the hearer. Truth learned from others is of no value, the only truth which is effective and of value is self-discovered ... the teacher can only guide to the point of discovery." In the end, "the only secret is that there is no secret." As Kato Tokuro, arguably the finest potter of the last century, a great art scholar, and the teacher of Pablo Picasso said: "The sole cause of secrets in craftsmanship is the student's inability to learn."

To find out what karate-do means to you, what it does for you, and what it holds for you, is a deeply personal process. Each path is different and we all have to find a personal rhythm that fit us individually, according to what surround us.

As human beings, we are always tempted to follow linear logic towards ultimate self-improvement—but the truth is that there are no absolute truths. You have to find your own way in life whether it be in martial arts, business or cherry picking. Whatever path you pursue, you have to distill the personal truths that are right for you, according to your own nature. The quest for perfection is very imperfect, and not in tune with human nature or experience. To have any hope of attaining even a single perfection, you have to concentrate on a single pursuit and direct all your energy towards it. In this sense, perfection comes from appreciating endeavors for their own sake—not to impress anyone—but for your own inner satisfaction and sense of accomplishment.

It is important to have a feeling of responsibility; and putting yourself into an art as genuinely as you can, without any sense that you are going to get something back in return, reverberates throughout time and space. We need to honor those who came before us, as well as nurture those who will come after, so the art can grow and expand—you've got to send the elevator back down.

Martial arts are a large part of my life and I draw inspiration from them. I really don't know the "how" or the "why" of their effect on me, but I feel their influence in even my most mundane activities. All human beings have sources or principles that keep them grounded, and martial arts are mine. That is when the term "way of life" becomes real. In bushido, the self-discipline required to pursue mastery is more important than mastery itself—the struggle is more important than the reward. A common thread throughout the lives of all the masters is their constant struggle towards self-mastery. They realized that life is an ongoing process, and once you achieve all your goals you are as good as dead. But this process is not all driven by action. Often the greatest action is inaction, and the hardest voice to hear is the sound of your own thoughts. You need to sit alone and collect yourself, free from technology and distraction, and just think. This is perhaps the only way to achieve mental and spiritual clarity.

I don't believe that books are meant to be read fast. I've always thought that writing is timeless and that reading is not a detraction. So take your time. Approach this book with the Zen "beginner's mind" and "empty cup" mentality and soak up the words of these great teachers. They will help you to not only grow as a martial artist but as a human being as well. O

Contents

1 James Fields — DARE TO CHALLENGE

13 Jerry Figgiani — A LOYAL LEADER

27 Robert Graves — REFLECTING BUDO

37 Yoshimine Inoue — RETURNING TO THE SOURCE

47 Genzo Iwata — THE SHITO KAI LEGACY

53 Nobuaki Kanazawa — ON A GIANT'S SHOULDERS

63 Pascal LeCourt — POINTING NORTH

73 Jim Mather — A TRUE GIFT

95 Masaru Miura — SLICES OF BUDO

103 Hideo Ochi — WISDOM OF AGE

111 Takemase Okuyama — TRUE PERCEPTION

119 Antonio Oliva — THE MASTER TACTICIAN

135 Toshihiro Oshiro — EDUCATING THE MASSES

149 Tomasz Piotrkowicz — BUDO INHERITANCE

167 Akira Saito	**179** Yasuyoshi Saito	**191** Sadaaki Sakagami
BEING PRESENT	A LIFE VISION	IN THE NAME OF ITOSU

199 Kensei Taba	**205** Ted Tabura	**213** Shunsuke Takahashi	**221** Takeshi Tamaki
AN OKINAWAN LEGEND	THE SICKLE MAN	UNDIVIDED PAST	CYCLES OF SHADING
225 Pemba Tamang	**237** George Tan	**247** Allen Tanzadeh	**267** Masahiko Tokashiki
KARATE'S CLOUDS AND WAVES	KARATE PILLARS	A WEALTH OF KNOWLEDGE	LIGHT IN THE DARKNESS
271 Gary Tsutsui	**281** Katsuhiro Tsuyama	**289** Vern Vaden	**295** Robert Weinberg
THE SPIRIT WITHIN	CHANGING LIVES	UNCOMMON WISDOM	INTEGRATING INTUITION

JAMES FIELDS

DARE TO CHALLENGE

SENSEI JAMES FIELD IS ONE OF THE MOST SENIOR AND EXPERIENCED AMERICAN KARA-TEKA. WITH A VERY SUCCESSFUL REPUTATION AND CAREER AS A COMPETITOR FOR MANY YEARS, HE CAPTAINED THE US INTERNATIONAL KARATE TEAM, HE WAS MANY TIMES NATIONAL COLLEGIATE CHAMPION, TWO-TIME NATIONAL GRAND CHAMPION, TWO-TIME PAN AMERICAN CHAMPION, US REPRESENTATIVE TO THE OLYMPIC GAMES IN MEXICO AND MEDALIST IN THE 1976 WORLD TOURNAMENT. AS ONE OF THE FIRST FOUR AMERICANS CERTIFIED AS JKA INSTRUCTORS, SENSEI FIELD IS A TRUE REPOSITORY OF KARATE KNOWLEDGE AND AN EXAMPLE OF BUDO ETIQUETTE AND MASTERY.

Could you please tell us a little about how and why you first started karate?

I was rehabilitating from a football injury. A good friend suggested that karate would make my knees stronger. He had trained in Japan and told me to look for a place with an instructor named Nishiyama.

So was Nishiyama Sensei the first person you trained under?

No. I first trained in Hawaii under one of Mr. Kanazawa's students for about 7 months. I found Mr. Nishiyama's dojo by accident while riding my motorcycle past it. I stopped to check it out. I saw pictures of Mr. Kanazawa displayed on the wall, so I decided to try training there.

You have experienced the teachings of many masters living in America, including Nishiyama Sensei, Okazaki Sensei and Yaguchi Sensei. How do you reflect back on the fact that you have trained with such world renown masters?

I feel very fortunate. I also feel that this experience gives me an advantage in understanding karate by having 3 different perspectives. Each had different applications, though similar explanations.

Do they differ at all in their approaches and in what ways?

I think that Mr. Okazaki and Mr. Yaguchi teach more of the budo aspect.

Karate Masters

"Mr. Nishiyama had us do more tournament sparring. Mr. Okazaki and Mr. Yaguchi emphasized application of techniques."

Budo can be used in competition. Mr. Nishiyama called his teachings traditional, but it seems more like sports karate to me. Mr. Okazaki and Mr. Yaguchi gave more application training. You would learn a technique, and then practice it with a partner. Each one had his own way of teaching individual techniques.

In what ways do you believe Nishiyama Sensei's was in fact more of a sport karate than budo karate? Has it always been this way with his teaching or it has it become this way over time?

Mr. Nishiyama had us do more tournament sparring. Mr. Okazaki and Mr. Yaguchi emphasized application of techniques. They were always this way.

Who influenced you most in Karate?

Two people: Takeshi Aoki and Yutaka Yaguchi. Aoki was a senior Nidan when I was a brown belt. He encouraged me to continue and was very inspirational. Mr. Yaguchi was my instructor. He had no prejudice about him. If you liked karate then he would teach you. I wanted to be like him in many ways. He was kind to people. He's the type of person that would give you his last penny. When my mother passed away, he was the only one to console me in a meaningful way.

As you have stated, Yaguchi Sensei was your instructor. Technically speaking, what would you say was so great about him as a karateka, and also as an instructor?

Yaguchi Sensei is technically very good, just like all JKA instructors. He was easier for me to communicate with. He is a very approachable person. Mr Yaguchi is technically a very diverse person with a great depth of understanding. He can teach a small person or large person to excel with whatever talents they have individually. If you like karate, he likes you and will teach you.

You mentioned that there was no prejudice with Yaguchi Sensei. Have you ever experienced prejudice of any sort with any instructors you've ever trained under, or other karateka?

Yes, I did.

How has karate changed you?

It changed a belief: Through teaching I learned that karate is for everybody, not just athletes and competitors. Everybody can get something out of it, unlike football. And you can do karate forever – it's an individual thing. To me, outside of my family, karate is the most important thing in my life. If not for karate I would probably be in jail or dead. It took me away from the thugs I was hanging out with. Karate made me the person I am today.

What do you enjoy most about karate?

I love teaching. It's rewarding to see improvements in individuals. I loved competition when I was in it. Now I get the same thrill watching my students compete.

What's the best advice you have for improvement in karate?

Just do it. The biggest problem that everyone has both new and old students is doing things their way. They need to forget everything they think is and just listen to what the instructor says and just do that, that day in that class – practicing as if with tunnel vision. Everybody thinks their way is better. Keep training, there are so many more levels to karate, and they usually take a little longer than you think to reach them.

In the 70's you spent time in Japan. Where exactly did you train whilst in Japan and who taught there?

I trained at the Honbu dojo and at the Hoitsugan with Master Nakayama. Instructors rotated at the Honbu dojo. All the ranking instructors taught. Training was 5 days a week, 3 times a day, sometimes 4.

Whilst on the Instructors Class at the Hombu Dojo, who were the main instructors who taught at that time?

All the ranking instructors taught.

Do you remember any specific session from the instructors class that you could tell our readers as I'm sure they'd love to hear about them.

These are personal experiences that I'd rather not share on this public a scale.

Karate Masters

"I love teaching. It's rewarding to see improvements in individuals. I loved competition when I was in it."

How did the classes at the Hoitsugan differ to those on the Instructors Course?

The Hoitsugan had regular classes with Master Nakayama. The regular classes there consisted of almost all foreigners. I trained in these as well. The instructors classes were very serious. They were the elite of the elite, and you'd better be serious too. Regular classes were serious, but there was a big step between the regular class and the instructor's class. In the instructor's class, the students were the future instructors of the JKA and they were dead serious and did their very best all the time. The spirit of the group was very high when they were all together. You would get a lot of lift out of being with them, like being pulled into a tornado. It made you want to try harder and be better.

Who were your peers in some of the classes, and in what ways did they influence your experience of karate in Japan?

Please let me clarify that the word "peer" means equal to me. I certainly don't consider myself equal to anyone there. The instructor trainees were very good. Some were former all-Japan and all-collegiate champions. Some of the people I trained with (that is, we were in the same class) from the 70's to the 80's were: Mr. Tanaka, Mr. Osaka, Mr. Ida, Mr. Yahara, Mr. Yano, Mr. Yamamoto, Mr. Sakata, Mr. Ogata, Mr. Kagawa, Mr. Imamura, Mr. Isaka and Ms. Abe. There were many others.

Also I realized that people training in the U.S. didn't train a quarter as much as they [the Japanese] did. I realized that we have to train as much or more to catch up. Most Westerners that go to train in Japan figure all they have to do is fight. But they don't fight using karate techniques. That's the point.

How would they fight, and who would you say impressed you most?

They would use a lot of roughhousing, wrestling you to the ground, trying to out-muscle you. A lot of techniques would just be swinging. The Japanese would use a lot of form and control and wouldn't turn into wild gorillas like the

"Yaguchi Sensei is technically very good, just like all JKA instructors. He was easier for me to communicate with."

Westerners. I don't understand the other question- do you mean what Westerners impressed me or what Japanese?

The person that impressed me most in the US was Mr. Frank Smith. I think he was the best American karate person ever in this country. In Japan, there were many great karateka when I was there, too many to pick just one.

As a very successful competitor you have collected many titles and trophies. How did your experiences of competition influence your approach to Karate?

I found that in order to conquer the title of kata champion it took a lot more work than winning at kumite. You really have to work at perfecting your techniques. You can cover mistakes in technique in kumite, but in kata every little technical point is important. In kumite, you have one opponent coming at you from one direction. You "just" need to figure out how to defeat that opponent's attack. But in kata you have multiple opponents

Karate Masters

"I trained at the Honbu dojo and at the Hoitsugan with Master Nakayama."

attacking from multiple directions. You have to be exact in what you do.

What are the most memorable trips you've taken for karate?

Three events stand out in my mind: When I won my first Pan American Championship, when I won my first collegiate championship and when I participated in the World Tournament in Cairo, Egypt.

What happened at the Pan American Championships?

The Pan American Championship was in Rio de Janeiro, Brazil. Although the US team had won team kumite, all my teammates had lost out in the individual events, leaving me fighting with the Brazilian Champion, Ugo Aregone. The crowd was roaring. I beat him. The crowd roared louder. Then I beat the current World Champion Luis Watanabe, also from Brazil. I was Grand Champion [1st place in both kata and kumite]. The trip ended up all right. I was actually made an honorary Okinawan [I even have a certificate], because the Okinawans claimed that no one except an Okinawan could do techniques the way I did them. It was very complimentary.

What stands out about your first Collegiate Championship?

This was in San Diego, California. Again, my team had lost and I was the only one left competing. I had actually won everything I had competed in that year, but for some reason did not feel confident about that tournament. I was up against Yamagami, the All-Western Collegiate champion from Japan, and I beat him. I must have been really lucky that year. He was really nice and invited me to come to his school.

What about Egypt?

Well, that was quite a different experience. President Anwar Sadat personally invited me to participate in the World Championship in Cairo, Egypt. He paid for my whole trip. I lived in a castle, had my own private trainer and was chauffeured by a Lieutenant General! I was the only one invited from the United States. Unfortunately, I unknowingly drank the water and got very ill. I didn't think I would be able to compete, but I put on my gi and tried anyway. It was a huge tournament and somehow I got 3rd place in both kata and kumite. I had to be hospitalized when I got back home.

Why did President Sadat invite you?

I don't know why I was invited. Apparently they had been studying films of me. I've never seen these films but I heard about them once when I won a US Championship. Afterwards a person came up to me and said, 'Everyone knows you for your front kick. We've been studying films of you, but tonight you beat everyone with different techniques. Why didn't you use your front kick?' I admitted to him that I had been competing with a fractured ankle and couldn't kick, but my favorite technique was not front kick, but whatever worked for a particular opponent in a particular situation.

"The person that impressed me most in the US was Mr. Frank Smith. I think he was the best American karate person ever in this country."

You are well known for being one of the first four Americans certified as a JKA instructor under the American Instructor Training Program am I correct?

Yes, I was told that I was the 4th.

Can you please tell us about your experiences as a trainee instructor before passing? Who taught most of the classes at the time and what did the sessions mainly consist of?

Instruction in the U.S. was evenly divided between Mr. Nishiyama and Mr. Yaguchi. I spent 6 weeks at a time in Japan, visiting every other year between 1966 and 1987. There I trained in the instructor's training, regular training, and I was assigned to train in the Hoitsugan for kata with Master Nakayama where I was the only private student. Training consisted of basics, basic combinations, kumite, and academics. We had to write papers on 43 different subjects. It was very difficult.

What were the main things Nakayama Sensei emphasized in your private Kata sessions with him, and what kata did he work on with you? Could you also please share some fond memories of Nakayama Sensei with our readers?

We worked on all the kata. The one that stands out the most was Heian

Karate Masters

"You can cover mistakes in technique in kumite, but in kata every little technical point is important."

Godan because we worked so long on it. His emphasis was the correct timing of each kata and small points like exact eye and hand positions. Small points were very important. He told me stories about himself when he was a little boy and times when he was practicing, but these are private stories. Sorry.

Would you care to share any memories from your time in the Instructor Program with us?

Mr. Yaguchi would spar with you 'til you were dead. He was the most educational person I ever dealt with. He was so much better than me, he would tell me things as we were sparring. He would say what technique he was going to use and where he was going to hit me with it and then do it, and there was little I could do about it.

Mr. Nakayama was a real perfectionist. I remember one time he had me practice Heian Godan for two hours and I never even got to the first kiai.

What was special was that I really learned what karate is and learned to appreciate it. I learned to see it as budo – which is so much more than sports karate and sparring. I learned this from Mr. Yaguchi and Mr. Okazaki. Unfortunately, ninety percent of Americans think karate is just sports karate and sparring.

And what would you say was the biggest significant improvement you made as a technical instructor from that time in your karate training?

Truly understanding techniques and their application.

You spend a great deal of time teaching in and out of America. Do you enjoy this lifestyle of teaching, and in what was is it rewarding?

I enjoy it very, very much. What I enjoy most is when people say that they have gained a lot of knowledge from the way I teach or do things.

What about your travels after you became an instructor?

Strangely, I find the same people wherever I go, just with different names, but people are great wherever I go.

I met a real godfather in Italy. We rode in his car and other cars would stop for us to pass by. He would stop his car in the middle of the street and go into stores where people would fawn over him just like in the movies. He opened a huge restaurant, which was closed, just so our small party could eat there. He presented me with a key to the city of Corado, but didn't need to use it, as I was treated as a celebrity just by following him around.

"Instruction in the U.S. was evenly divided between Mr. Nishiyama and Mr. Yaguchi. I spent 6 weeks at a time in Japan, visiting every other year between 1966 and 1987."

Were you treated as a celebrity in other places?

I did live TV interviews in Antigua and Dominica as well as Downtown Fresno! I was written up in Newspapers and Magazines in Italy and Norway. And I'm always treated well in Japan.

Any other reflections?

You know, I was born very poor, yet I have been able to travel the world due to karate. I see the importance and difference karate makes in the lives of people and feel fortunate to help be a part of that change. I always wanted to be known for doing something special and now I feel I have accomplished this through karate. I feel I am a very lucky person.

Coming back to your competitive interests, as we have already discussed, you were a very successful competitor. How did you make the transition from competitor to coach? Smoothly or did you get itchy feet to get back on the tatami?

I have never had itchy feet. Once I opened a dojo and began teaching, my sensei [Yaguchi] said to me, "The most important person in the dojo, James,

Karate Masters

"Mr. Yaguchi would spar with you 'til you were dead. He was the most educational person I ever dealt with."

is the student." From that day, I put my efforts into coaching students. I get just as much thrill from my students winning as when I won. Sometimes it's even more rewarding, as I might have more than one student competing and I can see what they are doing right or wrong and can correct them almost instantly and I understand what my instructor experienced with me.

What skills that you developed from your competitive years have you now seriously promoted with your competitors? Any skills or methods you found worked well that you still practice with your competitors today?

Timing is the most important skill. The idea of working toward a perfect technique in any situation is very difficult. The dojo kun says, "endeavor"' and so you just have to keep going and keep trying with this in mind. There are no secret techniques. What works for one person doesn't always work for another.

And what do you think is the key to effective coaching, what makes a good coach?

A good coach needs to know his competitors/students. You need to understand their strong and weak points, their psychological make-up, their personality, what motivates them, what depresses them. With some people you have to understand their personal life as well. You can't treat everyone the same.

What is your favorite kata and why?

I have two favorite kata. First, Heian Godan, because I spent so much time learning it with Master Nakayama. I realized that I had never done it right in my life. Now I hate to watch people "ruin" it.

I also like Nijushiho. When I perform it, I have a real feeling of fighting. I feel as if I'm in a small area being attacked by a group of people. I feel that I must put my opponent on the ground so I can face the next one.

"Mr. Nakayama was a real perfectionist."

In 2001 you passed an exam for 7th Dan. What do you believe at the outstanding characteristics of people who passed this test?

I believe people of this level have dedicated their lives to the study, practice, teaching, physical applications and mental understandings of the art. They have come to understand the essence of karate after many years of study. The actual definition is 'Nana-dan: Individuals who have devoted mentally and physically into karate-do training and attained high level expertise morally and technically'.

Did you ever believe you would reach this rank?

Never. I only had two goals: one was to black belt someday and the other was to maybe place 3rd in the National Championships. Everything else looked too hard. O

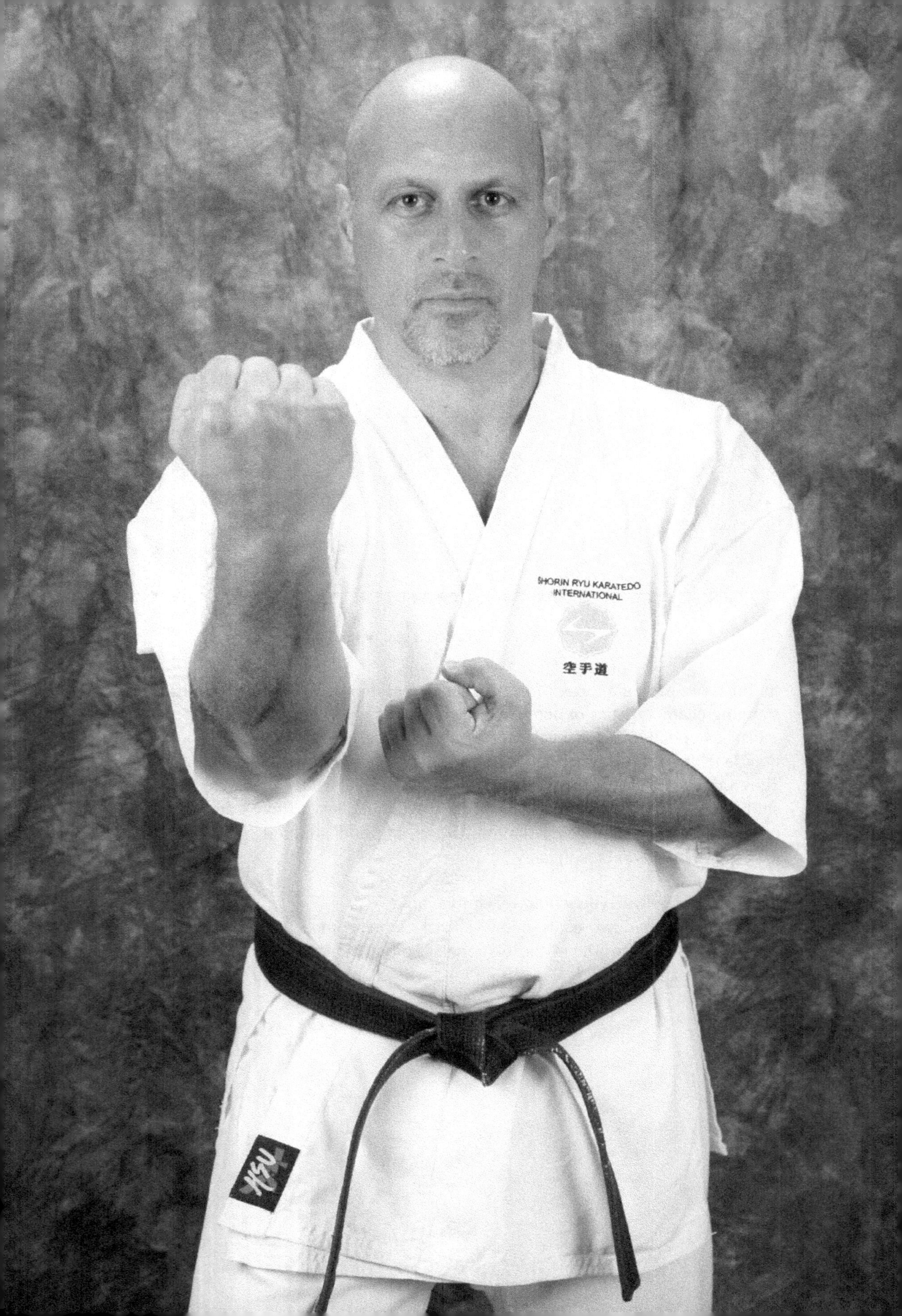
SHORIN RYU KARATEDO
INTERNATIONAL
空手道

JERRY FIGGIANI

A LOYAL LEADER

SENSEI JERRY FIGGIANI, HAS BEEN TRAINING IN THE MARTIAL ARTS SINCE EARLY 1970S. AS A NATIONALLY RATED FORMS AND FIGHTING CHAMPION, SENSEI FIGGIANI HAS WON TOURNAMENTS FROM 1988 TO 1996. IN 1995, HE WAS RATED THE NUMBER ONE FIGHTER BY THE PROFESSIONAL KARATE LEAGUE (P.K.L.). HE WAS ALSO INDUCTED INTO THE P.K.L. "HALL OF FAME" FOR THE "COMPETITOR OF THE YEAR" IN 1996. THAT SAME YEAR, HE WAS INDUCTED INTO THE "WORLD MARTIAL ARTS HALL OF FAME" FOR OUTSTANDING MARTIAL ARTS INSTRUCTION.

IN NOVEMBER OF 2009, SENSEI FIGGIANI FOUNDED THE "SHORIN RYU KARATEDO INTERNATIONAL" WHICH PROMOTES THE STUDY OF OKINAWAN KARATE.

ON JUNE 6, 2009, SENSEI FIGGIANI WAS PROMOTED TO 7TH DAN BY THE "ALL MATSUBAYASHI SHORIN RYU ASSOCIATION" UNDER THE DIRECTION OF HANSHI JOSEPH CARBONARA. SENSEI FIGGIANI HAS ALSO TRAINED WITH GRANDMASTER SHOSHIN NAGAMINE AND IN 1991 WAS A PARTICIPANT IN THE DEMONSTRATION CEREMONY FOR HIS 85TH BIRTHDAY AND THE 55TH ANNIVERSARY OF NAGAMINE DOJO.

IN 2009, SENSEI FIGGIANI AND HIS STUDENTS TRAVELED TO OKINAWA, WHERE HE WAS INVITED BY GRANDMASTER KENSIE TABA, 10TH DAN, TO BE PART OF THE WORLD CHAMPIONSHIP CEREMONIES. HE CONTINUALLY WORKS TO HELP KARATEKA UNDERSTAND THE DEPTH OF OKINAWAN KARATE, ITS HISTORY AND CULTURE.

How long have you been practicing karate?
I have been practicing karate for 35 years.

Who were your teachers in Shorin Ryu, and do you practice any other art in conjunction with karate?
The two Senseis that have made the biggest impact on my martial arts career are Sensei Joseph Carbonara and Sensei Terry Maccarrone. Both Senseis laid the foundation for Shorin Ryu here on the East Coast; they both received their shodans from Ansei Ueshiro. Ueshiro Sensei was the first of the Matsubayashi black belts to be sent over from Okinawa from Grandmaster Nagamine in 1962. In 1969, when Chotoku Omine Sensei

Karate Masters

"The two Senseis that have made the biggest impact on my martial arts career are Sensei Joseph Carbonara and Sensei Terry Maccarrone."

was sent to the United States, there was a split in the organization. Sensei Maccarrone stayed with Ueshiro Sensei, and Sensei Carbonara decided to go with Omine Sensei. It was Sensei Carbonara who encouraged me to start my own organization "Shorin Ryu Karatedo International" in 2009. My goal is to keep a strong Shorin Ryu presence here in the Northeast area. At one time, Shorin Ryu was a very popular style especially here on Long Island. I have been pleasantly surprised by the amount of interest this organization has sparked in a short period of time, not only here in the United States, but overseas as well.

I have also had the opportunity to study with Soke Takayoshi Nagamine many times when he use to stay here in the New York area and when I traveled to Okinawa. In 2009 when I traveled to Okinawa, I spent time with Kensei Taba Sensei of Shogen Ryu. Shogen Ryu is a break-off of the Matsubayashi Shorin Ryu System.

I hold a Nidan in Judo with the United States Judo Association. My sensei is Joseph Turchiano, 6th dan promoted from the Kodokan. I owe a lot to these Senseis who have contributed greatly to my success in the martial arts.

Presently, I am studying the arts of Iaido and Matayoshi Kobudo.

Would you tell us some interesting stories of your early days in karate?

An interesting story is how I first met my Sensei, Joseph Carbonara. I had only been studying for a short period of time when I was at a tournament in Kings Park, New York. While watching an open kata division, I was standing next to an older gentleman not realizing who he was. He was getting upset and voicing his displeasure at the way the kata was being performed. I thought he was pretty amusing. He was going on and on complaining. At one point, he turned to me and said, "This will be the ruination of karate." I didn't understand what he was so mad about; I soon found out who he was and how he had a reputation for being a traditionalist. Who would have known back then that one day that he would be my sensei? An appreciation for traditionalism is what drew me to the Shorin Ryu system.

Another memorable highlight of my earlier days of karate was when I attended the 85th birthday celebration for Grandmaster Shoshin Nagamine in Okinawa. Grandmaster Nagamine's birthday celebration was in conjunction with the 55th anniversary of the World Shorin Ryu Karatedo Federation. It was during this time when the Grandmaster passed the system down to his son, Takayoshi, and awarded him the title of Soke. During this initial visit, I also had the opportunity to train with many of the Okinawans from the Honbu dojo. It was an inspirational experience.

Were you a natural at karate? Did the movements come easily to you?
I was very athletic when I took up karate. Sports were already an integral part of my life. I really excelled in football. I was a running back for my high school football team and had set some team records. Running track and lifting weights were also activities I participated in when I was in high school. In college, I also played football. However, due to a back injury, my playing days ended. Even though I was athletic and coordinated, the movements of karate did not come easy to me. In the beginning when I started karate, I always tried to rely on my strength. I made progress when I started to understand the principles involved in karate, especially relaxation in the techniques. It was at this point I started to excel.

Please explain the main points of Shorin Ryu and its differences from other styles.
On the island of Okinawa, karate was divided into three major categories—Shuri-te and Naha-te, as well as Tomari-te. These districts in Okinawa were very influential in the development of the art of karate. Don't forget that before the word karate came about, the word te was used to classify the Okinawan fighting arts and the Okinawan fighting arts was heavily influenced by the Chinese culture as well as some areas from Southeast Asia. The karate from Shuri and Tomari, known as Shorin Ryu, is considered to be more natural in its movement and breathing techniques. Movements are relaxed, quick, and whip-like in their delivery. Some of

the styles that fall into the category of Shorin Ryu are Matsubayashi, Kobayashi, Shobayashi, and Matsumura Seito. Shoshin Nagamine Sensei, in his style of Matsubayashi Shorin Ryu, combined the techniques from Shuri and Tomari. Master Nagamine stated in his book, "The Essence of Okinawan Karatedo" that, "because of the secrecy in which te had to be practiced, there exists no evidence to indicate any clear-cut classifications of the various styles and types of karate during its formative years in the 18th century. This is also an indication that early martial art instructors really were influenced by people who they came in contact with and what areas in Okinawa they lived. The early instructors were influenced by the origins of their instructors as well as their instructors' methodologies. The styles and their names were developed into what we have come to know today.

The style of karate which developed from Naha is known as Naha-te. This style tends to be more rooted and steady in its movements. Naha-te also incorporates more intense breathing techniques which are used to create energy. Goju Ryu and Uechi Ryu fall into this category.

After so many years of training, what is it for you that is so appealing in this style of karate?

Shorin Ryu karate appeals to me because of its natural movements which also includes foot positioning and stances that aren't overly exaggerated. The breathing is very natural, as well. When the stances are not over-exaggerated; the practitioner is able to transition easier from move to move. These concepts I understand now. When I first started studying, I was drawn to karate because of the physical movements, but there was no understanding of the principles, theories, and even styles. It wasn't until I started looking into the history that I started to enjoy it even more.

Now I see how Grandmaster Shoshin Nagamine took the best from his teachers when he put together his style of Shorin Ryu which is Matsubayashi. It also connects us to the teachings of the great masters Motobu Choki, Kyan Chotoku, and Arakaki Ankichi.

As I continue to look deeper into the katas, I find that there are an abundance of techniques such as take downs, joint manipulations, choking, and even ground techniques that are applicable for self-defense as well as the principles of zanshin, go no sen, sen no sen, maai, and tai sabaki to name a few.

For example, when I first started taking judo, I came to realize a lot of the throwing movements were close or even associated with the movements of the Shorin Ryu katas. That opened my mind up to search deeper into the kata. Another aspect find appealing in studying Shorin Ryu is its rich history of Okinawan culture and its traditions.

What can karate offer to the individual in these troubling times we are living in?

Karate can give a person a sense of direction. Besides the physical techniques, there are many psychological benefits with studying the art of karate. Karate also teaches us about developing patience, focus, confidence, and perseverance, which are qualities that can help us deal with everyday stress. As far as giving one a sense of direction, I know from personal experience in working with high school children here on Long Island that this is another positive result.

"I made progress when I started to understand the principles involved in karate, especially relaxation in the techniques."

Since 2003, I have been teaching an anti-gang, anti-bullying program here on Long Island. This program has been implemented within high schools here in Suffolk County. I have seen much success in the program; it has changed many young lives for the better. What people don't understand is that karate can help an introverted person to be more assertive, yet at the same time, it can also take someone who is already aggressive and help them change their attitude to a more positive demeanor. This is a win-win for society.

Karate nowadays is often referred to as a sport. Would you agree with this definition or is it a martial art?

No. I believe it is a martial art; a martial art has no season. True karate is a way of life. One has to learn to apply the lessons they learn in the dojo to everyday life experiences. As far as self-defense, there are no rules. Whatever the practitioner needs to apply to escape a situation, that is what they must use.

Karate Masters

"Shorin Ryu karate appeals to me because of its natural movements which also includes foot positioning and stances that aren't overly exaggerated."

Now, as far as the "sport" of karate goes, it is separate. Am I against it? No. However as far as karate being a sport, one has to understand it is for show and performance as well as being rule bound. There is a big difference between the two.

What are the most important qualities for a student to become proficient in karate?

Effort and humility are two very important qualities for a practitioner to learn the martial arts. Very often in the dojo, the students who show little effort are the first to drop out. I have also seen people who make an effort but still show no humility. An example would be, thinking they can't learn from someone else. I have a couple of women instructors in my dojo who are very proficient in their study of karate. I have seen some men not take their advice or critiquing. These people will never get it. There is always something you can learn from someone else. I learn from my students every day and feel it is important to keep an open mind as well as a white belt, mentally. This means always wanting to learn more.

When teaching the art of karate, what is the most important element, self-defense or sport?

I feel self-defense is more important. You have to ask yourself this question: What is more important...your life or a trophy?

Kihon, kata, and kumite...what is the proper ratio in training?

For me that has changed over the years. I think it changes a lot for instructors who continually seek out knowledge. These instructors, in the long run, come to have a better understanding of karate. In my earlier days, I liked to do a lot more kumite. I still enjoy it, but kata is still the essence of karate. These three components are all interconnected.

Without kihon, you have no kata. Kumite techniques can be pulled from the kata as well. Today, I base my classes on what I feel my students need to work on. Sometimes you just have to go back to the basics.

How has your personal expression of karate developed over the years? What keeps you motivated after all these years?

I have a few thoughts on this. My personal understanding of karate in the beginning stages was just very physical. I was drawn to the kumite aspect of the art. I just felt kata was just a base of techniques pieced together. I had no understanding of kata nor the principles and theories which went with it. Questioning my senseis was not ever thought of; I just followed the instruction that was given to me at that time. What was taught to me was what I accepted.

As I progressed in my studies, I went through a stage where I started questioning and seeking more answers. I was questioning why I was doing things a certain way especially when I started training with other people. An example of this is when I started studying Judo. Judo really opened my eyes to some of the movements that were familiar to me in my Shorin Ryu kata. Here I was applying techniques where I'm throwing somebody or choking somebody out, and I could see a connection to the karate. It was an eye opener and a pivotal point for me in my studies.

One time, after a judo session at my dojo with Okada Toshikazu Sensei who was visiting from Tokyo, we had the opportunity to go out for a bite to eat. He taught me a very important lesson: He grabbed a napkin and began to draw a circle in the middle. He drew about eight lines coming out from the center of the circle. He asked me what I thought it was. I responded, thinking it was the Japanese flag. Inside each of the lines, he wrote a different martial art...karatedo, kendo, iaido, judo, aikido, etc. In the center, he wrote the word, "budo," explaining that all martial arts are interconnected. The principles never change. The teaching methodologies and the origins are the only differences.

Because I have been a practitioner for so long, sometimes, I can see techniques that are applicable for me as a martial artist without the technique being shown to me by an instructor. This can only come with many years of practice.

My karate has also developed through the teaching of my students. It is through them as I correct their mistakes that I can see and understand principles and theories a lot better. In turn, that helps me develop as a martial artist as well. Working with people of different abilities, body types, and physical limitations keeps me creative in helping them achieve ways to understand and execute techniques. Depending on the situation of the individual, modifications can be adapted to help them achieve their goal. Figuring out variations of techniques, depends on the limitations of the student who is trying to apply it. If you have two people, of different degrees of flexibility, you still have to get them to understand the outcome of the physical act of violence being performed against them. Both need to understand how to deal with that physical act of violence. One person may be able to pick up the technique the way it's shown, while the other may have to pick up the technique with a modification. It can be easy for any instructor working with a gifted, talented individual who picks up on techniques fairly easy. The challenge for an instructor is being able to work with all types of people and bring out the best of their abilities. This is very rewarding as well.

Going back to the second part of the question: What still motivates me? I really try to educate my students about the benefits of studying karate. When you teach it long enough to see your students' progress and recognize their development both physically and mentally, this can be very rewarding. Making a difference in someone's life is also very motivating to me.

Another motivating factor for me is keeping up with my training. I still attend seminars, as well as teach seminars, and meet great people worldwide who share in this common bond.

I also understand perfection is something we all strive for in karate but can never achieve it. If you keep chasing it, it keeps you hungry. I still approach every day with a white belt mentality wanting to learn more. I am also very aware of my strengths as well as my weaknesses.

How important is tournament competition in the evolution of a karate practitioner?

To me, the way I look at tournament competition is this: It can be good for some, and not so good for others. This has to be up to the individual. I have taken students to tournaments who have done very well. I have taken some students to tournaments who have not done well and it has affected them mentally. Students have to understand that although they might "lose," they should not lose the lessons that they learned in the dojo. Students who understand this continue to do quite well and show improvement. I also have students who do not compete but would do very well in competition because they have the right attitude—self-discipline and confidence in themselves. It is just that. Getting a trophy is not important to them.

Gichin Funakoshi said it best, "The ultimate aim in karate lies not in victory or defeat, but in the perfection of character of its participants." The real competition should always be with yourself.

What really means ikken hissatsu? How does it apply when used in karate?

To kill with one blow. That's fine, but you better have something else to back it up if that one blow fails.

Another way I could look at ikken hissatsu is by putting one's all into something you're doing, the best you can-whether it be a punch, throw, or a choke. Or, it could be approaching something in your life in which you have to just give it your all.

"The human body only moves certain ways regardless of what style."

How do you see the art of karate evolve in the future?

Since there are so many great martial artists out there today, it has to evolve. Especially with so many martial artists cross training and trying to become well rounded, this makes it easier for somebody who is studying karate to apply the principles from another art whether it's a throwing art, grappling art, etc. Somebody will always find a way to do things better, but it is also important not to forget the rich history and traditions of karate. One of my favorite phrases is, "On ko chi shin," to learn from the old is to understand the new.

Do you feel you still have further to go in your studies?

Absolutely. If I didn't, it would be a disservice to my students. One can never learn all there is to learn in a lifetime. As I look back and reflect on my studies, I have learned some valuable lessons along the way and not just the physical skill. Again, I am always looking to better myself as a martial artist.

Karate Masters

"Kobudo training is an extension of one's body whether you're using the bo, sai, etc."

What advice would you give to students on the question of supplementary training?

Personally, from experience, weight training, running, yoga, and swimming are all beneficial to the practitioner. Cross training will keep you stronger, more flexible, and in better condition. Nothing can be better for your development in karate than supplementary training especially as one gets older. It is important to find different means to improve upon certain areas such as more flexibility or better conditioning. This also aids in injury prevention.

What advice would you give to an instructor who is struggling with his or her own development?

I would suggest that they set new goals. The great thing about the study of the martial arts is that it always gives us a new opportunity to take ourselves to another level. Three goals to start with would be: 1. Define your purpose. 2. Educate yourself, and 3. Keep an open mind.

These goals will open more doors for you and, most important, never stop training for yourself.

Have there been times when you felt fear in your training?

In my training, never. I approach my training with the right mindset when I train whether it be at a different dojo or attending a seminar. Competing in a tournament or testing in front of my Senseis, yes. I think that is natural.

Do you think the Olympics will be positive for the art of karate-do?

I would like to think so, but did it really help Judo or Tae Kwon do? People have to understand these are two separate areas. One is an art while the other is just a pure, rule-bound sport.

I think it could be if it is done right. A lot of people have to come together to make this happen. There has to be a clear definition of the rules for the competitors. Though not everyone can compete on an Olympic level or national level, it may be good to get people involved in studying karate. It will also be great exposure for karate. Respect has to play a major role if it has to succeed. Respect is a foundation in all martial arts. Any lack of it could be detrimental to its success. Also, the athletes will need funding. As long as there is no mismanagement of the funds, the athletes will benefit greatly.

What are your views on kata bunkai? Is bunkai really important?
Kata bunkai is very valuable in understanding karate. The katas are the templates for the practitioner to understand the self-defense techniques that are hidden within these forms. I feel this is a very important part of the study of karate. To just do the physical movements of the kata without understanding the movement is an injustice to the practitioner. To understand the art is to dig deep into the kata for its hidden meanings. Working bunkai and understanding its principles helps bring the kata to life. It opens the mind of the practitioner to help give them a clearer understanding of that particular kata. It also helps us to understand the art of physical violence that one may encounter. When one explores bunkai, they can find that the kata is not just a set of punching, blocking, and kicking techniques. They will find an abundance of principles and techniques that deal with throwing, grabbing, joint manipulation, pressure points, trapping, ground techniques, and so on. This also aids the practitioner in understanding that the study of karate is really endless.

How important is it for a Shorin Ryu practitioner to know all of the kata in the curriculum?
It is not important to know all the katas. However, a practitioner has a responsibility to know whatever kata they are working on. For example, it's about knowing the kata bunkai as well; understanding the stances and how they are applied in a self defense situation. There are many facets to kata: the different heights in a kata, the different angles, and body shifting. All this gives the practitioner a more well-rounded approach to their training. More kata is not necessarily better. It's performing the kata and understanding the kata with accuracy.

How do you like to train yourself? Has that changed over the years?
When I am by myself, my best workouts are kata, followed by some type of conditioning exercise between the katas. I might do one kata followed

by some plyometric exercise and another kata followed by bag work or some type of weight training exercise.

When I get to workout with a partner, there is nothing better than two-person sets or Judo randori. My personal training has changed over the years. At my age, I look to avoid injury. I know how far I can push myself, but I also know when to back off. I still have good strength, flexibility, and endurance; I want to maintain that. I supplement my training with yoga, running, walking, light weight training, and in the summer, swimming.

Shorin Ryu, Shotokan, Shito Ryu, Goju Ryu, etc. How do you think the different styles affect the art of karate?

The human body only moves certain ways regardless of what style. So, whatever style one studies, they will find all the arts have something to offer. I think it is important for the practitioner to understand that there is always something to learn from any system of karate. Also, each system is rich in its own history, culture, and traditions. The styles' origins and methodologies bring us a uniqueness that we can all draw from and benefit. People have to feel comfortable with the style or system they are training in. This also aids in the longevity of one continuing their study of karate.

Do you think kobudo training is beneficial for the karate practitioner?

It can definitely help, but that is up to the individual. Kobudo training is an extension of one's body whether you're using the bo, sai, etc. This is an area that I would like to study more of. I have seen some excellent karate people who have never have picked up a weapon. So, again, it really comes down to the individual.

What is your opinion about the Shobu Ippon division in karate competition?

I never competed or had one of my students compete in Shobu Ippon, so I am not qualified to answer this question.

What are the most important points in your teaching method today?

Being honest with my students and not misleading them. I will never ask them to do something that I can't do myself. Leading by example will help to give the students more confidence in their abilities. My goal is to make them very well-rounded and life-long students of the art of karate.

Finally, what advice would you like to give to all karate practitioners?

Actually a few things. I like to educate people about the benefits of karate training. The public still needs to be educated about how karate

"Kata bunkai is very valuable in understanding karate. The katas are the templates for the practitioner to understand the self-defense techniques that are hidden within these forms."

can really help our society. It builds respect, confidence, and self-esteem. These traits are important for people in order to cope with life. Karate strengthens our minds and builds our bodies. This is very important for instructors to pass down to their students as well as the public.

Also, don't worry about being the best. Just do your best and everything will take care of itself. Keep a beginner's mind and realize there is always something to learn. And, most important, never give up! C

ROBERT GRAVES

REFLECTING BUDO

SENSEI ROBERT GRAVES CAN BE DESCRIBED AS NOTHING LESS THAN A 'SHOTOKAN LEGEND'. AS A STUDENT OF NISHIYAMA SENSEI, AND SPENDING TIME TRAINING IN JAPAN TRAINING UNDER WELL-KNOWN KARATE MASTERS, HE HAS GAINED A POWERFUL REPUTATION AS ONE OF THE MOST SIGNIFICANT FIGURES IN THE ART OF SHOTOKAN KARATE.

SENSEI GRAVE'S MAIN ESSENCE IS HIS SINGLE MINDEDNESS AS A KARATE-KA. HE HAS AN OUTSTANDING DETERMINATION AND TENACITY IN EVERYTHING HE DOES. IN THIS INTERVIEW HE TALKS ABOUT THESE EXPERIENCES, AND GOES ON TO DISCUSS HIS TIME SPENT TRAINING IN JAPAN AND HIS THOUGHTS ON 'SPORT' KARATE. WITH A BIG HEART AND A VERY OUTSPOKEN PERSONALITY, THIS HUMBLE AND QUIET MASTER CONTINUES TO DEDICATE HIS LIFE TO TEACHING SHOTOKAN KARATE AS TAUGHT TO HIM BY THE LEGENDARY HIDETAKA NISHIYAMA.

How long have you been training?

I started first in April of 1957. My arrival in Japan the month before saw me start with Judo on the base "Atsugi" in a gym taught by a Mr. Ito. He was from the Kodokan as it was common those days. As it turned out he also taught Mr. Nishiyama in an earlier time.

How many styles of karate or other Martial Arts have you trained in?

Well, of course the basic Judo by Ito Sensei. I was not the Judo type really. While I liked it very much, I am tall and skinny so any type of wrestling was not good for my body type. Also as a Marine, I was interested in a more lethal type of training. Remember, Martial Arts training in Japan was not allowed at that time. Only Judo was permitted because it was a sport. So we kept it a secret. I obtained a letter from Ito San introducing me as his student. With this letter in hand, I went to a school in Honatsugi - a little way by train from the Atsugu Air Station. This was not a very good dojo for me because the Sensei there did not want white guys in his school. He did have some service men from the base but I saw they were Hawaiians. I guess they were ok... but not me. Except for my letter, I would never have been accepted. This school was a line down from a man named Kyan from Okinawa. He had been dead since 1945, so I never saw him but his picture was in the dojo. Then, there was an article in a paper showing a karate demonstration. The punch line was that the instructor spoke English! That had been a problem before so I went to Yokohama to find this school. The address was not correct and to get it right I went to a police station for help. My last school required my registering my fingerprints before I could start training. So it followed that the police didn't know where this new school was located. They sent me instead to Fryers Gym. There, I met Richard Kim teaching three students the "Jion" kata. He only held class in the mornings as he ran a bar in Chinatown at night. But he knew where this school was and gave me the correct address. I began training at "Kawaguchi" Dojo on 4th street in Yokohama. This was a method taught by Ohtsuka Sensei. It was called Wado Ryu. It was really rough and tumble, almost all was based in free style work. I simply loved it. I went every day except when I had duty and all day on Saturdays. I did quite well there and one year later I took my Shodan exam at Keio University along with 130 other students from all over Japan. This was totally based in freestyle. There was some great experience there and I learned a great deal about fighting with respect to timing and distance. However, I didn't get much information about just how to create really big power in my movements. Years went by and there were always people from everywhere being on military bases so of course we saw each other and trained together. I used to be criticized for being sloppy with my control. You see, we hit each other a "little". Not to injure but to sting a bit. There was another thing that took place every so often. It was called a "Testing Exchange". I guess this was a practice between Universities in Japan. We went to a grade school near Opama base and two University clubs faced off the regular way, corner judges, referees, etc. Then the windows were curtained and front door was locked. All judges took off their ties and rolled up their sleeves. All equipment was cleared away. We lined up in three columns across from the other club. I think it was Tokyo University against Kawaguchi Dojo. A real donnybrook took place; a kick full force to the testicles producing urine all over the floor. A fist or kick to the face and blood all over the floor. Now that was a real problem for Japanese. Blood could not be allowed to be on the floor so towels quickly came out to clean things. I was cut in the face and had to have stitches. The base medical was close by so I ran over there with a phony story about a train pole hitting my head. The Japanese guards on the gate for civilian people were laughing at my story. They knew very well what was going on at the grade school!

I was the only white guy there. The fear was that I would blow their cover. Matches of this type were against the law in Japan at that time. I was never of that mind and when they saw that, I became one of them at last. We were a sight afterward all together singing Japanese songs covered in bandages walking up the street to the train station in Opama. It was such a great time. I've never forgotten that day. I was only a white belt then but I know that when later I tested for Dan it was a factor.

Some things at the training were natural to me. Others were not so. Spirit or Ki was very natural. I'm from a farming background. By working around animals a lot one learns about the sense of spirit connection in all things. Also my grandfather on dad's side was from Scotland and the genes there are a bit over the line if you know what I mean. Scottish simply love a good fight. On the other side, it's Irish so I m hopeless really. The physical action, at least in some of the techniques were not very easy for me. I am sort of obsessive though and spent lots of time on the makiwara.

"What I see generally now is not Karate to me. Martial Art is not a sport."

How do you see the style of Shotokan compared to Wado Ryu, Shito Ryu or Goju Ryu ?

Sensei Funakoshi had no name for what he meant to do. His plan, at least at first, seems to have been to show a little of all of the karate of Okinawa. He selected Kata from everyone and made a type of composite style. It was just "Karate Do" and he did not use Ryu as such. He modified his methods however and it seems that "Gigo', one of his sons, was taught a little differently than the regular classes. All this peaked in about 1935. His retirement

Karate Masters

"I don't see a great deal of truly traditional karate training in the future. I'm sorry about that but what's out there is not what I studied all my life."

put Gigo in the chief instructor spot. Gigo set up a dojo with his father's pen name over the door. You see, Sensei Funakoshi never really had a dojo of his own. Konichi, a kendo teacher, set up Funakoshi in a kendo school. Later, he taught in various University clubs. Gigo wanted to give his father a real dojo of his own. Shoto-Kan said "The place of Shoto", (Funakoshi). So his was a composite of Okinawa "To-De" (China Hand). The change to "Empty-Hand" was the result of a change to the character by students of Waseda University that he "certified " and then was given credit for. Shoto-Kan was based on blocking. Most kata were modified to emphasize a "blocking" structure. Also he had a "no first-attack idea". "Karate- Do has no offense". Much of this was mostly his own personality. Gichin Funakoshi was no "fighter" after all. Side snap, side thrust kicks and also to some degree the roundhouse kick came out after Gigo became Chief Instructor. Now of course everyone is doing these kicks so there have been many versions. They are not good orthopedic actions and we see much hip damage because of them.

Goju-Ryu I was told at least as the name suggests, was given by Miyagi Sensei early on. When asked if his "(Karate) was hard or soft?", he was to have said "little hard, little soft". I guess that is the character we call Goju. Nakayama Sensei said this style comes from South China. It's been said that it was practiced in Naha from around 1880 on. I have been in classes taught by a teacher named Kisakii who was from Yamaguchi Gogen's school. He also taught Nishiyama Sensei in his early years. Nishiyama-San told me Kisakii was the most powerful karate-ka he had ever met early on. The foundation stance is an inside tension action in China but it's a little inside as well as twisted out at the leg like we do with kiba-dachi in Shoto Kan when seen in Japan. As an overview, Goju starts with a study of the "core" of the body. Strong use of air pressure aids in this study. I personally teach this and I know it's very important to creating the really big shocking power of the Karate "punch". After all, if the core of the body is not the center of the movement we are just boxing. One punch - one death, requires much more.

Shito Ryu was at first a half way between Shuri Te and Naha Te systems. So when I studied at times with Mabuni Sensei it was a little strange to me. What I saw was more Shorin (Shuri) than Goju (Naha) at least when I was there. They were a lot like my older school under Ohtsuka Sensei. So having only a short experience, I can't really give an accurate opinion.

How was your relationship with Nishiyama Sensei?
He was a very complex person. I would say that few people really understood him. He was a product of the war, being born in 1928. He came from a rather upper middle class of Japan. My ability to communicate with him was I believe due to us both being military.

We knew many of the same things that only military people know. It was the same with Kawaguchi Sensei before. Also, he never really got his English very good and was able to freely talk in the "middle language" (Pigeon), so we could understand each other better. It wasn't that he didn't understand English, he did. It was that his ear for phonics was so bad that no one ever knew what he had said. His words were not recognized by most people. I always had to re-teach every seminar to my students. But on the bright side, we had a great review. I took him to a hot spring up in the mountains and there was six inches of snow. Of course, we were naked running around in the snow and in and out of the hot water. It was no big deal to me but his secretary called me and asked what it was about. He had told everyone about it. She said he really liked it and that "Japanese really like that kind of place". Bottom line is that he was not just a Sensei, but also an interesting friend.

I greatly miss him and always will.

Karate: Sport or Martial Art?
Frankly what I see generally now is not Karate to me. Martial Art is not a sport. Various aspects of any martial art method can be used in a copy of martial art. Some type of rule system established and yet it isn't even close to martial art. Karate, when practiced as Martial Art, is very dangerous. Sometimes accidents happen. We try to keep safety a priority but things happen. Competition is not easy because when there are rules, it no longer is real "Martial Art". When there are no rules it is not accepted by our society. A real sword is not Kendo, Judo is not Jujitsu and so on. I think Kata is

the highest level of training when done with extreme seriousness. There is a reason why all martial arts have "Kata".

I see very limited use of the sport aspect of any martial art. It has its use, but it's not the end result. Self-defense is a very close quarter activity. Some Sensei's study and teach this and I am one of them. However the model commonly seen in Japan is the dueling model. Coming from a long war less period, over 250 years with only sword fights with each other, the duel, where two face off at ten feet or so and fight, is anything but self-defense. In the street under ambush the aggressor will get as close as possible without raising any alarm in the victim. When the attack happens, it's a surprise. Kata if studied closely, will show a very likely response. Everything should be finished in three counts or less. Hopefully, the first half count! There should be no further action. Now I just described a perfect world. Nothing ever happens that way. So it's probable that it will decay into a dual requiring much more action. I teach both and I encourage sparring but it is very important to keep it in perspective.

What do you think are the most important qualities of a student?
Correct attitude. All students come to the dojo with baggage. But they must begin to see a different path and leave that baggage behind. The Dojo doesn't care about anyone's 'baggage'. They must show patience and perseverance. Above all what is seen in the Dojo stays in the Dojo. No street testing is aloud. All Sensei's must be charged with the responsibility of stopping the training of persons who show bad intent.

What is the correct ratio of Kihon, Kata and Kumite?
In a class not limited to beginners, I like an even balance. For special training, I give more emphasis to one or the other. For the seniors, over sixty, it is Kata and its Bunkai for self-defense.

How important is competition?
If it could represent the real life side of Karate, I would embrace it more. What I see, unfortunately, is something else.

How do you see Karate in the future?
I don't see a great deal of truly traditional karate training in the future. I'm sorry about that but what's out there is not what I studied all my life.. I love Karate. It has never stopped growing and changing. I don't think it is ever mastered as such. I don't even like the term "master". As in any art there is no limit to human growth. Some of us get really good but even they fall vic-

tim to age. Don't stop, shift gears and come at it from another perspective. It's too interesting to ever put down I think. But maybe that's just me. I am over 75. Progress is maybe only an illusion now. Still, I've had a very healthy life and had the chance to meet and get to know some really great people. You could say I am a happy man.

Did you ever feel fear in training?

Yes, at different times and for different reasons. Nishiyama Sensei in his early years was very scary. The potential for extreme damage was exceptional. He was a bit 'demonic' at times [laughs].

How important is understanding Bunkai?

Kata is Bunkai. It never stops changing and growing. What s seen at white belt is not what is seen at the black belt level. What you see at twenty years old is nothing like fifty and not at all like when you are seventy. It is very important but it is never the same.

"Kata is Bunkai. It never stops changing and growing."

How important do you think it is to know a high number of Kata?

Shotokan reached its peak in 1935 and what came after continues to grow. Today, we still reach for more but we are standing on big shoulders. If you teach karate you will know many kata but you will only really like maybe three or four because they fit exactly to you. You have to be balanced in your teaching and in your personal choices.

How has your personal training changed over the years?

I like to wear training in everyday life. Karate training doesn't only happen in the dojo. As I like to say, I'm retired, but everyone knows you can't put this stuff down. I teach workshops and clinics around various dojos.

Karate Masters

"I like to wear training in everyday life. Karate training doesn't only happen in the dojo."

Do you practice Kobudo?

Yes, but I don't use tonfa, nunchaku or sai. I train only two weapons, Bo and Jo. These can be very helpful. I think that in the distant past all Kata as such were weapon kata. I've been told the kata all had two versions, weapon and non-weapon. I've used any kata for a Bo Kata as such and they work nicely.

Is the concept of Shobu-Ippon important?

Those who came from the JKA system [we] only use this system. If there is an exception it would be in a training mode only. Then, we use just flags, or even if the contestants are young or very new to karate. "Todome", is the basis for "Ippon" and that ends the match at a full point. However, I have seen many tournaments in which no "full point" is ever seen; many times the contestants are not capable of even generating a full point and it comes down to a half point or other reasons to win by decision only.

What do you think are the most important points in Karate technique?

Foundation of power; stance and posture; course of action and center of balance. Then, impact time with the transfer of shock to target.

Lastly recover time and unbroken connection of mind (Zan Shin).

All this is Kihon - of course - but I teach it in all three areas of Kihon, Kata, Kumite. It's also necessary to point out the difference between the principles of "pushing weight" versus "shock unloading". I like to use the comparison of equal weight, cotton and steel. Same weight but if you throw them at a glass window, steel goes through and cotton does not. What's the difference? Cotton unloads its energy in maybe a 5th of a second. Steel in maybe a 10,000th of a second. If the fastest man alive can only move at the rate of cotton, how is it we can generate our own energy at one 100th of a second? Maybe we have a secret. This makes new students perk up and think. What's the secret?

How do you see the influences of your teachers today?

I guess the many persons I've met along the way have had an effect on me. While I began in Japan under Kawaguchi Yoshio Sensei, when in California, I met the great Sensei Dan Ivan and he introduced me to a newly arrived Nishiyama Sensei. I felt conflicted and sent a letter back to Japan to my old dojo. Kawaguchi San set my attitude for life. "If Nishiyama is there and you can train but don't, you would be the fool!"

I took off my black belt and rank and put on a white belt so there would not be anything in the way. I never looked back. I also never regretted the lessons I got training in other styles.

Finally, what would be your main advice to others?

We who train all know the keen awareness that develops through Martial Arts. This awareness can keep us out of harms way if we let it. There is always that person or that situation that can harm us but something alerts us to it and we can take a different action. Go a different way. Stop short of danger. I wish I had a nickel for the times that has happened to me. Also keeping a stable emotion under great stress can be very valuable.

On the physical side, work hard with a serious attitude. Don't take yourself too serious. Listen to your instructor but don't put him on a tall white tower. We are all just humans and we do the best we can. Be patient with yourself. Karate is like the mating of elephants. Much stamping and trumpeting. Results take a long time. Make your haste "slowly". O

YOSHIMI INOUE

RETURNING TO THE SOURCE

THIS QUIET AND REVERENT SENSEI IS ONE OF THE MOST IMPORTANT SHITO RYU INSTRUCTORS IN THE WORLD TODAY. HIS POSITION AS DIRECTOR OF JKF "INOUE-HA SHITO RYU KEISHI-KAI" DEMANDS OF HIM A CONSTANT TRAVEL SCHEDULE. WITH AN EXCEPTIONAL LEVEL OF SKILL SECOND TO NONE, SENSEI INOUE DISPLAYS ALL THE MAJOR PRINCIPLES OF THE SHITO RYU-HA DEVELOPED BY THE GREAT TERUO HAYASHI.

HE HAS TAUGHT EXTENSIVELY IN JAPAN AND EUROPE AND RECENTLY IN THE U.S., AND TRAINED PRIVATELY SOME KATA WORLD CHAMPIONS WHO LOOKED FOR IMPROVING THEIR TECHNICAL PERFORMANCE IN COMPETITION. CURRENTLY LIVING IN JAPAN, YOSHIMI INOUE SENSEI IS ALWAYS GENEROUS WITH HIS TIME AND AGREED TO SPEAK FREELY ABOUT THE PRESENT STATE OF KARATE-DO. HE HAS WALKED THE PATH OF BUDO FOR MANY DECADES AND IS ONE OF THE FEW MASTERS IN THE WORLD WHO CAN TRANSCEND STYLE AND POLITICS. IF SOME MEN POSSESS A PHILOSOPHICAL APPROACH TO LIFE AND CAN SUFFER IN AGONIZING PAIN AND STILL FIND SOME GREAT INSTRUCTION FROM THE LESSON LEARNED, INOUE SENSEI IS WITHOUT DOUBT ONE OF THEM. "THE GOAL OF KARATE SHOULD NOT ONLY BE SELF-DEFENSE," EXPLAINS INOUE. "THE ART SHOULD PROVIDE A GUIDE FOR LIVING AND THIS ENCOMPASSES THE STRIVING FOR SELF-CONTROL THROUGH THE DISCIPLINE OF DEDICATED PRACTICE."

IN AN AGE OF MEANINGLESS SUPERLATIVES, IT IS DIFFICULT TO DESCRIBE THE DEBT OF GRATITUDE KARATE OWES TO SENSEI YOSHIMI INOUE.

Sensei, how does Hayashi-ha Shito Ryu differ from other karate styles?

Hayashi Teruo Sensei trained in different styles (including Kobudo) and finally decided what was the best approach to combat. He developed a series of principles that should be used in combat, and his main idea was not to face strength with pure strength. His approach was substantially different from other masters who emphasized more kata over kumite. Hayashi Sensei realized the limitation of some traditional techniques in actual combat and began to modify the technical structure of the techniques to better fit into a realistic fighting situation. He studied with great masters to learn new things and eventually to mold what it would be his

Karate Masters

"All Karate styles use the principle of balancing the "hard" and "soft"."

creation: the Hayashi-ha style of Shito Ryu karate.

What can you tell us about the balance of the opposites [soft and hard]?

In the universe, all is based on the balance of opposites: day and night, cold and hot, etc. Karate is the same: relaxation and tension, hard and soft, body and mind ... it is all in there. No Karate style is "hard" or "soft" per se if you truly understand Karate. Some people say Goju is "soft," Shotokan is "hard," etc... that makes no sense. All Karate styles use the principle of balancing the "hard" and "soft". It is just a matter of the level of understanding and knowledge of the person or karateka who is talking.

What is your opinion about trying to make [in Kata] the external technique perfect from a visual point of view?

With the possibility of including Karate in the Olympics, there has been an attempt to standardize not only the actual kata but also make the physical movements "prettier," to say at least. The idea of a perfect "outside" visual form has become the goal. But there is a big problem here because Karate kata is not gymnastics. Kata is not about the external technique only but about the "philosophy" and "meaning" of the actual technique. If we change the outside form to make it look better but lose elements that "show" the real meaning of the technique, we are losing a great deal of understanding. If we don't maintain the "function" of the technical movement, then it is no longer kata. It's gymnastics. Once kata is only visual (as we see these days), it has no point. The visual of the kata must represent technically the "bunkai application" of the movement. We have to consider the "bunkai" when we do kata.

Can you give us an example?

For instance, in some kata when performed in competition, the karateka jumps higher than what the actual technique requires; they slow down the techniques breaking the actual rhythm of the form, etc. Why? To impress judges. Every movement can be used and it has to be performed as it works. That is a choice you have to make: perform kata for looks or for true Karate. Real Karate kata may not be more beautiful but certainly is way more meaningful.

What about Kihon training?

Kihon training, although it may be boring is extremely important. If the foundations of a house are weak, as the house gets older, problems will arise. This is the same for all Karate styles, no matter their origins. A lot of people spend many years training to realize later on, after 30 years of karate practice, that they don't have a solid foundation and their technique is not "polished" at all – that they lack solid basic, clean Karate technique and they feel embarrassed because they have a high rank. You find this situation mainly among karateka who have devoted their training mainly to kumite. Don't misunderstand my words; kumite is not easy but it is not what makes a good karateka. Kihon and kata are the foundation for Karate. Kumite is a "personalized" way of using Karate technique. But you should get that [technique] first. Unfortunately, you see high ranks who lack good Karate basics and they try to cover it up focusing on kumite. This shows what kind of "atitude" and "personality" these practitioners have.

How can these practitioners who focus mainly on kumite correct that?

Well, that is a little bit difficult. They will realize this problem later on in their Karate training; they may be 5th, 6th or 7th Dan already. They have a reputation at stake [some may be Asian, European, American or world champions] and it is hard for them to acknowledge what they truly lack in their Karate. They never had the motivation, patience, and sense of detail to begin with and that is why their Karate is like it is. So, it is very hard for them to accept that fact and go back and do thousands of basics to catch up with the deficiencies of their past Karate training. Karate's basic movements are incredibly difficult to perform correctly and it takes a certain attitude and personality to focus on details. Kata is kumite at its most complex form. All the techniques and strategies used in kumite and also in self-defense are contained in the fundamental kata. You just need to know "where" to look and "how" to uncode them. In traditional Karate, kata equals kumite but kumite doesn't equal kata.

Some people may argue that good technique is alright…but Karate is about "if you can fight or not." What do you have to say about that?

Very simple; that show how little these people know Karate and their level of understanding. That mentality shows why they lack technique. And no, Karate is not about "if you can fight or not." Mike Tyson at his best could probably have knocked down 90% or more of the karate practitioners around the world, but that doesn't mean he knows Karate. Fighting is a part of Karate but it is not Karate. People use this excuse to justify they own inabilities. MMA champions can really fight, but it has nothing to do with Karate or true Martial Arts. So, if these people only are interested in fighting, why do they do Karate and not MMA?

What can you tell us about kumite?
Kumite is based on two principles: distance and timing. Without these two, nothing else matters. Not matter how good your primary elements (techniques) are, they will be useless. But even with a lousy technique, if you have developed a decent amount of ability in using distance and timing, you can be very good in sparring. You won't have a "good" Karate but you can win competitions, even world championships.

Would you elaborate, please?
If you don't have the right distance, your attacks will fail and your defenses will be useless. The right technique without the right [delivery] distance is useless. Then, if you have the right distance but the technique (attack or defense) is not delivered at the right time, it will either fall short in execution or won't be done to its fullest potential. The "when" to move is at least as important as the "how." It is useless to have a powerful technique if your body movement can't put you in exactly the right place and at the right time to use it effectively.

How we can develop the "right" distance?
Let me begin by saying that there is no one "right" distance. It is true that the "basic" kumite distance is the one that is slightly farther than the reach of the rear leg of the opponent. For instance, if you opponent is facing you, he won't be able to reach you with a kick from the back leg without taking a preliminary step toward you. That is your basic "safety" or "critical" distance. During a kumite match, the distance alters constantly so the key to obtain the right distance is "correct footwork." If you don't have the right kind of footwork, you won't be able to attain the right distance efficiently during the match.

What do you mean by the right kind of footwork?
You need to know what kind of footwork you should use to defend, to attack, to intercept, to shorten the distance, to create distance when

defending, or to create distance in order to simply create space, etc. Not all footwork patterns are the same and shouldn't be used randomly. Right footwork "gets" you there and gets you "out."

What about timing?
Timing is a very complex element because it requires a sense of rhythm – not only of the correct [intrinsic] rhythm of how the technique must be used and works but also of the rhythm of the fight. Then, you need to have an understanding of the opponent's rhythm and the tempo and cadence of his movements. Distance can be drilled and developed by Sanbon and Gohon kumite but timing only through actual jyu kumite.

And …?
Then, it is when you can actually find a certain pattern in your opponent's rhythm and find out how to break it. You can create it, too, and force it into your opponent, but that is more complex. You can read the opponent's rhythm and then break it to hit efficiently.

"Kata is not about the external technique only but about the "philosophy" and "meaning" of the actual technique."

You mentioned Sanbon and Gohon Kumite but some modern practitioners might argue that attacking someone with Oi Tsuki is not "realistic." What do you say?
That they don't know what they are talking about. Oi Tsuki as a technique in itself shows a lot about the practitioner's technical level. If you can actually hit somebody with a full Oi Tsuki, that tells a lot about us as karateka. But let me say that for prearranged kumite drills like Sanbon and Gohon Kumite, many people don't actually do it right. The right starting distance is when you place yourself with your fist actually touching the partner's face. Then, you take one leg back to Zenkutsu-dachi. From there, you initiate the Oi Tsuki It is not a long distance but an actual "striking

Karate Masters

"Karate's basic movements are incredibly difficult to perform correctly and it takes a certain attitude and personality to focus on details."

distance." Your intention is to "hit" the training partner, not just pose the punch. The fact that Oi Tsuki is more "visible" allows the trainee to coordinate his reaction and timing better. This is a training process; it is not a fighting drill, but a training drill to learn how to time the defense, the counterattack, and the tempo of the response. If you don't understand the actual use of the drill, then you may make nonsense statements because of lack of understanding on what you are talking about.

It is believed by many that the power comes from the hip but studies proved different. What can you tell us about this?

It is true that people say that the power in Karate "comes from the hip." Let's start using the words correctly. Power comes from the ground up. It doesn't come or originate from the hip. This is pure physics. A Karate punch [or kick] does not begin with the hip rotation. It passes cleanly through the hips into the torso, but it is not the hips that cause the power or the turn. The power that starts/originates or comes from the ground is transmitted to the upper body [and eventually to the punch or kick] by the correct use of the hip and then directed to the target via the arm or the leg. Our hips will impede the progress of the leg force/thrust if we don't know how to open them loosely as pivot points. Why the legs? Because if you have no base, you have no power. Once again, pure physics. Your connection with the ground is the base for the power. Studies have been made in universities where professional boxers and karateka have been placed in the air hanging, with no base or contact to the ground whatsoever. The result? Their punching power was gone, decreased to the simple arm power. Why? Because they had no base. Those studies proved that the power originates from the ground up, not from the hips. It is impossible to deliver a powerful punch without a strong stance to launch it from, as you cannot use the rotation of your hips without being rooted to the ground. This is the right way to express it. What is important to the body mass and the way the hip is used.

Body mass?

Yes. The real driver behind power in any punch or kick is the amount of mass behind the movement and the direction of that mass. Check all the physics equations for force, momentum, and impulse. The way to maximize the amount of mass behind your attack is to get as much of your body moving in the direction of your attack as possible.

So what is the role of the hip?

As I said, the hip is the transmitter of the power that originates from the ground and from your "rooted" stance. Hip rotation is an accelerator that adds speed, and of course, increasing the speed of your body mass will increase the amount of power. But hip rotation is only one way of increasing the speed of your body mass and never is a substitute for proper application of your body mass to your techniques – which involves the whole body. You also need to know how to use the counter-rotation of the joint and when to use it properly. Hips are where the body's center of gravity is located; our center point of mass is at the hip level and we should learn how to use our hips to increase velocity of the body mass – not necessarily speed. The right use of the hips helps to keep posture, balance, and stability for every move, but at the same time, being used incorrectly may shut off the powerful thrust of the legs. Hip rotation – not hip shifting – is used for adding speed to the body mass and therefore develop maximum power in karate techniques. That is why we say that in karate we always try to punch with the hips and kick with the hips, etc.

One more thing, the hips bones can't generate power. Power is generated by the muscles around the hip. Two of the largest muscle groups in the body are the buttocks and the abdominal muscles; therefore, utilizing their strength, as well as rotating or shifting the hips, will add power to any techniques. As the hips turn, the torso and buttocks are added to the force of the technique. The hips are part of the bone/skeletal structure. A bone does not generate power ... muscles do. The real power comes from the buttock and the abdomen muscles. But a tight hip with no flexibility will decrease the potential power that you can use from your body mass and technique.

What about hip shifting? What is the difference from hip rotating?

These are two different things and should be used in different ways. Shifting is the movement of the entire body from one point to another in a straight line. Shifting includes both stepping and sliding the feet. And this is how the hips should be used because if you don't move, you simply can't hit your opponent. So shifting your hips is the real key.

Shifting the hips and not rotating the hips is the method which allows the karate-ka to develop the greatest amount of force. This is possible because we use the maximum amount of body mass by using the legs driving against the floor [origin of the power] to push forward against the hips.

The rotation is developed by the circular motion of the body mass. Control of rotation is centered on the use of the hips. The outside hip joint moves forward and backward, while the inside hip acts as a hinge. This can be practiced without technique, and then with techniques added. It is very important that the knees remain locked in place without moving. The pivot point in hip rotation changes depending upon the situation. It is always either one hip joint or the other, never the center of the body. Rotating on the center of the body would mean that one leg is retreating while the other is moving forward, eliminating the effect of the rotation. With the use of hip rotation, it is possible to create very powerful techniques in a small space.

Another important aspect is to fully understand the hip rotation around a central axis and the application of the hip shifting in the same motion. This is a completely different concept and a more realistic way of using body torque to use the technique effectively. One aspect we should be aware of is that different styles tend to use or move the hips differently, although they are based on the same principles. Shotokan uses a very "wide" application of hanmi and shomen and Shito Ryu, Goju, and Wado use the same principle but with more emphasis on shifting.

Why you think people explain it incorrectly?

They are misinformed. Hip shifting and hip rotating are both important. Hip rotating by itself won't do anything to your punch unless you are punching a stationary object and your distance is already there. It is like rotating the tap of a bottle ... it doesn't move/shift forward to reach the target. You need to use hip shifting and body mass, and then you finalize the movement with full hip rotation that concludes at the moment of impact, not before. And this has to be syncronized and not divided in parts or different movement sections.

What do you mean by "divided in parts"?

You see many people snapping the hips back and forth. They really get good at "hitting" and snapping the hips but this is useless in real Karate. It is just showing off. When they punch, you see clearly when the hip movement (rotating) starts and when it ends. You can actually see the "separation" between the hips and the rest of the body movement. Well, this is wrong. The hip movement or rotating should be "hidden" along with the punch [or kick]. It should be "one" with the punch [or kick]. These people snap the hips and then punch. This is ridiculous. The hip movement should be coordinated with the rest of the body and not be visible. It is like the separate parts of a whip ... when snapped in the air, you see just one single action, not several segments moving one after the other. Only one single perfectly coordinated movement, that is what a karate technique should be. So drop that hip snap. It may look "impressive" to a beginner and fellow karateka's, but not to someone who knows and understands Karate.

"Kumite is based on two principles: distance and timing. Without these two, nothing else matters."

What would be your final advice for the readers?

In Karate you never stand still. You always have to try to move forward, to get better and improve what you are doing. When you go to train every day, you have to go far beyond the idea of simply "training" and use your mind when you train. That is the only way to really progress. O

GENZO IWATA

THE SHITO KAI LEGACY

When you meet Sensei Genzo Iwata – the Technical Director of the "World Shito Kai Federation', you will feel nothing less than the energy of someone seriously devoted to the study of karate-do. Although Genzo Iwata started his training a very early age, he is extremely understanding, approachable and respectful – not only as a karate instructor but as a human being as well. His long years of experience and training under the guide of his father, the legendary Manzo Iwata, have allowed him to internalize the important moral aspects of the art and use them in his daily life. Internationally recognized as a Shito Kai authority, he found a way of life in karate and became obsessed with sharing his knowledge and expreiences with students both young and old, regardless of their ability. What sets him apart is that he is ready and willing to not only train hardcore karatekas, but also individuals interested in personal development as well. He is a knowledgeable and fascinating man, full of interesting stories, and brimming with a positive attitude towards teaching and to life.

What was your father Manzo Iwata Sensei as an instructor?

He was very serious. He trained us very hard and always encouraged us to not only train hard, but to intellectually study what we were training as well. He always stressed understanding ourselves as human beings and to strive to be productive not only as karatekas but also as members of our society. Karate is not only about the Martial Art. Karate is also about the relationship between the Sensei and the student, which is similar to the relationship between a father and child. But children cannot choose their father, but in Budo, a student can choose his teacher (father).

Did you have any other Sensei?

Obviously I had the chance of receiving knowledge from my Senpai but I would only call my father my "sensei". By being able to see with my own eyes and experience with my own body so many great teachers and sempai capable of such a high level of Karate represents a huge source of wealth and experience for me.

Karate Masters

"Karate is about the relationship between the Sensei and the student, which is similar to the relationship between a father and child."

Do you think that Sport Karate is destroying the spirit of Karate-Do?

It's important to have a balance. The true path lies in a balance between training Karate for health, training Karate for Sport and Recreation and training Karate for Budo (Karate for a life and death self-defense situation). Technically these things are very different. You must not mistake the true path as being only one of these aspects of Karate. Training Karate for health will allow your body to defend against illness and you will live a longer higher quality life. Real Budo Karate training for self-defense will have ramifications of serious injuries to you and your training partners. You must be very careful in Budo training. Besides, you should never have an occasion to use Karate in a real situation anyway. You should develop the intuition, character and ability to avoid a fight. Training Karate as Budo has little to no application in our society. Avoiding a fight is the best self-defense. If you lived in a time of war where real combat would be used, your training would be drastically different.

Sport Karate training allows you to develop without serious injury, to a physical level not possible before. The attitude in your training is most important. If the spirit of Karate-Do is being destroyed, it is happening because of people and attitudes, not because of sport competition. No matter what you are training, you should always train with the idea of becoming a better human being. Train to understand your strengths and weaknesses. Train to be a good, honest and trustworthy human being. Train to perfect your character. This is the spirit of Karate-Do.

What were Iwata Sensei's feelings about Sport Karate?

He understood that our Karate would grow and change. He understood that it would be influenced by many people and many things. The perfection of one's character was the most important thing. I think this should be our concern and more important goal in training.

Do you think that fear in the Dojo is positive or negative?

Every instructor creates different level of "fear" or "tension" in the Dojo and every student feel different level of fear in the dojo. Fear could make the mind focused and enhance the development of mental strength. Fear is not always good and it could make people weaker. But when you overcome the fear, you develop the confidence and turning it into strength Training makes you physically stronger. When the body gets stronger you feel more confidence and also mentally you get stronger. When you mentally get stronger, you can push more and work harder. And it will relate to you life style. It will relate and affect your relationship with your family or at work. When you work at the edge of your limit, your mind and mental strength at the time changes your performance. From an instructor point of view it is important to make a class where students can focus on what they do during the class.

What is your opinion about "Ippon Shobu?

"Ippon Shobu" teaches the karateka to maintain a heightened awareness and superior concentration because there are no second chances when your life is on the line. We need that intense mental and emotional pressure to remain in the correct frame of mind. Traditional "Ippon Shobu" also helps to promote and maintain a high standard of technique. We should keep the traditional approach of the idea of making our Karate effective in a real situation. Training with this intent raises your spiritual awareness and appreciation of life. Modern day Karate has lost the "Ikken Hisatsu Spirit."

Would the different principles of the different styles promote confusion or conflict in the student?

If a Martial Art is being taught properly, all the essential principles should be the same and compliment each other. There is only one human body. When I say become familiar with many arts, I don't mean to practice Shotokan on Monday, Goju on Tuesday, Jujutsu on Wednesday, etc… etc… I mean that you should have an open mind to exploring principles, techniques and training methods taught in other styles. Study the Budo with an open mind.

Karate Masters

Would you recommend that Shito Ryu karateka study some of the original Okinawan versions of our Katas and some other Okinawan Katas that are not found in the style?

Shito Ryu has a great number of katas within the style but any additional study is positive. The study of old Okinawan Katas is a must for the advanced only. It will allow you to see and better understand the evolution of our modern day Kata. The Katas were originally designed for Budo. Kata was a library of techniques to incapacitate and even kill the opponents. Remember, the origin of many Kata and techniques were Chinese. These fighting methods eventually found their way to Okinawa and Okinawa was involved in wars. These fights were all hand-to-hand combat. Killing was face to face.

This developed a mental focus in the warrior that is indescribable and most probably unattainable unless you were in the terrifying reality of hand-to-hand, face to face warfare. The techniques found in Kata came from actual battlefield experience where killing and killing quickly was necessary.

Modern masters modified the Katas to be more physically demanding and more focused on body dynamics and beauty. This allows the student to focus on defeating his most dangerous modern day opponent, himself.

Are there philosophical lessons taught and represented by the physical techniques of Kata?

Yes. The deep practice of Kata is linked to interpreting opponents and reading and understanding human beings. You must also understand the relationship between Kihon, Kata and Kumite. The mental focus and image training taught in serious Kata training will help you to anticipate the thoughts and movements of others and will bring a greater focus to your life in general. You must study this very hard for a very long time.

Shito Kai is known for the natural high stances, how this approach fits into the regular kihon training?

We practice moving from a high stance when we do drills that require you to begin from a Shizen Tai, then shift into a stance to block and counter. In this training you start from a high stance. You don't really need to practice a high stance because it's much easier than a low stance. Everything depends on the situation. You should use the appropriate stance for what is happening at the moment. In a fight, height will naturally vary. Tai Sabaki (Body Shifting) is better from a high stance because higher stances provide more mobility than low stances. Lower stances provide more stability because of their shape and the low center of gravity.

Because the situation should dictate the height of the stance, a karateka must be able to generate power from a stance of any height. Power only comes after a person is an expert at generating power from body rotation. We must understand how they make power. One can generate great power if they understand proper body dynamics. One of the most important things emphasize is pushing from the hips and to keep the rotation of the hips smoothly, always keeping the direction of the rotation parallel to the floor. The idea training to develop instant or instantaneous power comes through training the body with slow movements. In order to be able to develop the body so that it can accelerate, you must be able to understand how the body moves, and this understanding can be developed through slow motion training.

"The true path lies in a balance between training Karate for health, training Karate for Sport and Recreation and training Karate for Budo."

Would you please describe the concept of Kime?

Kime is the same as control; some say focus, but it is the same as control. When we punch, some muscles are for pushing and some are for pulling. If they are working at the same time, then you cannot punch. So, when punching, the pulling muscles should be relaxed to allow you to punch. If the muscles work together, then the technique will be more efficient. For me, Kime is when the muscles, tendons, ligaments and spirit, intention etc. locks for a split second. There is no waste.

When you are travelling it must be difficult to find time for your own training?

Even when I am teaching, I try to do the techniques as many times as possible, demonstrating them to the class. So, I must show strong techniques and do them correctly. O

NOBUAKI KANAZAWA

ON A GIANT'S SHOULDERS

HE IS ONE OF THE MOST ACCLAIMED YOUNG TEACHERS OF OUR TIME, NOBUAKI KANAZAWA, SON OF THE LEGENDARY MASTER HIROKAZU KANAZAWA, IS WORLDCLASS EMERGING SENSEI THAT WILL TAKE THE ART OF KARATE INTO THE FUTURE GENERATIONS. BY COMBINING THE POSITIVE ELEMENTS OF MODERN THINKING WITH THE DEEPER ASPECTS AND LESSONS OF TRADITIONAL KARATE INSTRUCTION RECEIVED FROM HIS FATHER, NOBUAKI KANAZAWA HAS TRULY TRANSFORMED HIMSELF INTO "ONE OF THE ELITE." HUMBLENESS, ACCORDING TO NOBUAKI, IS THE TRUE QUALITY OF A KARATEKA: "BEING HUMBLE MEANS HAVING AN OPEN ATTITUDE TO LEARN AND GAIN KNOWLEDGE, AND TO ENDURE SWEAT AND PAIN WHILE TRYING TO IMPROVE YOUR KARATE SKILLS. IT MEANS THINKING THAT YOU ARE STILL A BEGINNER AND STILL HAVE A LOT TO LEARN. IF YOU HAVE THAT IMPORTANT QUALITY, EVERYTHING ELSE WILL BE POSSIBLE BECAUSE YOU'VE GOT A STRONG FOUNDATION TO BUILD ON."

How long have you been practicing martial arts?

I started when I was 17 years old. Considering that my father is Hirokazu Kanazawa you would think that I should have started as soon as I could walk but my father didn't imposed the art of karate on me and I think this was a very intelligent thing to do. He allowed me to actually develop my own interest in Karate and it came in a very natural way, without pressure as a kid.

How many styles (karate or other methods) have you trained in and who were your teachers?

My college days were spent at the JKA and directed by great teachers such as Iida Toshihiko Sensei, Ogura Yasunori Sensei, Hanzaki. Yasuo Sensei. They all made sure that I was getting the right training but they were really hard on me and today I really thank them very much their time and dedication to my Karate development. They set up a very strong foundation for the rest of my evolution.

Karate Masters

"My training was normal but very hard and dedicated."

Would you tell us some interesting stories of your early days in karate?

Believe or not I really don't have interesting stories, at least no more interesting than any other practitioner could have. But obviously there were times when accidents happened and those are never fun. My training was normal but very hard and dedicated. I have been always very focused on what I was trying to accomplish in Karate.

Were you a 'natural' at karate – did the movements come easily to you?

I would like to say that I was. I believe I had some natural skill that helped me in the beginning – but if I hadn't trained every day I still wouldn't have progressed. Since I was very young I saw my father doing Karate so even as a little kid I used to play. The Karate movements were not strange to me since I had 'at home' on a daily basis. My father spent a lot of time traveling and teaching all over the world but the art of Karate perspired in everything that we had at home. So Karate has always been natural for me and from a physical point of view I can say that I have been always very athletic and that helped me in Karate training. Also physically I can say that my father had a great body for Karate and I would like to believe that I have received 'part' of this in my DNA and in my genes. Now it is up to me to work hard to be the best I can be.

How has your personal expression karate developed over the years?

I am still very young and my Karate is still growing in a physical level. I am putting all my time is improving my skills and learning not only from my father but also from every single person I met when I travel around the world. There is so much knowledge that I honestly don't see the end of the road. I don't think that there is an actual 'end' in Karate training. After you do your best for your evolution I think you reach a point when the art actually 'emerges' from inside of you. I believe that it is when one start to understand Karate as part of you as human being.

What are the most important points in your teaching methods today?

I teach Karate as an art and not only as a physical activity. Karate has many different 'slides' or aspects that can be used for many purposes; sport, education, discipline, etc. It is important to understand that not every student comes to the teacher looking for the same goals. Therefore a good instructor needs to understand how to use these different 'slices' of the art of Karate create a passion and dedication in the student and later on, start adding the other aspects in a progressive manner.

How do you manage the pressure of being Kancho Kanazawa's son?

I simply do not think about it. If I did that would be way too much pressure. Imagine being John Lennon or Elvis Presley' son and being a musician! I know that people compare me to my father but

"There is so much knowledge that I honestly don't see the end of the road."

he is a true legend of Karate, very few people can actually be next to him and hold their own. I am better off by not thinking about it and giving my best every single day, by taking his knowledge and experience and adding my own for future development.

Karate is nowadays often referred to as a sport... would you agree with this definition or is a martial art?

As I said before all the aspects of the art of Karate are important. The times are different, the society is different, our values have changed and people look for different things. We need to use Karate as a total art to help people to develop themselves. As far as myself I like to focus on Karate as a Martial Art and the development of principles of Budo.

What are the most important qualities for a student to become proficient in karate?

First of all you need to put yourself in your teacher's hands and trust him. Obey what he tells you and have confidence that that is the best for you. Once you have a total trust in your teacher, train and hard and as often as you can. Don't try to intellectualize everything you do in your training, simply train and your body will learn and eventually the technical understanding of the art will come to you.

When teaching the art of karate – what is the most important element; self-defense or sport?

For me it is Karate as Budo, therefore self-defense in my main focus when it comes to the application of karate techniques. Sport competition is important, interesting and a very good growing experience the goal as karateka for me is to have the ability to efficiently protect myself.

Kihon, Kata and Kumite, what's the proper ratio in training?

Kihon should be half of your training and then kata and finally kumite, but with a little more emphasis on kata. So I would break it down in something like 5-3-2.

Who would you like to have trained with that you have not?

Sensei Funakoshi Gichin.

How important is competition in the evolution of a karate practitioner?

Sport competition is a stepping stone and a growing experience, but you have to know how to use it properly for your further development in Karate as a martial art. You can learn a lot of things for competition and from facing other karateka that you don't know and are not your usual opponents at your dojo. Some people think that if you compete you are not doing Budo Karate but this is not correct. Many great JKA sensei were very active competitors; Sensei Mikami, Sensei Osaka, Sensei Yahara, my father, etc…all of them competed but they used competition as a part of their training and evolution in the art of Karate-do. You can compete and at the same time do real traditional karate.

How do you think practitioners can increase their understanding of the spiritual aspects of the art?

Be patient but consistent in your training. Don't think that you will have an understanding on the deeper aspects of Karate in few years. It takes time and dedication. Understanding comes after many year of training and a patient spirit. As years pass, you will understand the simplicity of the philosophy of Karate. When we start we want to learn a lot of techniques and kata but after many years you find yourself trying to master the basic and just a small number of katas. You realize that 'less is more' when you reach a certain level of understanding, It is all about quality training and quality knowledge.

Is there anything lacking in the way martial arts are taught today?

Courtesy and respect. Respect brigs courtesy and how we approach things in life and training. When you respect your teacher, your dojo and your senpai and kohai, you act in a 'classy' way. You are an example. But this affects all things and areas of your life. I don't like some of this important things being lost in Karate and life. These days young people lack courtesy.... we are in times where there is a collapse in manners in young people. Respectful, courteous and well-mannered individuals are important for our modern society and traditional Martial Arts teach these qualities.

Do you feel that you still have further to go in your studies?

Absolutely! Karate is a life-long journey, you only stop when you die.

"We need to use Karate as a total art to help people to develop themselves."

In my mind, I feel that I'm just beginning – that I'm still growing and learning and developing.

As a teacher, I have to be able of explaining clearly the principles of techniques of the art in a way that people can understand. I see teaching as an art within an art! You have something inside you, which you know, and your goal is to get another person to know what you know and do what you do. For me this is an art!

What advice would you give to students on the question of supplementary training?

From a Budo point of view, if you want to be good at Karate, practice

Karate Masters

"Karate has many different 'slides' or aspects that can be used for many purposes; sport, education, discipline, etc."

Karate. Period. But from a physical conditioning perspective, do running for your cardio and heart, do weight training or resistance training for your muscles and stretch for limberness.

It is interesting to notice that when we are young we have strength, good resistance and some degree of flexibility and limberness. I believe at the time, Karate training should be 90% of your training. Your body will get stronger simply with Karate practice. Later on, when we get older, we lose our cardiovascular resistance, the strength in our muscles and the flexibility in our limbs. Then we need to dedicate more time to the physical part of out training to keep the body healthy...and that also implies a good diet and a correct nutrition. Don't forget we are what we eat.

Why is it, in your opinion, that a lot of students start falling away after a couple of years of training?

I think it is a lack of understanding of what Karate training is all about. I think they come with the wrong idea of what Karate is and represents and when one or two years pass, and they are not seeing their 'goal' close at a hand reach...they lose motivation and decide to leave. They realize that what they were looking for they wont find in in a karate dojo. Also let's not forget that some may join a dojo just for physical exercise and Karate is much more than that and requires a deeper and more profound dedication than an Aerobics class.

Have been times when you felt fear in your training?

Yes, many times, specially at College. The senpai were very hard on us and the kumite training was really tough. In the beginning you don't have a lot of technical resources so your techniques are limited. The senpai test your spirit not your body. They know that you can't do much because of your limited training but the spirit has to be built and that why they push you and push you extremely hard. And this sessions may be a little bit scary depending of the level of pressure in training.

What are your views on kata bunkai?

It is important to understand the meaning and the significance of the kata because it is part of our tradition and there are many important principles and knowledge in these 'time capsules'. The application of the movements obviously is important but we need to understand that 'bunkai' has different levels and the depth of it will depend of the practitioner's level of understanding and experience in Karate.

What is your idea about incorporating kata from other styles [shito and goju] in Shotokan Karate?

My father incorporated kata from Shito and Goju in our curriculum. Shito kata uses small and short movements that are very effective, very natural. Goju uses a 'closed' approach to positions and movements that we don't have in Shotokan. Our style, Shotokan, uses long and wide movements, so I think the combinations of these three different concepts of hot to use the body and the physical techniques is very positive. They provide different approaches to the use of the body that are al beneficial for the karateka.

What are your thoughts about doing thousands of repetitions of one single technique in training as in the old days? Is it a good training method?

It is important to remember that without hard training and constant dedication we simply can't master the Karate techniques. It takes a strong spirit to do 1,000 repetitions of a punch or a kick but at the same time we have to be reasonable in our training. This type of training is good for the spirit and when you are young but when you get older you have to be careful with your joints and quality is more important than quantity.

How do you think the splits have impacted in the Shotokan style of Karate around the world?

In the vocabulary of traditional Martial Arts we have the principle of "Shu" (To protect and obey), "Ha" (To break or diverge) and "Ri" (To depart or leave). Shu means to keep teacher' spirits and lessons; Ha means to master the teacher's doctrine with strong disciple and total dedication. And Ri means create and establish our own way through those lesson and teachings from our Sensei.

In this sense, I can understand and approve those different 'paths' but if those are based on politics and self-interests, then it is regrettable behavior and I don't agree with it.

How do you see the art SKIF evolving in the future?
The SKIF's objectives are diverse and involves friendship and brotherhood between all its members regardless their nationality. We want to feel like a family and this is being accomplished by Karate training. SKIF is pursuing the spiritual aspects of Karate and the harmony amongst all its practitioners.

How important Dojo Kun is to the art of Karate-do?
I would like to say that Dojo Kun is the foundation and essence of traditional Karate training. It gives us the principles that we should follow in and out the Dojo. It teaches how to perfect out character and how to become better human beings. Dojo Kun is not about Karate but about life. A lot of Karate schools do not do Dojo Kun and that I think it is not good. Dojo Kun is good for everybody.

What karate can offer to the individual in these troubled times we are living in?
Traditional Karate teaches patience, courtesy and strong spirit. All these are very important to become a good human being.

After so many years of training, what is it for you that is so appealing in this style of karate and why?
Its dynamism. I think Shotokan is a very dynamic and powerful style of Karate.

How do you like to train yourself? Has this changed over the years?
Yes, it has changed and changes according to my age and I know that it will change as my body changes. That's normal and it is the way it should be. Your personal training has to fit you body and your physical limitations and potential.

How do you see your own karate as opposed to say ten or fifteen years ago?
I don't think that it will be a big change from a physical point of view but I am sure that from a spiritual and mental approach I will be different.

"Sport competition is a stepping stone and a growing experience, but you have to know how to use it properly for your further development in Karate as a martial art."

What advice would you give to an instructor who is struggling with his or her won development?

I would recommend them to keep the tradition of Karate preserving the Dojo Kun and to train hard in Kihon, the essence of Karate technique.

Finally, what advise would you like to give to all Karate practitioners and martial artists in general?

Listen to your Sensei and give your best effort in every training session. O

PASCAL LECOURT

POINTING NORTH

PASCAL LECOURT IS ONE OF THE LATE SENSEI TAIJI KASE'S MOST DEDICATED AND LOYAL PROTÉGÉS. FOR MORE THAN 30 YEARS, HE FOLLOWED HIS TEACHER AND WAS COMMITTED TO FOLLOWING THE 'KASE' WAY OF SHOTOKAN KARATE-DO. IN 2004 HOWEVER, SENSEI KASE PASSED AWAY AND SENSEI LECOURT REMEMBER THE LAST MOMENTS NEXT TO HIS MASTER: 'I ACCOMPANIED MY SENSEI IN HIS DEATH, I ATTENDED HIS LAST BREATH AND I TOOK HIS HAND AS HE LEFT FOR THE AFTERLIFE, MAKING HIM THE OATH TO FORWARD HIS WORK UNTIL MY LAST BREATH'.

AT AGE 26 SENSEI KASÉ SAID TO HIM: "PASCAL, SINCE WHEN YOU TRAIN?" AND HE SAID: "10 YEARS SENSEI" AND HE ANSWERED ME "I SEE, IF YOU CONTINUE TO TRAIN LIKE THAT, YOU WILL STOP IN NEXT FIVE YEARS". THIS WAS LIKE A BOMB... AN EXPLOSION IN PASCAL LECOURT MIND. "HE WAS RIGHT" LECOURT SAYS, "BECAUSE A FEW YEARS LATER I HAD A LOT OF PHYSICAL PROBLEMS WITH MY KNEES, SPINE AND LIGAMENTS. SO I STARTED TRAINING DIFFERENTLY, WITH GREATER FLUIDITY. SO I COULD BE FASTER AND MORE POWERFUL WITHOUT RISK TO MY BODY. I CHANGED 'MY' APPROACH TO KARATE."

THROUGH MANY YEARS, SENSEI LECOURT DEDICATED HIMSELF TO TRAIN UNDER MASTER KASE AND GATHER AS MUCH AS KNOWLEDGE HE COULD. SEMINARS, PRIVATE TRAINING SESSIONS, TRIPS TO JAPAN TO STAY WITH SENSEI KASE IN HIS LITTLE DOJO, ETC BECAME THE 'TOOLS' USED TO ABSORB AS MUCH AS KARATE HE COULD FROM ONE OF THE LEGENDARY TEACHER OF OUR TIME.

TODAY SENSEI PASCAL LECOURT IS WORKING TIRELESSLY TO FURTHER DEVELOP AND PROMOTE THE TEACHINGS OF MASTER KASE.

How long have you been practicing karate and who was your teacher?

I started karate in 1975, so I am in my 39th year. My first teacher was Sensei Gerald Dumont, himself a student of Sensei Kase. Sensei Dumont remained a year in my town and then moved to the West of France. I naturally turned to Seminars Sensei Kase used to give two to three times per month across France and then following him all over Europe.

Karate Masters

"The Kase Ha School is primarily characterized by a freer style in its expression, which is why the "fudo-dashi" is the reference position of our style."

How many styles have you trained in? Do you practice any other art in conjunction with karate?

Before starting karate I practiced judo for several years and later kyudo for a decade. Today, I practice karate only, because I consider it takes a lifetime of practice to understand the essence of art, I want to stay focused on the path of Karate Do Shotokan Ryu Kase Ha.

Would you tell us some interesting stories of your early days in karate?

During one of my first training with Sensei Kase, I was a white belt then, I saw one of the assistants of the master, breaking a makiwara with one gyaku-tsuki. I was 16 and I thought then that karate was all I wanted to do and nothing else ... Then Master Kase demonstrated with one of the highest level students there and all were trembling at the idea of being in front of him, because he could be unpredictable and so powerful. I was a teenager and therefore without financial resources, but I always found with my companions, a solution to travel hundreds of kilometers and participate in Seminars with Master Kase. Sometimes "hitchhiking" too! At first we had a tent, then we arranged a van to be able to eat and sleep even in winter. Nothing could stop us! It was the beginning of a long journey that I will start again if it was necessary!

Were you a 'natural' at karate – did the movements come easily to you?

I was an impulsive teenager and not very flexible. My body was not very willing to adapt to the techniques of karate. So I had to work a long time to relax my body and mind. Sensei Kase in 1989, while I was in his home in Japan, laughed at me about my inability to do what he asked me to in private lessons, in his personal little dojo. But I did my best, but his advice has pushed me to reconsider my practice.

Please, explain for us the main points of Kase-Ha and its differences with other styles like JKA Shotokan, Shito Ryu or Goju Ryu?

The Kase Ha School is primarily characterized by a freer style in its expression, which is why the "fudo-dashi" is the reference position of our style; it is powerful, low, fluid and free, allowing stability and perfect body control. He thought it was a better position for fast moving in all directions because we don't stretch our back leg and we are ready to move all around ourselves. Moreover we can be able to push down our center of gravity more carefully than Zenkutsu Dachi. Fudo Dachi is a free position without physical restraint. Energy flowing more easily through the entire body. Sensei Kase developed techniques with open hands, both defensive and offensive, based on the use of Katana "school of two swords" from Miyamoto Musashi. Our school also offers four major respiratory principles themselves broken down into different options. The Hente (attacks and defenses of the same arm) and different angles of blockages or different principles of "timing" in action amending the intervention or initiative in different contexts or kumite approaches, are typical of our school. The circular movements (Tai No Sen) are among the main principles of the Kase Ha Shotokan Ryu Karate Do. All degrees of rotation, pivot forward or backwards are studied, giving access to a full control of the space around us. Master Kase had a unique way of treating kata, including his study different aspects: "Omote, Ura, Go and Go Ura" and various application systems: Bunkai, Bunkai Kumite, Oyo and Oyo Kumite. He always insisted on rooting in the ground and he wanted for us to always have the back heel in contact with the ground. "Take energy from the universe and keep contact with the ground, be fast and strong and still have deep technique". The energy and spirit of determination, essential in Budo as in everyday life, are the main roots of school of Sensei Kase.

Please tell us a little about your relationship with your teacher Sensei Taiji Kase?

I stayed alongside Kase Sensei from 1975 until his death in 2004. Very early he asked me to participate in the demonstrations during trainings he did. I considered him as a father, and his invitation in 1989 to spend a few days with him and his family, allowed me to discover in part the man he was, beyond the Master I knew. Throughout my life he was a reference, as Master of course, but also as a man.

There was a moment after the death of Nakayama Sensei that many people look at Sensei Kase as the new leader of the JKA. What happened?

I really don't know because I was very young but in 1985 in Japan, when I asked him if he would become the head of the JKA, he looked at me with an amused smile and he said that if he took that position, he should exchange his kimono for a pen!

How do you remember him?

I remember him as a good man, listening to others, patient and tolerant. He loved people and regarded his students as his children. He often said that we were his family ... Each stage with him was a source of inspiration and motivation. They were moments of great intensity and happiness. Even if sometimes, because the fatigue or for financial reasons, I had difficulties getting to training, to see him give me the energy to continue going forward. During some seminars he asked me to demonstrate exercises that he proposed, which allowed me to show my loyalty and gratitude. I wanted him to be satisfied with my demonstrations. Each course was an unforgettable experience and an important lesson that is engraved in me as an indelible imprint. He was truly a free man. He wanted above all to convey the story of his art and his research but without political concessions. The legacy of a master is the transmission of his school and his research. That's why he left all official organization, and created his own academy. The person who can speak more deeply of him is, of course his wife. Ms. Chieko Kase.

Karate is nowadays often referred to as a sport… would you agree with this definition or is a martial art and what it was Sensei Kase's perception of the sportive aspect of Karate?

What is defines a sport? Is it the technical or the spirit which animates it? Kyudo, Aikido, Iaido and others, cannot be sports, because they rely on the spirit of Budo, a lifestyle that connects people and not in a spirit of competition. Karate can be practiced as a sport or an art. But I think that these two approaches are not mutually exclusive. Many practitioners have to first practice as a sport and then, over time turned to the research of the art. Sensei Kase said that the competition is technically and mentally reductive. Technically because very few techniques are used, and mentally, because the protections and especially the rules, alter the approach of the element of fighting.

What are the most important qualities for a student to become proficient in Sensei Kase method of karate?

Perseverance in the effort, patience, selflessness, openness, humility and sincerity.

As a teacher of the art of karate – what is the most important element of your teachings?

The respect of the different steps or phases that all students must pass in their progress, without haste, because each of them at a different rhythms which are a function of age, morphology and personality, but with serious discipline.

Kihon, Kata and Kumite, what's the proper ratio in training?

For me, the training of these three themes should be equal. Each is important and interacting with the other two, inseparable. The harmony of three reveals the entire practice.

How has your personal expression karate has developed over the years and what is it that keeps you motivated after all these years?

"What is defines a sport? Is it the technical or the spirit which animates it?"

My motivation is intact. I would say it is enhanced with the passing of the years. Exploring for nearly 40 years the richness of this art, I discovered its benefits on my personality, but also that of my students. I teach in many countries in Europe and elsewhere in the world and I can say that across cultures, the personality of all everyone is enriched by the practice of Karate. As an unstable and impulsive teenager, I grew up and became capable to controlling the bulk of my being and my life and destiny, and it is a privilege that I wish everyone.

How important is competition in the evolution of a karate practitioner?

I'm not sure that competition is essential in the development of a practitioner. The competition must be considered a game, nothing more. There is therefore, in my view, no practical impact in the Art as such.

What really means "Ikken Hissatsu" and how it applies when used in Kase-ha Karate?

"Ikken Hissatsu" means defeating or killing in one hit. To achieve it, we must bring together various principles such as the speed, power, accuracy, and a willingness to strike beyond the impact, called "Atobaya" and expressed physically by the depth of movement beyond form. All these features are worked in the school Kase-Ha. The karate of Sensei Kase was influenced by the art of the samurai sword, it comes from the history of feudal Japan and his karate is very different to the modern karate as practiced in the JKA. This practice requires of us the power and spirit, as he said "to kill an enemy with a single attack or break those of our opponent by a single block." We see here that the sport aspect of karate, of Sensei Kase is far from what is practiced today in most schools of karate.

How do you see the art of Karate evolve in the future?

Traditions are the roots of our civilization. They often remain confidential, but essential to the stability of the world. The whole evolution of humanity is based on these foundations. This is why I do not see changes in the future, but continuity.

Do you feel that you still have further to go in your studies?

Yes! Sensei Kase said: "Karate is for a lifetime." Life is not over, practice, research and progression remain my goal ... When the body loses his youth, we must turn to a more internal practice. But the time is not coming yet for me, and my body still needs to develop and use its energy!

What advice would you give to students on the question of supplementary training?

Karate is a great wealth and contrary to other practices it is very complete. I do not think there's any additional training to have. However, I would say it is necessary to have regular and balanced training program, daily in the dojo, but also seminars and personal training. These three forms of combined training are essential to fully explore our art.

What advice would you give to the instructors whom are struggling with their own development?

Our students progress constantly. The instructor must always evolve too. A true teacher cannot stop their progression, He shall be in search of his own development. My advice to them would be to continue their practice with sincerity and honesty with their research. His determination and passion for teaching must be strong and intact. And humility is the requirement to transmit with sincerity.

Have been times when you felt fear in your training?

Sincerity in realistic training environment leads inevitably to a feeling of fear. But it is through this kind of emotion that we learn about ourselves, our personality and to improve our behavior. Fear can be useful when tamed and controlled. Anyone who is never afraid is dangerous to himself.

Do you think that Olympics will be positive for the art of karate-do?
Probably one day, karate will become Olympic. The traditional karate as Budo will become a little more confidential and personal then. But the media will be more important and there will have much more students in the dojos.

What are your views on kata bunkai? Is it bunkai really important?
It would probably take me many pages to talk about the importance of bunkai! There are actually different types of applications and different steps that are the result and mark the progression of the practitioner: bunkai, bunkai kumite, oyo and oyo kumite which is the ultimate expression. And the large variety of options that explain each theme of each kata, enriches the understanding of the practitioner. Without forgetting the training to omote, ura, go and go ura, that facilitate and justify the applications, and they are essential in the practice of karate.

How important is for a Kase-ha Shotokan practitioner to know all the Kata of the style?
The extent of the knowledge acquired through all kata and different ways to study, make that all kata are indispensable. They bring together all the techniques employed and allow to the practitioners to study all. Master Kase has also created others, as the "Heian Oyo" kata, which is the synthesis of the all Heian kata.

How do you like to train yourself? Has this changed over the years?
When I was young I was looking for strength, but I was too slow, I then had to work the speed, but I lost strength. I realized that I was too contracted and stiff, which slowed me and brought me a relative strength. Then when I got older, I could not work under constant tension. So I searched the flow and availability of the body, freedom techniques to find technical spontaneous vibration. And it is through the work of the hips, the internal energy, breath, I focused my training. Anything that helps to release the tension became my daily work, my research and teaching...

Shotokan, Shito Ryu, Goju, Ryu etc...How do you think the different styles affect the complete art of Karate?
Styles exist in their specificity and the interest they generate. I think that in all things, diversity is an asset, it does not affect the art in any case, I

think on the contrary, it enriches it. This is the case in the art of painting, floral art, music, etc.... I am convinced that the arts have the interest it generates by the different approach they propose.

Do you think Kobudo training is beneficial for a Karate practitioners in general?

There are similarities in the techniques of Karate and Kobudo, which can be complementary. Budo practitioners often have a look interested in other close martial arts. However, when I was practicing Kyudo, and at my request, Master Kase told me one day that two arts can be compatible only when they develop different energies. Internal for one, and external for the other.

What is your opinion about the "Shobu Ippon" division in Karate competition?

Before to be a game, karate is a fighting art, and "Shobu Ippon" reflects the fighting spirit. I think it is very unfortunate to move away a little more of the values of our art, forgetting that originally, one blow would be fatal. But competitive sport is generally deaf to traditional values in favor of the media.

What are the most important points in your personal training these days?

The work of breathing is essential in my practice, it often reflects our feelings, expressing our determination, our energies and frees our tensions ... Shortly before his death, Master Kase sensitized me to pursue this research, he spoke also very often during internships, private trainings and seminars. But I also have different forms of training on the mechanisms of the hips and repercussions in the techniques and movements. And this particular research on what Master Kase called "Ten-Shi-Jin" and the fusion it generates...it really fascinates me.

What karate can offer to the individual in these troubled times we are living in?

Now you know that karate Kase-Ha is an access to the energy development. This is the spirit of determination, willing and passion that lead to this research, and it is in my opinion, what the individual needs to believe in his destiny and will achieve its objectives. Life is a battle that must be won, and this is not a game, this is our reality and we need to develop and believe in our strength to rise to the hope that this 'energy' is the key to our success.

After so many years of training, what is it for you that is so appealing in Kase-ha Shotokan and why?

A lot of things, but I'd say, the emotion from our body, transmitted through the techniques and through it, our history, our roots and what our human existence wants to express. Also the quest for a "bright, intelligent" karate, I mean constantly changing. The "Fudoshin" the harmony of body and spirit which makes it a real Art... and so much more!

Finally, what advice would you like to give to all Karate practitioners?

Continue the practice, whatever happens! Sensei Kase said: 'Karate... that's life, life is karate." So we have to think of "karate for a lifetime" to discover all the intricacies of this art so rigorous, but so exciting and so rich, which leads man to the depths of his being and the quest to find himself. Kase Ha Karate-do is more than a sport, it's a lifestyle. There is a little of Sensei Kase in each one of his students! O

"Karate is a great wealth and contrary to other practices it is very complete. I do not think there's any additional training to have."

JIM MATHER

A TRUE GIFT

JIM MATHER IS RECOGNIZED AS ONE OF THE WORLD'S LEADING KARATE-DO EXPERTS. HE HAS DEVOTED MORE THAN FOUR DECADES TO PERFECTING AND TEACHING THE MARTIAL ARTS AND IS ONE OF ONLY A SMALL NUMBER OF MARTIAL ARTISTS IN THE WORLD TO BE AWARDED THE TITLE OF "HANSHI", WHICH IS THE HIGHEST IN KARATE.

FORMER NATIONAL KARATE CHAMPION, SENSEI MATHER HAS GONE ON TO BECOME ONE OF THE COUNTRY'S TOP COACHES. HE WAS SELECTED AS ONE OF ONLY THREE MARTIAL ARTISTS IN THE COUNTRY WHO WERE ALLOWED TO TRAIN THE OFFICIAL UNITED STATES NATIONAL KARATE TEAM AT THE UNITED STATES OLYMPIC TRAINING CENTER (USOTC) IN COLORADO SPRINGS. AS A NATIONAL COACH, HE HAS LED THE OFFICIAL UNITED STATE KARATE TEAM IN HIGH-LEVEL INTERNATIONAL COMPETITION. MANY OF HIS STUDENTS HAVE BEEN SELECTED TO REPRESENT THE UNITED STATES AT MANY SUCH EVENTS.

IN KEEPING WITH TRUE JAPANESE MARTIAL ARTS TRADITION, HIS QUEST FOR PHYSICAL MASTERY HAS GONE HAND-IN-HAND WITH HIS PURSUIT OF INTELLECTUAL EXCELLENCE. SENSEI JIM MATHER CONTINUES TO TEACH AT HIS DOJO. HIS LOVE OF THE MARTIAL ARTS IS AS STRONG AS EVER.

How long have you been practicing karate?
I started in 1955 so it's been over six decades.

How many styles have you trained in and who were your teachers?
My first instructor (more like a workout partner) was a Shotokan black belt and San Jose State College grad student. When he returned to Japan, the only martial arts instruction available was in judo and jujitsu. So I trained at Pacific Judo Academy under a great sensei, Bill Montero, who had been a student of the legendary Henry Okazaki, trainer of Wally Jay, Sig Kufferath, and Willy Cahill. A few months later, Sensei Montero introduced a young Hawaiian kenpo instructor, Sam Brown, at one of our classes. I trained with him for a couple of years before joining the Army. While in the service, I trained briefly with a bunch of other people, whoever was teaching on whichever base I was assigned. I spent my last 13

Karate Masters

"My karate life has passed through many significant stages, each contributing towards forming my present philosophy."

months of military service in Korea, where I trained in old style taekwondo (which was more like Shotokan back then) and kung fu. I met Soke Takayuki Kubota after I returned to the States. He became my primary life-time teacher and mentor.

In the 80s, I was named one of the national coaches and co-chair of the National Coaches Education Committee for the USAKF, then the national governing body (NGB) for karate under the U.S. Olympic Committee. Through my various positions and close friendship with USAKF head/WUKO 1st VP George Anderson, I learned a huge amount. And it opened many doors of opportunity around the world, enabling me to train with pretty much anyone I wanted – and I took advantage of it. I also had many friends in a variety of arts and styles over the years, including some great Chinese and Filipino martial artists such as Brendan Lai, Jimmy Yim Lee, Bruce Lee, Angel Cabales, and Al Dacascos. I also studied judo and jujitsu from Montero, Tamura, and Kitaura along the way. Plus, I'm very fortunate to have Dan Smith as a friend. He took me to Okinawa twice and opened many doors there. He and I still communicate regularly. Those trips were extremely enlightening and I hope to do more in the future. I traveled a lot at one time with both Takayuki Mikami and Osamu Ozawa and was able to tap their long histories and participation in the early formation of karate in Japan. We share information and video clips, so I'm essentially now learning from many more people. The amount of information within the martial arts is almost infinite and almost everyone who's spent any length of time in them has something to offer, something I could benefit from learning, and I've always tried to take advantage of it. So I've learned from many, many people, including some who thought they were learning from me.

Would you tell us some interesting stories of your early days in karate?

I met Soke Kubota and two of his students, Tonny Tulleners and John Gehlsen, in 1965 at Parker's International Championships in Long Beach. John and Soke did a short demonstration for the instructors that afternoon in the basement of the old LaFayette Hotel, Ed's tournament headquarters back then. Then, Soke also performed a longer demo that night during the finals. He did the thing where he beat his hands and shins with a sledgehammer. Then, he sparred with three finalists from black belt division, individually and then all three at once. It was very impressive – not just his skill but that he had no problem putting it all on the line, while others did well-rehearsed self-defense or kata demos. Tonny won his division. I don't know how John did as he was only a green belt at the time. When I hosted the United States Winter Karate Championships in San Jose in February of 1966, I invited Soke to demonstrate. He came and brought John with him. Chuck Norris drove up with Chris Wells and one of his other students. I asked a young, unknown kung fu friend, Bruce Lee, to demonstrate, which he did. Chuck won the Grand Championship, his first I think, defeating Roy Castro, Ralph's brother, in a great match.

When I first began training with Soke Kubota, his Hollywood dojo was an apartment above a Russian restaurant on Vine Street, if I remember right. I was a black belt and ran my own dojo but wore a white belt when I started training with Soke as I wasn't a black belt at the time with him. Anyway, my first class was what they called their Kamikaze Class, teen-aged Japanese brown belts. We sparred near the end, probably as a test for me. I beat the first one. The next one was more determined not to be beaten by a white belt. But I beat him too. I went up the line, each one attacking harder and harder, fighting for dojo honor. But I lost to none of them. After class, we were getting dressed in the changing room. They all keep looking over at me but I ignored them. Finally one asked "How long have you been doing karate, anyway?" I told him several years. There was this great sign of relief. He said "Man, I thought you were the toughest white belt I ever saw." After that, Soke told me to wear my black belt.

Were you a 'natural' at karate – did the movements come easily to you?

I had always been athletic and picked up physical things quickly. But I found karate to be more challenging, much more complex and possessing more depth and breadth, than anything I had undertaken before. It was clear right from the start that it couldn't be mastered easily or quickly. It was this, never feeling I had it mastered, which has kept me happily struggling with it for over 55 years.

Karate Masters

How your personal expression karate has developed over the years and what is it that keeps you motivated after all these years?

My karate life has passed through many significant stages, each contributing towards forming my present philosophy. When I was young, all I wanted to do was spar. It kept my eye sharp and my reflexes finely honed. We had a saying back then, "Those who can, spar. Those who can't, do kata." But as I got older, I came to see the value of kata and why the old masters held them in such high regard – and thankfully left them so their voices can still instruct us today.

As I moved through each of these stages, I didn't discard any of what I had learned along the way. I just expanded the list – put more tools into my martial toolbox.

I practiced only Shotokan and Gosoku kata back then. Soke Kubota developed several unique kata – such as Tamashii, Denko Getsu, Rikyu, etc. – that contain very quick ashi and tai sabaki and unique defense that carries directly over into fighting. The Shotokan kata have become more refined over time, more precise. But back then, their actions were still large and full powered. Sensei Nakayama likened them to the explosion of a hand grenade – in a split second things go from nothing to bone crushing, brick breaking power. And I liked that. Hit and penetrate, regardless of what an opponent might try to put between you and your target. Go through their blocks, breaking their arms if necessary, penetrating their natural body defenses, like muscles and bones, and damage internal organs. That, to me, was karate.

Whereas the Gosoku kata were very practically oriented, the Shotokan bunkai back then was always a little suspect – spear hands to the solar plexus, and such, stuff you'd never use in a real fight. When I was flying back from the WUKO Championships in Cairo, Egypt, in 1988, I was fortunate to be seated next to the legendary Takayuki Mikami. I was soon named one of the U.S. coaches and traveled often with him, as he was senior coach. He told me there wasn't any real bunkai in Shotokan kata at that time, that to learn the true bunkai I'd have to look to Shorin Ryu or jujitsu, which I did.

My experiences as one of the national coaches opened many doors, allowing me to study with pretty much whoever I wanted. Dan Smith took me to Okinawa twice in the early 90s. As I mentioned earlier, it was eye-opening. As a former student of Zenryo Shimabukuro and Shinpo Matayoshi and still an active student of Zenpo Shimabukuro, he opened doors for me to train with whoever I wanted on the island. They were great experiences. I also learned a huge amount from George Anderson, who was a great friend and mentor.

All of this expanded my knowledge and contributed towards forming what I practice and teach today.

What are the most important points in your teaching methods today?

My teaching methods evolved over 50 years of teaching karate plus what I picked up while working on my M.A. then PhD degree in Education at Stanford. But I think the single most important point is seeing students as the treasures they are. What greater gift or responsibility could we possibly be given than having people put their trust in us? Each student is unique and possesses sometimes very different strengths and weaknesses.

"My experiences as one of the national coaches opened many doors, allowing me to study with pretty much whoever I wanted."

So I approach each differently. My first goal is to get to know each student well enough to determine the instructional approach best suited to their individual nature. A teacher is one who teaches. If a teacher can't instill knowledge in his students, then by definition, they are not a teacher. So I feel a responsibility to find a way to get through to each student.

I generally begin new students in a less structured manner, leading them patiently, overlooking misbehavior, but tightening things up as I go. Many who come to karate lack stick-to-itness so if I attempted to apply traditional etiquette and discipline at the start, most would quit, especially those who most needed what we have to teach them. As a result, I begin by instilling in them value for what they are learning, pride in themselves and their progress, and hopefully a desire to do what is necessary to advance further, while also teaching them basic kihon. Then, I become far more firm and advance them in the traditional manner.

Karate Masters

"A teacher is one who teaches. If a teacher can't instill knowledge in his students, then by definition, they are not a teacher."

What is opinion of fighting events such as the UFC and Mixed Martial Arts events?

I don't watch much of it. But I can appreciate what they are doing, especially their strength, stamina, grappling skill, and tamashi. I think they've made contributions to the more traditional martial arts by making us more aware of their entering techniques and the need to cover grappling techniques and defense in our curriculum.

Karate is nowadays often referred to as a sport... would you agree with this definition or is a martial art?

Karate can be modified and practiced as a sport. But that is only one aspect of it, and a small one. One of the great things about karate is its potential to be practiced for any of a large variety of reasons. It can be something people study as a competitive sport but more often for self defense, self betterment, physical fitness, philosophy, and so on. I can't think of any other activity that offers as wide a range of physical benefits – strength, speed, balance, flexibility, and so on. Perhaps only gymnastics and ballet offer anywhere near as many. But when you add the mental and spiritual benefits – self discipline, self control, self confidence, self actualization, and so on – gained through both instruction and the difficulty of the journey, nothing else comes even close, and takes it far beyond a mere sport.

What are the most important qualities for a student to become proficient in karate?

The most important is perseverance. They once asked a Nobel Prize winner what it felt like to be the smartest guy in the world. He said he was far from the smartest guy. There were, according to him, many smarter within his field. How, then, did he explain why he won the Nobel Prize and one of the others didn't? He replied that it was because he had persevered in the face of adversity longer than the others. He said his win might even be due to him being stupider than the others, not being smart enough to know when to quit. Few of my students over the years who came into karate with great natural talent went anywhere near as far as they could have. It was the pluggers – those who persevered – who went the furthest.

When teaching the art of karate – what is the most important element; self-defense or sport?

Self defense. Even when I was one of the national coaches, I seldom trained my personal students for sport. Maybe I would have been a better coach, although surely a worse instructor, if I had spent more time teaching them how to play tag. But my teacher trained some great competitors – John Gehlsen, Tonny Tulleners, Val Mijailovic, Boban Petkovich, George Byrd, and others, all members of the national team – and never taught tournament type sparring in the dojo. Tonny easily beat Chuck Norris three out of three times, when Chuck was at the top of his game, and tied for third with Dominique Va era at the first WUKO World Karate Championships in Tokyo in 1970. I can't remember anyone ever stopping the action at Soke's dojo and awarding points. Most of his students in the early days, including Tonny and John, were cops, FBI agents, undercover narcotic agents, Secret Service, and so on. On the street, you hit someone in a serious fight and they try to hit you back. So you can never hit and relax. You hit and defend, then hit again. That's life and that's how training has to be. You also never give up the first point on the street as it may be all you get. While all this helps in the ring, tag type competitive sparring seldom translates well to the street against tough opponents.

Close fighting techniques were always a part of our training as fights often end up at that range. So Soke worked us extensively on elbows, knees, headbutts, take downs, sweeps, attacks to vulnerable points, and so on. Having trained directly under Kanken Toyama, Soke understood all of this from the start. Plus, his father was a high level jujitsu master, specializing in taiho jitsu. He trained the Kumamoto police. So he was also very expert in grappling and joint locks. Sparring at his dojo was always very tough. It could probably be classified as closer to semi-contact than non-contact. We were supposed to control our techniques but it often didn't happen. So you always fought with that in mind. Soke always said "Little touch okay" but never explained exactly what that meant. "Little" definitely included a far wider interpretation than most would have made. But the upside was you learned to protect yourself.

Karate Masters

Kihon, Kata and Kumite, what's the proper ratio in training?

Kihon is critical as it's the basic building blocks from which everything else is constructed. Correct form in the execution of our kicks, punches, strikes, and blocks not only enables us to deliver maximum power but to do so safely. Proper stances become the platforms from which maximally powerful techniques can be launched. Waza teaches us proper distancing and to mix and match various combinations of our kihon in rapid succession. Kata takes things even further, while teaching deeper applications of the specialized kihon for closer range fighting. Kumite teaches us to apply kihon spontaneously, training our eyes to see weaknesses in an opponent's defenses and capitalize on them, while keeping our opponents from capitalizing on our weaknesses.

Who would you like to have trained with that you have not?

I was extremely fortunate in that I was able to train with pretty much everyone I would have liked to. As one of the national coaches, Vice President of the World Students Karate Union, member of the WUKO medical committee, and so on, doors were opened to me as I traveled around the world. But there are many past masters who I would have liked to have trained with – Kanken Toyama (one of my instructor's instructors), Gichin Funakoshi, Anko Itosu, Asato, Kyan, Matsumura, Sakagawa, and a long list of others.

How important is competition in the evolution of a karate practitioner?

Knowing what to do and being able to do it in a stressful situation are two separate and unrelated things. Sparring is certainly not fighting but, especially if dojo-sparring is intense and the possibility of being injured is always present, it can help bridge some of that gap. The alternative is to get into actual fights, which is clearly unacceptable for a variety of reasons. (I had instructors in the early days who encouraged us to practice what we'd learned on the street as often as we could.)

Jacques Delcourt, George Anderson, and I stayed at the same beach house on the French island of Guadeloupe many years ago, while Delcourt was still head of WUKO. We were there for a small competition between the USA Karate Team and members of the French national team. While together one day, Delcourt and I discussed the value of competition. He felt that it helped a karateka learn to apply his techniques against another trained fighter and to gain better control of his emotions. He said in a karateka's first tournament, he is often only able to execute at perhaps 20% of his capability because of nervousness. He doesn't see openings, doesn't execute his techniques properly, etc. At the next tournament, he or she has a better idea what to expect and is a little more relaxed. So, they can now perform up to say 40% of their capability. And so on until they are approaching 100%.

Obviously, if a karateka isn't able to control his nervousness in a non-contact tournament, what will happen in a real fight, when his life could be at stake and the stress level astronomically higher? This is certainly not to say that becoming a good tournament fighter will necessarily make one a good fighter on the street. There are far too many examples of good tournament fighters getting their butts kicked on the street. But it can be useful in helping a person gain a better insight into how he will react in a real fight and to become potentially better able to function efficiently.

"Karate can be modified and practiced as a sport. But that is only one aspect of it."

What really means "Ikken Hissatsu" and how it applies when used in Karate?

I think its original meaning was the ability to kill with one strike. But I use it to mean the ability to finish a fight with a single technique, one so powerful and directed towards a body target so vulnerable that the person struck would be rendered unable to continue fighting, either temporarily or permanently.

While at Stanford, I was required to take a very intensive human anatomy class. It was taught at the Stanford Hospital and covered the same material as was taught to first year medical students. Only 12 students were allowed in the class. And it was taught by two surgeons and a PhD in Anatomy. Four students were assigned to each of the three dissection tables. The instructors rotated tables on a weekly basis, so one was with us at all times to guide us and answer any questions we had. We spent entire afternoons, five days per week, dissecting the fresh cadaver assigned to our table. It gave me a very good look at the human body. What I found was our bodies are well engineered to withstand a lot in some ways but are surprisingly fragile in other ways, when hit in the right places with the right body weapon.

How much influence you think has the Zen philosophy in the art of Karate?

Fifteen or twenty years ago, I invited writer, martial artist, and Asian scholar Thomas Cleary to speak to my senior students. Cleary had translated many famous texts, including "Book of Five Rings", "The Art of War", and many religious/spiritual texts. I asked him to discuss Zen mental concepts and their application to combat. I had read much about this subject and it always seemed each writer – Takuan, Shosan, Musashi, Yagyu, etc. – had a different view relative to its application. Plus, there was the major dilemma – Zen, and Buddhism in general, doesn't believe in taking a life. And here some of the greatest takers of life in history were using it to take even more, to become even more efficient killers. I thought maybe I was missing something. But Cleary said it wasn't my lack of understanding. Each did, in fact, have a different view as to how to apply it, or how much of it to apply. He said samurai used what he called "utilitarian Zen", taking from it what they found useful and ignoring the rest – especially the prescription against killing and other religious parts.

He believed samurai studied Zen for four reasons: 1) to "learn the secret of learning itself". 2) to free the mind from fear, doubt, and hesitation so they could act efficiently and spontaneously regardless of what they faced, even death itself. 3) to see things clearly, without any distortion from extraneous factors. And 4) to become able to "see into the future", to become more finely aware of the subtlest of signs in their opponents in order to read their intent.

Of course, Zen is only one method for acquiring emotional control and mind clearing qualities. While at Stanford, I also worked on a concurrent M.A. in Physiological Psychology and did a lot of work in developing methods for increasing mental speed. Some of the techniques I ended up with were very similar to ones traditionally practiced in Zen but with results achieved in far less time and without the religious attachments – probably much as the samurai used Zen.

Do you feel that you still have further to go in your studies?

Of course, a great deal further. There is no possible end to the things one can learn about the martial arts. It's wonderfully infinite.

What advice would you give to students on the question of supplementary training (running, weights, et cetera)?

Those things can be beneficial if one has the time these days. But I think, if taught or practiced properly, karate needs nothing additional for the average student. I've always liked natural training methods over machines, mainly because they can be practiced at home or the dojo. Having to get into your car and drive to a gym can become one more impediment to training. So I generally push natural methods, exercises one can do at home without equipment, or very basic equipment.

I was fortunate to be among those selected to work with the U.S. team at karate's first training session at the U.S. Olympic Training Center. The U.S. women's team kata team – made up of the Tang sisters (Mimi and Debbie) and Melanie Genung and coached by Kathy Jones – had been 2nd in the world for several years. So I was very interested in seeing how they prepared themselves. They were extremely disciplined in their approach. But what amazed me was their level of physical conditioning. Both the sparring and kata teams were doing three workouts per day. But the women put everyone to shame. They showed up the first morning, warmed up, and then did 150 perfect pushups in unison – backs, legs, and necks perfectly straight, dropping to one fist's distance of the floor, then up again. Then, they did the same with situps. And they repeated the same number at all three workouts that day for a total of 450 of both situps and pushups. They came back the next day and did the same. In addition, they did a good deal of cardio on the track – in the thin, 7,000 foot altitude Colorado Springs air.

What advice would you give to an instructor who is struggling with his or her own development?

Over 45 years ago, I made a conscious decision to devote my life to the study and teaching of the martial arts. I based my decision on a logical analysis of the pros and cons. I thought it good to have the constant need to stay technically and cognitively ahead of my students, to keep myself in top shape, to live my life carefully so as to always be a proper role model for my students, and so on. In return, I hoped I'd receive the gifts of being able to continue to serve a useful purpose and enjoy greater self sufficiency in my old age. In America, old is bad and new is good. Here, if a fence gets weathered, we slap an ugly coat of redwood stain on it. In Japan, they find beauty in the effect nature and the years have had on the wood. I believed that, as a martial artist, I'd become more valued as I got older – not less valued, as is the case with most senior citizens in this country. And now, I see that things have worked out exactly as I had hoped. I would recommend everyone follow a similar path.

Have been times when you felt fear in your training?

I had never really given it any thought until you posed the question. But I can't remember a time when I was afraid during training. I remember times when I was very alert and careful. There was often that guy in the dojo who kept everyone honest – the student who didn't have any control and tried to hit you with every technique he threw, regardless of what he was supposed to do. These kinds of guys are often an asset. When you're paired with them, you get a good reality check as to how things would go on the street, as they always go full bore.

I trained myself from an early age to keep totally focused on whatever I was doing, disassociating myself from pain, and not allowing emotional stuff to clutter my mind. My wife will sometimes ask me where I got a big bruise on my leg or arm or body. I can seldom remember as I didn't pay any attention to it at the time so it didn't get transferred to long term memory. When someone attacked me during sparring, I seldom thought about what they had in mind or where they intended to attack. I generally only focused on the targets they left unprotected and would attack "on motion". Now, of course, I'm much older and sen-no-sen has been replaced more and more with go-no-sen, unless I'm fighting another old guy.

Do you think that Olympics will be positive for the art of karate-do?

Only 10% at most who register at my dojo, or even contact us about lessons, have any interest whatsoever in competition. And that number seems to be dropping. So I think it would be helpful but not significantly so. I was with George Anderson when he got karate accepted into the Pan Am Games. I know what he went through to get even that. Plus, I had conversations with him and Jacques Delcourt about the Olympic movement and the manipulations and payoffs by others in the past. So I'm not holding my breath. But there are new people running the movement now, so who knows?

What are your views on kata bunkai?

Direct students of Chojin Miyagi were once asked about the bunkai for a particular kata. In their discussion, they found they had all been taught different versions. One, in fact, was never taught bunkai. Sensei Miyagi required him to come up with his own as part of his promotion requirements.

Instructors who teach for many years go through many cycles, emphasizing different areas at different times. This is natural. They also recognize that students have different body types and different physical and mental strengths and weaknesses. And the old masters surely took that into consideration as good modern ones do today.

I don't believe there is a correct bunkai. There are many correct bunkai, just as there are often several correct versions of a kata in question. "Itosu no Passai", "Matsumura no Passai", or "Oyadomari no Passai" are significantly different. Which is correct? None of us were there when the original version was created so we don't know what the originator intended or even taught.

"Kihon is critical as it's the basic building blocks from which everything else is constructed."

Some claim the bunkai is only for close fighting, for the utilization of the kyusho and tuite within the old forms, and that competitive training and the Japanese versions of the kata are useless in real situations. There seems to be sufficient evidence that the original versions of Okinawan kata did focus on close fighting techniques. Perhaps so did the Chinese kata from which they were derived. But, for me at least, that doesn't mean everything else should be discarded and declared useless. What the detractors forget is the Okinawans weren't introducing karate to the Swiss. They were adding it to the fighting arts of a nation with a very, very strong and legendary warrior tradition. I think those who claim what the Japanese contributed to be useless on the street would get a very rude awakening if they tested that theory against people like Mikio Yahara, Frank Smith, Ray Dalke, Terry O'Neill, Val Mijailovic, and many more.

I don't see it as an either/or situation. I teach my students both the close fighting kyusho and tuite and also the medium and long distance techniques. Some argue the kata bunkai wasn't intended to be used against another trained man. And perhaps that was true back then. But times change and true martial artists have always changed with it. Now, the

Karate Masters

"Zen is only one method for acquiring emotional control and mind clearing qualities."

probability of running into another trained fighter on the street is higher than not. So I think it's all good – close, medium, and long range applications – as long as we always keep riai in mind, that they be realistic and effective responses to realistic attack scenarios.

What are your ideas to improve judging and referring in Karate competitions and what are the main problems you see in sport karate referring these days?

I haven't been to a tournament in a few years. But I competed in many and attended hundreds over the years and I'd imagine the problems haven't changed. Hanshi Anderson, former head of the WUKO Referees Committee, said the greatest sin an official can commit is allowing the outcome to be incorrect – for someone other than the best man or woman to win. The best person must take first, the second best take second, and so on down the line. You also don't want anything other than the actual fighting to affect the outcome – such as the officials stopping a match too often or too quickly, throwing off the strategy of a competitor. You don't want competitors feigning injury or exiting the ring to buy time or prevent a valid technique from being recognized. You don't want coaches, competitors, and parents attempting to intimidate or sway the officials, etc. The officials and the event organizers must establish protocols to prevent any of these.

Another problem was officials calling techniques they couldn't possibly have seen unless they had x-ray vision. If their views are blocked, so they can't actually see if a technique is on target or within range at the end, they can't call it. In the old day, we took the position that when in doubt, don't call anything. Today, some seem to take the opposite position.

One of the things that will get me really angry is when an official repeatedly waves off good techniques because they supposedly aren't close enough, when they are, in fact, right on the money. That tells the fighter he has to bring his techniques closer still. But this often ends in him making contact. Then, the inferior official penalizes the fighter for doing what he forced him to do. Also, ai-uchi seldom happens in real life. One thing is always ahead of another. It's generally only a lack of skill, vision, or focus of an official that prevents them from being able to determine which technique was first. Sometimes they're actually too close even a good official can't make the call. But this should happen very seldom.

What are your thoughts about doing thousands of repetitions of one single technique in training as in the old days?

My master's degree from Stanford was in Motor Learning. I know of no other way to learn any complex physical skill, especially to a point where it can be applied spontaneously in a high pressure situation. They can't be learned intellectually. The reps have to be done. Too many people today mistake familiarity with mastery. They do ten or a hundred reps and think they've mastered a technique. I believe it takes a hundred just to smooth out the wrinkles in a new technique. One thousand for it to begin to have some degree of speed and power. Ten thousand to be executed somewhat automatically, with the supportive muscle groups coming into play at optimal points to generate maximum speed and power. To become world class, it could take hundreds of thousands. This is true for any physical activity. How many golf balls do you imagine Tiger Woods has hit to reach the point where he was at his peak? How many shots do you think Michael Jordan or Kobe Bryant have shot? Hundreds of thousands, perhaps millions. This doesn't just commit the action to memory but also strengthens the exact muscles and muscle groups employed, while learning to relax the antagonistic muscles, and develop proper sequencing.

Shotokan, Shito Ryu, Goju, Ryu etc...How do you think the different branches/styles affect the art of Karate?

I think they're all equally great, each moving karatedo forward in their own way. Many great minds working their entire lifetimes to find solutions and insights is far better than one. There's unfortunately a tendency for those at lower dan grades of a particular art or style to think theirs is the only way. But the highest, most knowledgeable and experienced martial artists know there are many paths to the top, not just one. This is not just restricted to the Japanese/Okinawan martial arts but also those from China, Korea, the Philippines, and so on. Those at the very top of every martial art I've ever encountered – and I've met many – all look surprisingly alike in how they generate power and execute their kihon.

Karate Masters

How do you see the art of Karate evolve in the future?

I think on whole they will proceed as they always have. There will surely be more of a blending of the lines between arts and styles as information gets shared. But this is nothing new.

One of Sensei Yamaguchi's shodans trained with me briefly many years ago. The Goju Kai organization always held closed tournaments, not allowing outsiders to compete in their events or vice versa. The shodan once asked Sensei Yamaguchi if this would ever change. He said it would. "Soon?" she asked. "Yes, soon," he responded. She was surprised so she asked how soon. "Probably in twenty years" was his response. To her look of disappointment, he added "Karate is 2,000 years old. Twenty years is nothing."

People have been attracted to the martial arts throughout the centuries as a response to the presence of the threat of violence in their environments. This hasn't diminished. In fact, the threat of violence has risen in many ways and will likely get worse over time. People are people and do the kinds of things – good and bad – that people have always done. I think the appeal of traditional dojos will rise, if we do a good enough job at educating people as to the benefits. We are all bombarded with information and demands for our time these days. As our societies become more hectic, traditional dojos offer islands of simplicity, a place where people can focus inward, an outlet for some of the rising clutter and stress in their lives. And they will become even more useful as science throws more and more gadgets at us over time.

What is your opinion about the "Shobu Ippon" division in Karate competition?

I prefer it. For me, sambon shobu and newer even worse versions break the rules of budo. One of these surely is "When you're dead, you're dead." Another is "And it doesn't matter how I kill you." I realize this is competition and they must make it acceptable to the Olympic Committee and national TV audiences. But I'm not concerned anymore with that. So I haven't much use for it as a training tool, and never did.

I don't want my students thinking it's ever okay to allow an opponent to score a couple of points on them, while they figure out how best to beat them, then coming from behind to win. That doesn't work on the street. In competition, they call them "slow starters". On the street, they call them "that guy who just got beat up". Students need to learn that everything may ride on that first technique.

What karate can offer to the individual in these troubled times we are living in?

Imagine you're a doctor in a backwards land where thousands of children are dying from a deadly disease which you could cure with a shot of antibiotics. But the people either didn't know they were sick or didn't have any faith in western medicine, thinking only a faith healer or whatever could cure them. Would you have a duty to find a way to get them to take the shot? Or would it be okay to just wash your hands of them and let them die?

Well, hundreds of thousands die each year in our own country from illnesses that could be cured with something we can give them.

Few of the almost 2.5 million who die each year from preventable causes were unaware of the risk they assumed when they chose to lead unhealthy lifestyles – smoking, eating poorly, getting insufficient exercise, abusing drugs or alcohol, and so on. They simply lacked the self discipline and self control necessary to make the right choices in life.

In the old days, children gained self discipline and self control in the home, school, and/or church. But the only place remaining in many parts of the United States today are martial arts schools – meaning us.

As such, I believe we have a duty to reach out to as many people as possible within our local communities and do whatever is necessary to get them to "take the shot", to get involved in our schools. Then, we must work equally hard to keep them there long enough to instill critically important self discipline and self control in them.

This is not in any way to downplay the value of instruction in self defense skills. In fact, we must make especially sure our young students become proficient in defending themselves. Without that ability, they are still vulnerable to potentially destructive peer pressure. But when a teenager, for example, is able to defend himself, he doesn't need the security of the group. He doesn't need to pacify his peers, to do what they want him to do in order to fit in or gain the approval or security of the group, who may lead him to drink, smoke, use drugs, join gangs, etc. His peer group should need to gain his approval, not vice versa. My teenage students have become the leaders within their peer groups, not one of the compliant followers. And since they possess the inner strength (from their self defense skill and their self discipline and self control) to make the right choices in life, they become positive role models for their peers to follow.

Wouldn't your local community become significantly better if a large percentage of your local residents were involved in your school? There would likely be huge improvements in the local fight against teen drug and alcohol problems, gangs, childhood obesity, and so on. They'd run the drug dealers and gangs out of town. So we have within our hands a life-saving gift and I personally feel an obligation to share it with as many people as possible.

After so many years of training, what is it for you that is so appealing in this style of karate and why?
I like the efficiency of it. It has a unique ashi and tai sabaki developed by Soke Kubota that offers great mobility, incorporates broken rhythm, and opens up many targets of opportunity. He is also one of our greatest tacticians. Gosoku, the name of Soke Kubota's style, means "hard and fast" and these two qualities play a significant part in his system. "Speed" applies not only to how fast you can extend a technique but also how fast you can bridge the gap between you and your opponent, or evade an attack. Also, if a technique lacks sufficient power, it's not only useless but can open you up to an immediate counterattack. Soke Kubota taught us an extremely powerful flat kick, its trajectory making it far more difficult to block or evade. We also worked on putting sufficient power in all of our techniques to break through whatever an opponent put between us and our targets and still penetrate deep enough to do serious damage. When you couple all this with Soke's unique soft and hard hand defense techniques, you have a very efficient and effective system.

How do you like to train yourself? Has this changed over the years?
You have to make adjustments as you get older. When you are young, your goal is to make progress – make yourself faster, stronger, more enduring, and so on. If you were rowing a boat, the goal of a young person is to move their position upstream, away from the falls. But when you get older, your goal becomes to hold your ground, to simply keep from going over the falls. Against the debilitating effects of advancing age, holding your position – resisting the pull of the current and that long fall – is like an improvement. So I'm more in that phase. I not only train almost daily in karate but also do a lot of hiking in Big Sur. It's beautiful country with very steep and challenging trails. So it's perfect for training at my age. I used to spar heavily in the early days. I still do, although far less frequently, and with a different focus. Now, my main goal is to assist my students eliminate weaknesses in their defense via a variety of sneaky, old guy tricks and techniques.

Do you think Kobudo training is beneficial for a Karate practitioner?

I've trained in kobudo since the early 60s. I initially added weapons to my instructional curriculum for a variety of reasons. First, there's obviously a long tradition of training in both karate and kobudo. So I taught it in order to make sure my students were able to pass this great art on to the next generation, to assist in making sure they survive. Second, each weapon requires the development of different strengths and skills. The nunchaku, for example, requires young students to gain better concentration. They move one end a little and the other end moves a lot. With the bo, they have to learn to extend their minds to the ends of a long weapon, and so on. Third, knowledge of kobudo enhances a student's self defense capabilities, enabling them to make better use of makeshift weapons found on the street during an attack. And fourth, kobudo offers students who desire to compete another option, which many have taken advantage of over the years.

"There is no possible end to the things one can learn about the martial arts. It's wonderfully infinite."

How do you see your own karate as opposed to say twenty years ago?

It's lost in speed and flexibility but gained in breadth and depth of knowledge.

Is your style of teaching the same as the traditional Japanese method or do you have your own ideas?

I pretty much follow the traditional method relative to training, eliminating only techniques that put students at permanent risk – duck walks, bunny hops, stance changes with people on their backs, etc. – to protect students, as these have been proven dangerous. I have, of course, added drills and approaches I've developed over 50 years. And, as with all instructors, I have my own areas of emphasis and ways I consider best able to deal with those.

Karate Masters

"I trained myself from an early age to keep totally focused on whatever I was doing, disassociating myself from pain, and not allowing emotional stuff to clutter my mind."

Do you practice any other art in conjunction with karate?

There's more than enough in any legitimate art or style to occupy an entire lifetime. I see karate as my primary area of specialization, but have studied other arts and styles briefly along the way. When I was one of the national coaches, I traveled almost every weekend, sometimes with the legendary Takayuki Mikami, one of the truly great men and martial artists of our time. He commented about this subject on two occasions. On one, he said "The hunter who chases two rabbits goes home hungry". On the second, he said "The broader the base of the pyramid, the lower the peak." Many years ago, I witnessed a kata demonstration by a well-respected instructor. He performed his style's version of an advanced kata. Then, he performed it as a Shotokan stylist would. There were many very high ranking people there. I knew the performer and was so embarrassed for him that I had to turn away. When he finished, he clearly thought he had done a great job. But he hadn't. I told myself, never consider yourself an expert in another man's art or style unless you've trained in it an equal length of time.

Many, many years ago, my young five-man team fought a team of dan grade competitors from a well-respected dojo whose style was a blend of karate and judo. My team was made up of two 6th kyus, one 5th kyu, one 4th kyu, and one 3rd kyu. The opposing team was made up of two shodan, two nidan, and a sandan. We beat them 5 to nothing. My brown belt kicked the sandan in the stomach so hard he broke a couple of his own toes. My assessment was they were spending half of their time on one art and the other half on another, while my students were spending all of their time on one. So I've cross-trained in other arts every chance I get in order to improve my art but kept it at that. That's not to deprecate other arts. It's just that many require body actions that aren't complementary. I can look at how someone moves and have a pretty good idea what art they study. A judo guy moves very differently than a Shotokan guy, for example. And even though you can learn the techniques, it's hard to get that core movement. I have trouble switching back and forth from kiba dachi to shiko dachi, from Shuri to Naha kata. I am, of course, only speaking for myself. Others may be able to make those switches but not me, at least not to my satisfaction. When I do a Naha kata, the movement isn't quite right. I can duplicate the stance but my hara doesn't flow as it should. So I keep myself pointed in one direction, with side excursions to broaden my perspective.

Finally, what advise would you like to give to all Karate practitioners?

Stick with it. Get yourself into a routine of training on a regular basis, even if it's only once per week. Never ask yourself "Should I go to the dojo tonight or should I stay home and watch the game?" Instead, tell yourself "It's Tuesday, time to go to the dojo." Also, never take a break from karate for a month or two. You'll never get back, no matter what you think or tell yourself. I once had a guy come in for a first lesson. This was probably 45 years ago. He told me he was going to come back in a couple of weeks, after he'd gotten himself in better shape. I'm still waiting for him. Don't stop training when life isn't going well for you, train harder. Focus your mind totally on your kata or kihon and your problems will have no place to exist in your mind. Keep training, it will change your life in more wonderful ways than you can imagine. O

MASARU MIURA

SLICES OF BUDO

SENSEI MIURA IS ONE OF THE DIRECT STUDENTS OF MASTER MASATOSHI NAKAYAMA. DURING HIS COLLEGE YEARS HE STUDIED KARATE AT THE TAKUSHOKU UNIVERSITY, WHICH IS THE JAPAN'S LEADING KARATE TRAINING CENTER. AFTER GRADUATING SENSEI MIURA CAME FIRST IN ENGLAND AND THEN IN ITALY. MIURA'S REPUTATION AND TECHNICAL SKILL LED TO MASTER NAKAYAMA SUGGESTING TO TRAVEL TO INSTRUCT IN EUROPE. THE PART HE PLAYED IN THE POPULARIZATION OF KARATE IN ITALY CANNOT BE DENIED, AND HE IS NOT ONLY A LIVING LEGEND, BUT A CREDIT TO HIS TEACHERS AND WILL ALWAYS BE RESPECTED AS ONE OF THE GREATEST KARATEKA TO HAVE EVER LIVED. ALL WHO TRAIN WITH SENSEI MIURA ARE MESMERIZED FOR HIS STYLE AND PERSONALITY. HE IS ONE OF THE MOST DYNAMIC SHOTOKAN TEACHERS TO HAVE EXISTED, AND HIS MOVEMENTS ARE BEAUTIFUL, PRECISE WITH FULL OF ENERGY AND ECONOMY OF MOTION. HE IS ONE OF THE MOST FAMOUS KARATE INSTRUCTORS TEACHING TODAY AND HIS DEEP SKILL AND EXTENSIVE KNOWLEDGE MAKE HIM A MARTIAL ARTS TREASURE.

Sensei, would you tell us about your current position and where you were born?

I have been teaching in Italy since 1964. I was born on April 22nd 1939 in Shizuoka prefecture, Japan, which is 150 miles west of Tokyo.

How were your beginnings in the Martial Arts?

When I was eight years old, I started practicing Judo. It was during World War II that my family had to move from the city to a country village to avoid the city bombing. Since I was very little and came from outside of the village, I was bullied by other kids every day. The reason I decided to take Judo lessons was very simple. I wanted to become strong and to avoid being bullied. I started taking Judo lessons at the local police station. Once I started learning Judo, the other kids stopped picking on me. After I knew some Judo techniques and gained confidence, I began challenging other kids, who were bigger than me.

Karate Masters

"After I graduated from Takushoku University, I worked at the local city government office for 6 months but I did not like the job."

When you started Karate training?

When I turned the age of thirteen, I started taking karate lessons. I thought that the karate techniques were fancier and stronger than the Judo techniques to defeat an opponent. I wanted to master some karate technique so that I could knock down the opponent with only a soft touch. I read about it in a martial arts magazine. I recalled that it must have been some acupressure techniques. The name of my first Karate Dojo was called "Shunpu-Kan".

Would you tell us some anecdote during your early days?

One day, when I went to the dojo, two guest instructors were visiting from Tokyo. They were Masters Nakayama and Kanazawa and they were in the middle of a karate demonstration tour. When the kumite practice began, I ended up facing Master Kanazawa. During the sparing drill, I swept Mr. Kanazawa by accident. My timing was perfect. At that moment, I thought that I had defeated the JKA instructor and I was very proud of myself. But at the same time, I had great fear and regretted that the other dojo senior students were going to punish me later. I felt very bad and tried to help Mr. Kanazawa get up. I apologized deeply and said, "I'm very sorry, sir!" I expected that Mr. Kanazawa would get revenge on me later in practice. However, Mr. Kanazawa was very gentle and whispered to me, "It was a good technique!" and tapped my shoulder with a nice smile. I was very impressed with Mr. Kanazawa's reaction and wanted to become like Mr. Kanazawa, who is a strong and gentle karateka. This was when I was a high school student.

How influential was Sensei Kanazawa in your life?

Soon after, I decided to go to Takushoku University, where Mr. Kanazawa had graduated. I would not be a Karate instructor today without this little incident with Master Kanazawa. When I was a member of the karate club in Takushoku University, during my junior year, Mr. Ochi was in my senior year and was the team captain of the karate club.

We have heard you did get in trouble there….is that true?

A little! One day, one of the club members caused a lot of trouble and the school suspended their club activities for a year. At that time, all the club members were living in the school dormitory, but they had to leave there during this suspension period. They needed to make some money to rent a new place to practice and to live in and

"I have a fond memory with Okazaki Shihan. I went to see him off at the Tokyo airport when Okazaki Shihan was departing to the United States in 1961."

all the members got a part time job. Me and other students worked at a department store. Our job was to deliver packages from the store to a store in another location. I was the only one who had a driver's license so I became the truck driver. The other members rode in the back of the truck and would carry the packages from the truck to the door. One day during the summer, it was very hot. I was driving the truck, the other members opened one of the gift packages and started drinking the cold drinks and eating the food. I thought that this was unfair. I was the only one who was not able to taste anything. One day, when I was by myself, I stopped the truck, sat down on the grass by a river, and was eating the sausage from one of the gift packages.

All of a sudden, someone hit my head so hard from behind and pushed me into the river water. I got so angry, turned around, and yelled at him, "Who are you? What are you doing?" After I wiped off my face and looked at that person, I realized that it was Mr. Ochi. Mr. Ochi punished me because I was skipping the job, and I was stealing the food from a business package. Mr. Ochi was monitoring everyone to check whether they were working hard or not. Since he was the captain of the club, he had a huge responsibility to raise the club money to get back their dojo space and dormitory. This is my best memory with Mr. Ochi.

What did you do after graduation?
After I graduated from Takushoku University, I worked at the local city government office for 6 months but I did not like the job. One day, I met Master Nakayama at the karate dojo again and he told me that I should go to Europe to teach karate. When I was in college, I had experienced many different types of jobs and had saved up enough money to travel to Europe so I was able to accept Master Nakayama's suggestion.

What it was your first impression in Europe?
In 1964, I arrived in London, United Kingdom. Before I arrived to England, I used to imagine that all the people in England were very gentle and polite, just like how the Royal family behave in public. However, when I rode a taxi in downtown London, I saw that the driver spat from the window. After I saw this, I wanted to travel around Europe to explore how the world acts. I had traveled for approximately 6 months in European countries until I spent all of my money. When my money was all gone, I was in Torino, Italy.

What happened then?
Since I spent all my money, I was sleeping under a bridge or shelter in the town. One morning, I was practicing karate by the river, and a man came up to me and asked me for karate instructions.

He was my first student in Italy. Of course, he did not have enough money to rent or buy a dojo, so I used a butcher shop and practiced in their kitchen. They had to move the machines to make enough room to train and move around. This is how I started teaching karate in Italy. Forty years later, the number of my students has increased to a very high number. My organization has become one of the largest in Europe today.

Tell us about Sensei Okazaki...
I have a fond memory with Okazaki Shihan. I went to see him off at the Tokyo airport when Okazaki Shihan was departing to the United States in 1961. Okazaki Shihan was my senior from the same college and he used

"My ideal vision for the future is for students to be able to visit each other more freely and frequently from different countries."

to come to teach at my school but I was not able to have any chance to talk to him while Okazaki Shihan was in Japan.

How do you see the future of Karate?

My ideal vision for the future is for students to be able to visit each other more freely and frequently from different countries. I think that we should develop this kind of close relationship between any organizations. In this way all students would be able to exchange goodwill and develop friendship.

How do we have to change the combat approach as we get older?

When we age we can't bounce back and forth and move like lighting anymore, we simply can't. We need to conserve energy and don't waste our energy in feints and fancy movements. We need to change the approach to combat and be decisive. We need to learn to move when we are sure that we are going to hit the opponent, remaining almost static the rest of the time. Speed is not the answer, timing is. The approach should

Karate Masters

"Karate belongs to everyone, not only young strong people, but also older and smaller people."

be very simple: to hit the opponent, to win. There is no need to be flashy, just get the job done. We need to reach the point of not having to have a guard. Master Funakoshi mentioned that guard is for the beginners. But to start fighting without a guard we need to change radically the way we fight and focus on real Budo fighting concepts.

What advise can you give to all practitioners regardless of style?

Karate belongs to everyone, not only young strong people, but also older and smaller people. My techniques show that you do not use muscle strength to defeat an opponent. I am always using physics or architectural knowledge and uses the entire body to execute the technique. To reach this level, would take a long time but there is no fast path in Budo. You must keep training every day. This is the only way that you can become a good technician. Of course, nobody can keep hardcore training forever. When you get older, your muscle strength decreases. You need to change your training method. And this is the most important point to study Budo. You need to keep having a clear mind and good attitude. You should be a humble person. For example, you must run when an instructor calls you. You must put your shoes together if you take them off. Those small things will develop your clear mind. That will help you develop good technique. Karate is lifetime training. You must keep training with the right mind.

I want students to learn the techniques so that a smaller and older person can defeat a bigger and stronger person. I have studied these for many years and want to share them with my students.

How much the concept of "change" should be part of the evolution of Karate?

I think flexibility to change is one of the most important qualities a good instructor should have. Please note that I am now referring to simply change things for the sake of change. Change should come after any years of study and a process of trial-and-error with experimentation. It is important to study the principles that the techniques are based on and then "adapt" things to the circumstances. The old way is good but we should not afraid of using "new" ways of doing things if these methods are proven to be correct. Karate is based on interaction and it should be no locked on one single way of doing things. Karate should be fun.

"The old way is good but we should not afraid of using "new" ways of doing things if these methods are proven to be correct."

Finally, what advise can you give to teachers and instructors in general?

I really think that school and dojo instructors should reflect dedication in all areas. For instance, some teachers are 30 or 40lbs over his standard bodyweight. This doesn't show a lot of physical dedication to keep training. In order to teach one should keep training and be an example for the students. Yes, a complete example by training and being in shape. Obviously at 55 years old we can't be the same than when we were 25 but you get my point. How many hours do you train "teacher"? How is your diet? Do you keep yourself in good physical condition that shows an example for the students or you are overweight?

Look at sensei like Okazaki, Kanazawa, the late Nakayama, Nishiyama, Asai, etc. they were in very good physical condition for their age. That shows respect for your teacher, for the art and for your students. Wearing that black belt, having a high rank and being called a sensei is not enough. O

HIDEO OCHI

WISDOM OF AGE

BORN IN 1940, HIDEO OCHI STARTED KARATE DURING HIS DAYS AT THE FAMOUS "TAKUSHOKU UNIVERSITY" IN TOKYO. A FORMER GRADUATE OF THE JKA'S INSTRUCTOR PROGRAM IN 1964, HE BEGAN TEACHING AT THE JKA HONBU DOJO ON A REGULAR BASIS AFTER PASSING HIS FINAL EXAMINATION.

AN ACTIVE COMPETITOR IN HIS YOUTH, SENSEI HIDEO OCHI WAS ALSO A FORMER ALL JAPAN GRAND CHAMPION PLACING FIRST ON NUMEROUS OCCASIONS. IN 1970, SENSEI OCHI WAS SENT OVERSEAS TO GERMANY AND IN 1993, HE FORMED HIS OWN ORGANIZATION "DEUTSCHE JAPAN KARATE BUND" (DJKB) TO HELP RETURN GERMAN KARATE TO MORE TRADITIONAL ROOTS AND AWAY FROM SPORT KARATE WHICH WAS BECOMING EVER MORE PREVALENT IN THAT COUNTRY. IN 1997, HE WAS AWARDED THE GERMAN MEDAL OF HONOR FOR HIS CONTRIBUTIONS TO THE DEVELOPMENT OF GERMAN KARATE.

Sensei Ochi, how were your early days in Germany?
It was hard because I had no idea of how to speak German so the communication was pretty much the same than other JKA instructors at that time...show the technique and use some basic Japanese words. I learnt few basic words in German to give directions during classes but I was far from being able of maintain a conversation of any kind! I had to teach by example and showing with my body. The students couldn't rely on their brains to try to "learn" my body movements since the "logical explanation" of the technique was impossible. They had to "copy" me. The body usually learns faster than the mind so I believe it was good that I couldn't speak German in the beginning!

Did you keep your connection with the JKA Headquarters in Japan?
I always maintained connection with the JKA Headquarters and with Nakayama Sensei in Japan and Okazaki Sensei in the U.S., although we were separated by thousands of miles. I remember the old days with a great feeling of happiness because I think it is fair to say that JKA had at that time the best group of karatekas in the world. I am not saying that

Karate Masters

"I always maintained connection with the JKA Headquarters and with Nakayama Sensei in Japan and Okazaki Sensei in the U.S., although we were separated by thousands of miles."

Shotokan was [or is] the best style but the way Nakayama Sensei structured the training, the instructors program and the vision of expansion of the style around the world was years ahead of any other and tat is the reason why Shotokan is spread all over the world the way it is.

How do you remember Sensei Nakayama?

He had a vision and knew how to make it happen. He knew what kind of blocks we were going to meet ahead because he used to travel to China and actually lived there for a while. Everybody respected him because he was a unique combination of seniority, knowledge, experience and practical wisdom.

How it was the training with Sensei Nakayama and Sensei Okazaki?

The training was very spirit oriented. Karate should be approached spirit first and technique second. This is the traditional way. You use basic techniques like oi-tsuki, gyaku-tsuki, mae-geri, etc...to build the spirit. Every technique was repeated thousands and thousands of times with no rest. Obviously you develop a very good basics but the main goal is to 'break' the students' spirit and then build it up from the scratch. Today the training in based on technique first and eventually the spirit will developed. The times are different and the society is different. I know that you can't push students as hard as we were pushed. It is that simple. Nowadays, you can't have people hitting the makiwara 1,000 times with blood in their hands. I feel that in general the technical aspect of karate has evolved a lot. People's technique are much better than ours when we were young, better conditioning, better training methods, etc...but the new generations are lacking of the 'spirit' that we had. I think you win some...you lose some.

Do you think that with the modern way of teaching – less hardcore - part of the traditional spirit is being lost?

Many karate-do instructors still have a traditional attitude. They like to teach and preserve the art in the old ways, like a treasure and the training is reserved to a few chosen students. On the other hand, other instructors are more progressive and think that the art has to be taught widely in our society to prevent it from dying. Both approaches are good and it depends on the teacher how he decides to share the art. There are good and bad aspects for both ways and that is normal. To be honest, karate is a very personalized art. It was developed by the masters based on their own perception of the old Okinawan methods. Masters like Funakoshi, Mabuni, Miyagi, etc…gave a personal expression of the material they learnt from their instructors and their styles are an example of that. Shotokan, Shito and Goju are different in concept and application because they are the personal expression of these masters. I believe they did a great job by studying and formatting their principles. I really don't think we have to "reinvent" the wheel and create more styles or combine any of the ones that already exist. Why? We have all the right set of tools in each style of karate, we simply need to understand which method or style fits better to our body type. And even then, I don't think that is a relevant point since you may like a style that may not be the best to match your body type. For instance, Goju Ryu seems to fit better for short people. I am not that tall and I have been doing Shotokan all my life! I think this is an example of how the style will mold the beginner's body to fit the demands of the particular style.

But I would like to say that Funakoshi Sensei never talked about styles or "ryu" when he talked about karate-do. Just karate-do. We should think about this.

What advise would you give to the instructors?

One of the things that leading instructors need to remember is that is their responsibility to teach the complete art. I will explain. We all, including instructors, develop our own preferences in kata, kihon and kumite. Things and techniques that fit better to us and we like and enjoy to train and therefore to teach more often. This is alright but we can't emphasize these kata and techniques more than the rest when we teach our students. Our preferences are "our" preferences and should not be imposed on our pupils. If we do that, eventually we are helping to develop an "style within an style" instead of teaching Shotokan, Shito, Goju, etc.

Karate Masters

Once you truly understand the art of karate-do, you realize that it is a very flexible art but certain principles should be followed and maintained because forcing the student to follow a rigid shape and fixed format is not truly the way of allowing the students to eventually express themselves. The art of karate-do provides a way to accommodate the need and abilities of every student. The existence of many styles is a fact but unfortunately not all the styles have a complete training system and progression. Some people are advocates of developing one single style or method of karate but I don't think this is the right direction to go. The principles of Shotokan not necessarily are compatible with the principles of Shito Ryu or Goju Ryu and vice versa. Instead of trying to unify karate we should be more preoccupied with unify the instructors who teach it!

How do you separate the students in your classes?

In my classes I have always separated the training into different levels. This gives to the students an idea where they are what they need to do to progress to the more advanced levels. Some students are too clever and they try to copy and practice the advanced movements and kata even before they are ready for them but their foundation od not good enough and eventually they will make big mistakes in the future, like trying to compensate the lack of technique with other physical elements. For instance, in kata you have different levels that you have to 'master' before learning kata from a more advanced level. Just because your body is capable of doing "Unsu" or "Gojushiho" and your brain can remember the sequence of movements it doesn't mean that those kata are meant to be practiced but someone of your level. Maturity is the key.

What do you mean when you say "karate techniques are not simple"?

It is important to remember that at an advanced level, karate techniques are not "simple" in application. What we can see as an attacking movement at a beginner's level it will become a defensive action at an advanced level. And vice versa. An attacking punch can be also a blocking move. The focus of the physical action must be changed as the situation demands and that is the reason why it takes a certain level of understanding and skill to make it happen.

Sensei Okazaki is a very important figure in your karate-do development. What can you tell us about him?

Training under Okazaki Sensei was very hard. He always wanted for us to give the most and the best we had within and never allowed us to give up. Giving up was simply not an option. He emphasized basics and spirit training. He knew how to build up our spirits and give us the necessary confidence to face many of the challenges that he knew were waiting for us abroad. Every class and training session was a serious feeling of strain without relaxing. But I was happily aware that I became stronger and stronger whenever I participated in a class.

You often mention of the "stillness" in training as a beneficial tool for the progress. What do you mean by that?

We tend to think that exercising is only based on moving the body but old masters discover that stationary activity brings a lot of benefits. The idea of no movement equals no exercises it is not true. For instance, get your "kiba-dachi" stance and hold it for fifteen minutes. Don't move. After few minutes your legs are getting a very serious workout…either you believe it or not. Maintaining the stance for thirty minutes not everybody can do, not even professional soccer or football players can hold it that long. Unfortunately we only understand physical training when is measured in sweat. It is important to appreciate other ways of developing the human body and how to better learn to use it for karate purposes. Nakayama Sensei traveled to China and discovered many other training methods used by Chinese martial artist that he knew were very interesting and effective for all practitioners. Also if you look at Funakoshi Sensei's stance and movement they were the same as that as Shito Ryu; short stance and higher. But young men must have wider, deeper stances.

"Karate should be approached spirit first and technique second. This is the traditional way."

Are those two training method complementary to each other or not?

They totally are. When doing physical exercise based on motion the individual focuses more on the external aspect of the activity. When we train with a static method like the "kiba-dachi" exercise I mentioned before, we need to calm down and focus on the internal aspect of the stance, the breathing, the tension, etc. It is a different aspect that is emphasized. These two methods do not conflict at all. They are complementary to each other and both are beneficial for the development of the karate practitioner.

You seem to emphasize very much stance training in you classes. Why?

The stances in karate are extremely important because they are responsible of the karateka's ability to move. The hips determine most of the body movement. Therefore, it is important that we develop new ways of stance training that can be used for the students' development so they can reach their true potential. The transition between stances is a very important aspect to train since they teach the student how to coordinate the body in a single, unified motion. All instructors should examine their training methods and develop creative ways of stance and body turning training.

What should be our goal in karate-do training?

Karate technique and kata should not be practiced with the intention of hurting another human being or destroying an opponent. The training should focus on perfection of character and betterment of the human beings. That's the true goal of karate-do training and its real value for the modern society. With the perspective of many year of training I can tell you that any practitioner that spend years of training trying to make of his body a killing machine or lethal weapon is missing the point of karate-do training. Your training should enhance and educate the body, the mind and the spirit.

What advise would you give to those looking for a karate school?

I would recommend seriously check the "DNA" of the teacher. Don't simply start training with someone because he or she is a champion or well-known. Make sure that that teacher has a solid base in all karate-do aspects including the moral aspects of the art.

How important do you think competition is in the development of the practitioner?

I think it is important to test yourself. We train everyday but it is hard to really know where we are and how much we are realistically improving when it comes to the actual use of karate techniques against others. "Shia" means "testing" and that is why it is a positive part of the development of the karateka, if used correctly. You test yourself and you test the opponent.

Do you think the Olympics would be a positive step in the evolution and development of karate for the future generations?

I do not think that karate is a sport although competition is important. I am seriously afraid that a big distortion will happen if karate-do enters in the Olympics — Judo is an example of it.

I don't like the attitude of players in the Olympic Games, which is to win, no matter what, by any means. I do not think winning is everything, definitely not in Budo training. The desire to win, when it becomes a hindrance of practice, is contrary to my philosophy. It should not be our goal the mere victory in a sportive competition.

What is you opinion of how the art of karate is being taught around the world?

I have to admit that many schools, not only in Japan but also around the world offer 'family friendly' karate. I am not against this "family-friendly" classes, because they may attract many people and lift up the 'grassroots' of karate in the world. But I also worry about how much of this approach can actually damage the true are and specially the spirit of karate-do. We also need "hard-spirited training" for karate to prosper Real karate-do trainingusing the Budo spirit is not a "joke", it is not "fun". Karate is martial arts on which the concepts of life and death should be present at all times. I demand that my black belts students train karate seriously and earnestly.

You moved to another country, to another culture…do you think karate-do is better understood by Japanese and therefore only Japanese should lead the art in the future?

Karate should be open to anyone, and the person who trains the most eagerly and have the right Budo attitude, should be qualified to take a leading position. Nationality or gender should not matter. O

TAKEMASA OKUYAMA

TRUE PERCEPTION

SENSEI OKUYAMA, BORN IN 1944, IS AN EXAMPLE OF SOMEONE WHO HAS RISEN TO THE TOP OF HIS DISCIPLINE BY A NEVER-ENDING DESIRE TO TRAIN AND EXPAND HIS KNOWLEDGE ABOUT KARATE. IT HAS TAKEN HIM TO FIVE CONTINENTS AS A TEACHER AND TOURNAMENT OFFICIAL, AND HE IS NOW RECOGNIZED INTERNATIONALLY FOR HIS KARATE INSTRUCTION.

HE STARTED TRAINING IN SUMO AND JUDO AS A SEVEN YEAR OLD, UNDER HIS FATHER, TAKEMI AND BROTHER TAKAO. YOUNG TAKEMASA OKUYAMA TRAINED HARD AND WAS EVENTUALLY MADE CAPTAIN OF THE "HACHIJO HIGH SCHOOL" JUDO TEAM. HIS INTRODUCTION TO KARATE CAME WHEN HE WAS 13, THROUGH A KARATEKA FROM OKINAWA NAMED MR. KINJO.

SENSEI OKUYAMA ENTERED THE FAMOUS TAKUSHOKU UNIVERSITY IN APRIL, 1960 AND STUDIED POLITICAL SCIENCE, RECEIVING A DEGREE IN FOREIGN TRADING. AT THE SAME TIME, HE STUDIED KARATE UNDER OUTSTANDING SENSEI LIKE TABATA, HAMANAKA, OZAWA, AND TSUYAMA. THIS UNIVERSITY HAS PRODUCED SOME OF THE FINEST INSTRUCTORS IN THE WORLD, AND HE TOOK ADVANTAGE OF THIS OPPORTUNITY TO LEARN THE ART OF THE "EMPTY HAND". OKUYAMA MOVED TO CANADA IN 1969 AND HE HAS BEEN A LEADING FORCE FOR KARATE EVER SINCE.

How long have you been practicing Karate?

Around six decades of my life I have dedicated to karate and martial arts training.

How many styles have you trained in and who were your teachers?

Over more than half a century of my martial arts journey, I have had many teachers and influences of different styles. Mr. Kinjo, came from Okinawa to the Hachijojima Island, where I was born. I first learned Karate from him. Mr. Tsuyama, Mr. Tabata, Mr. Hamanaka from the Takushoku University in Tokyo, Japan where I attended were my instructors. My spiritual influences were Mr. Yaguchi Yutaka and also Master Yamada. For Gosoku-ryu style, I studied directly from Master Kubota.

Karate Masters

"I find that in modern day Karate, the fighting styles have become more similar and not as different in character as they were in the past."

Also Hanshi Gustavo Gondra, who is a Uechi-ryu Master influenced me greatly. I observe and study him in detail when he trains with me and at the various Seminars he does at my Dojo and around the World. I was also a WUKO kata judge, so I had a chance to observe and learn many different styles such as Shito-ryu, Wado-ryu, Goju-ryu and many others.

How were your beginnings in the art of Karate and your early days in Karate?

I started training Judo first as a very young child. My brother, Takao Okuyama was a Judo Captain at the Nippon University, "Nojui Gakubu" team.

My father Takemi Okuyama was an amateur Sumo Wrestler. My father was an employer who helped many soldiers after the war. They could not go back to the mainland because there was no food and many places were all destroyed. Since my father had a lot of land on the Island, he cleared all the trees and planted potatoes, raised cows and produced milk for all these soldiers.

When I was 6 years old, I would watch many of the soldiers train Judo with my brother Takao. The soldiers enjoyed training Judo with my brother because it helped them use their energy as they were very hyper. I would constantly bother them because I wanted to try. I kept asking them and finally my brother gave me an "ashibarai" and I flew up almost 2 feet in the air; then dropped down very hard on the ground. The impact hurt me so much that I felt a great deal of pain for weeks. However, as I watched them train on the grass, I made a promise to myself that I would be a strong martial artist one day. My experience with the movement on the ground and on the grass during my early days of training of Judo, made me think about "existing space", between Judo and Karate.

At the Takushoku University that I attended, for Karate training, the training was based on a lot of kihon and kata. And for sparring, ippon kumite and jiyu ippon kumite. It was extremely hard and the basics and fundamentals were the 90% of the training.

In those days they had friendly tournaments or "Shiai" (small tournaments that honor religion and nature). There were many different styles represented like Wado-ryu, Goju-ryu, Shotokan, Shito-ryu, etc. Each style had its own character that was demonstrated, and each one was so noticeably different. It was so interesting for me to view the differences as a young student. Each participant had to demonstrate the best strengths of the style they are representing. I was amazed with each style's unique character. I find that in modern day Karate, the fighting styles have become more similar and not as different in character as it was back then. The differences are almost non-existent, especially in kumite competition.

Were you a "natural" at Karate?
As I mentioned, I first studied Judo from age 7 years old and years later I became the Judo Captain of the Hachiojojima High School. Judo is skin to skin, body to body. When I did train in Judo, the training felt "warm".

When I first started learning Karate, I felt it was "cold", because in kihon and kata, there is so much "space" with the opponent. In kumite, there is always space with the opponent, however in time and with more training, through this "space" I found that Karate is "harmony with the universe". Anything has to go throughout that "space" and I became comfortable with this harmony with my opponent.

It is important that we place emphasis on 'natural' everyday movement for human beings and connecting in harmony with sources of natural power like gravity, water, air, etc. These are the key elements. They all work together naturally as we should be aware of the "space" in relation to one's training and one's movement to nature. I am aware of myself in relationship to the flowers, to the sky, to the stars, to the mountains and to my opponent when I am training. All this should come through the natural movement.

What do you think are the most important characteristics of Shotokan Karate and Gosoku-ryu?
Shotokan Karate is composed of very big strong and wide movement, it is dynamic – "fudono seishin". Fudono (no movement) Seishin (spirit). The kata of Shotokan have many meanings. Gichin Funakoshi re-created many kata and named them like "Kanku Dai", "Jion", "Meikyo" and many of the Shotokan kata, there is a reason behind each name of the kata which I am always deeply searching.

Also within Shotokan, there are many differences that were seen in my University times. Takushoku University's Shotokan was different than Mr. Oshima's from Waseda University, which was different from the Shotokan of

Keio University. It was very interesting to see the differences within the same style. Not a lot of people are aware of this. There are many "ways" of Shotokan karate.

On the other side, Gosoku-ryu is a very unique style with Master Kubota's character. "Go" means strong, "Soku" means fast. He has a very strong body, and is very fast. He puts his love, all of his character and his passion into this style. You have to see him and train with him to fully grasp this personal and powerful style.

Karate is nowadays often referred to as a sport... would you agree with this definition?

I believe Karate-do is Budo. Karate has to have harmony with your daily life. Each moment, each action and thinking relates to your training. A human being's strongest time is when one is thinking, when in harmony movement with the spirit and also involving the breathing as they all come together.

Of course "sport" has a great spirit, it is also recreation and the aspect of the tournament, participation and sportsmanship is good for our modern society. Karate is not yet a "sport" in a sense because the rules are not perfect. An example of Budo, in ancient times, ancient generals or officers, when they are sleeping, they wear their official clothes. That tells you a lot about the right Budo attitude.

Do you think Kobudo training is beneficial for a Karate practitioner?

Yes! Many Shotokan katas incorporate defense movements with Kobudo weapons and also traditional sword. It is important to know how to defend from these weapons. I strongly recommend its study and practice.

When teaching the art of Karate - what is the most important element for you, self-defense or sport?

I believe when teaching the art of Karate, the most important element is not self-defense, not sport, but Budo. But of course, the spirit of sport and self-defense are important. However, for me Budo is the most important element.

Nowadays, sport does not have the same spirit as during the ancient Olympic Games. The ancient Olympic Games had a special spirit, however I feel a lot of modern day sports have lost the right spirit. It is all about winning instead of the spirit of participation and pride of whom one is representing. Of course, many modern day athletes do capture the ancient spirit of sport but it is not as prevalent now as it was in the past.

My father Takemi, used to organize tournaments or small friendly championships "Shiai", all the time through the Shrine. It is called "Hono" Sumo. These tournaments were in conjunction with "Nature" and "God". In these tournaments, the participants train and compete for spiritual reasons. We used our strength and knowledge to appreciate nature, to appreciate the rice growing in the field, the milk we drink etc.

At the present times, as I mentioned before, sport is about simply winning. Back then, it was more a celebration of demonstration, of seeing different styles, character and forms and to give thanks to what has been given to us through Nature.

Kihon, kata and kumite, what's the proper ratio in training?

Kihon uses the right side of the body and the left side of the body, identical movements. Left brain, right brain; then back brain organizes, it becomes natural control for the body, mind and spirit. In kata, all attacks and energy comes from 8 directions. For kata, you look toward the movement to those directions. Kata has philosophy, spirit and tactics. Kumite, gives you timing and thought of an opponent who in turns, makes you strong.

All these are important in training and they relate one to another in training.

How important is competition in the evolution of a Karate practitioner?

It is important because meeting different people will give you different energies and you will improve. This concept is important.

What really does "Ikken Hissatsu" mean and how does it apply when used in sport Karate?

"Ikken Hissatsu" literally translates as "one punch must kill". I believe in the spiritually aspect of this saying, "when training you must put your 100%". As in sport, you must focus, you must give all your power at the exact point.

The human body is not easy to be killed by one punch or even by a sword, but we should take this meaning spiritually. For me, it means to give your all, as if you are to kill or if you are in a situation where you might be killed, you must give your everything when training or giving your whole self when doing sport. It is the same to be in a dojo or in a competition. Give you best. Do or die. That's the right attitude.

Karate Masters

"It was very interesting to see the differences within the same style. Not a lot of people are aware of this. There are many ways of Shotokan karate."

How do you see the art of Karate evolve in the future?

It is very important to maintain the true meaning of karate for a good future. The world needs Karate-do and Budo education to make people strong and to teach love. We have to make and create good instructors and sensei to continue this tradition. A person can help someone in the XXII century by training now in Karate-do.

What advice would you do to those who want to focus on becoming a Karate teacher?

Human's most important work is to build. To make others strong and to love. This is why we exist. To continue our existence in this world to the future you have to realize that you are the center of this world. If you are not existing in this world, then there are no stars, no Mount Fuji, no flowers... your existence is very important in this world. We have to build Karate-do training and make everybody aware of this training especially kata training and breathing. There are many ways to breath.

What advice would you give to an instructor who is struggling with his or her own development?

It comes back to the beginning of spirit. When you start Karate, you should be searching for that spirit. You are the center of the world and must find inspiration within your world. Kihon, Kata, Ippon Kumite Training all are important.

For Kumite, you get your opponent's energy and you are given back the energy, therefore you receive 2 energies and your opponent receives 2 energies. As with a wife and husband, the 2 energies from both create a third energy, a child.

For me, I am always think back to my Island, Hachijojima, for my inspiration. The Pacific ocean's waves are very strong and give me power. I also think of the top of my head in relation to the stars. I imagine the stars when I train, I think of nature all the time when I train as nature connects to me.

When I train Kata, I always make the connection of my daily life to movement and great nature, I will give you a few examples, when I do Heian Nidan, I feel the deep. In Nijushiho, I feel the wave of the ocean. In Kankudai, I find the center, in Sochin, I feel the movements give me power to the earth/ground - like what I experienced when training Judo as a child - I also experience gravity power. I experience Heaven's power and power from the East, West, South, North, the feeling gives me power, all in relation to gravity.

What can Karate can offer to the individual in these troubled times we are living in?

You always have to have positive thinking and study, and search for love. Love has many stages, for example: 1. Normal love, family love, friend's love. 2. Next teaching love to educate, to build people. 3. Next is excuse love (forgiveness). This is very difficult. It is hard to excuse and forgive people but it is essential. 4. Next is existence, your existence is very important and when you make people happy, you enhance your existence. 5. Finally, approach the highest love, God's love or whichever higher power and spiritual power you believe in.

Karate training will give you guidance in these troubled times if you use and follow the principles above.

Finally, what advise would you like to give all Karate practitioners?

As I have mentioned throughout, you are the center of the Universe. You are in existence. It is very important in this world to acknowledge that the past, the present and the future are with you all the time. Make sure "kime" brings everything together.

The refinement of Karate-do is when a person trains 2 or 3 times a week, then one's body and the spirit get the benefit. When you train in Karate, you unite with those who trained long time ago. Those that trained in the past, help those who are training now, which in turn will prepare and help those who will train in the future.

Karate will increase and intensify in importance to many people. The spirit and scientific principles of Karate will be a great asset in the coming centuries. Therefore I teach those who are not born yet, so subtly, I teach the unborn. As the sun rises and the sun sets, in each moment in the world, we are all one. O

ANTONIO OLIVA

THE MASTER TACTICIAN

SENSEI ANTONIO OLIVA IS CONSIDERED A "MASTER COACH" AROUND THE WORLD. BASED ON THE NUMBERS, HE IS THE GREATEST COACH IN KARATE COMPETITION HISTORY. EQUIPPED WITH AN UNMATCHED ABILITY TO COMMUNICATE, INNOVATE AND LEAD HIS ATHLETES WITH INCREDIBLE DESIRE AND LEADERSHIP, HIS TEAMS AND COMPETITORS HAD WINNING RECORDS THAT EXPANDS FOR OVER THREE DECADES.

WHEN DIRECTLY COACHING A NATIONAL TEAM - AS HE DID WITH THE SPANISH SQUAD IN 1980 TO TAKE THE TEAM TO THE WORLD CHAMPIONSHIP - SETTING A TURNING POINT IN HISTORY, HE IS AN ELITE AND HIGH-LEVEL MOTIVATOR, DEMANDING A CONSTANT PURSUIT OF EXCELLENCE FROM EACH OF HIS COMPETITORS, CREATING AN ENVIRONMENT WHERE LOSING IS NOT AN OPTION. HE NEVER ALLOWS YOU TO MISS A TRAINING SESSION WHEN YOU ARE UNDER HIS COMMAND. I REMEMBER HIM SAYING, "A KARATE WORLD CHAMPION IS A WELL-OILED MACHINE. AND THE TRAINING IS WHEN YOU PUT IN THAT OIL!"

I COULD WRITE A BOOK ABOUT THIS MAN AND HIS MANY LESSONS — ON AND OFF THE MAT - BUT AN IMPORTANT ONE PEAKS ABOVE THE REST WHEN MANY YEARS AGO HE PULLED ME APART IN A COMPETITION ARENA AND SAID; "LIFE IS ABOUT ITS EVENTS; IT IS ABOUT CHALLENGES MET AND OVERCOME — OR NOT. IT'S ABOUT SUCCESSES AND FAILURES. BUT MORE THAN ANYTHING ELSE, IT'S ABOUT HOW WE TOUCH AND ARE TOUCHED BY THE PEOPLE WE MEET. IT IS ALL ABOUT THE PEOPLE."

IT TOOK ME DECADES OF TRAINING, ANALYSIS AND PERSONAL INTROSPECTION TO FULLY REALIZE THAT THE TEACHERS IN MY KARATE LIFE MADE ME WHAT AND WHO I AM TODAY. I HOPE THAT COMES THROUGH CLEARLY IN THIS INTERVIEW WITH SENSEI ANTONIO OLIVA.

How long have you been practicing martial arts? Would you tell us a little bit about your beginnings?

In 1966 I began my training in the art of Hapkido under the Korean Master Yong Hoon Cho. I trained with him until 1974 and during these years I combined my training with Tae kwon Do which I studied under Master Jae Won Kim. My contact with karate, in 1970, came through sport

Karate Masters

"I was five times national champion and I did reach a point when I saw things that I didn't like but it took a while to realize that competition is not bad."

competition because of the circumstances at the time and it was the great Dominique Valera who shared with me his deep knowledge and extensive experience in "shiai-kumite". My knowledge of what we can call 'traditional' karate came from Sensei Atsuo Hiruma (shoto-kai), Yoshinao Nanbu (shuko-kai) and Masatoshi Nakayama (shoto-kan).

From 1975 until 1980 I was in charge of the Technical Department of the National Federation in Spain and I was the Head Coach of the National Team. Because of my position I had the opportunity of sharing information and knowledge with other great international coaches of that time.

I don't think it is really important the quantity of arts or the name of my teachers but the 'quality' - as human beings - that my mentors had when they shared with love and dedication their knowledge with me. It is the memory of them and their dedication that still inspires me today and provides me enthusiasm and passion for what I do.

How was the competition in your day?

Traditional hardcore. It was pretty much "Ippon-shobu"; no weight division. Solid hits. No hand or foot protectors. Basically we went in there, hit hard, took the 'punishment', endured the pain and allowed the doctors do their job afterwards!

Have you been at any time discouraged with sport competition?

Five times I was national champion and I did reach a point when I saw things that I didn't like. It took a while to realize that competition is not bad. What is bad is the behavior of some individuals linked to the sport competition. I worked hard to leave those things behind and soon realized that these [type of] individuals are present in all fields and areas of life. There are dishonest people in every line of work; education, politics, healthcare, etc. Karate is not different.

I do love the competition and its elements; the challenge, the training, the sweat, the experience, the brotherhood, the trips, the excitement, the passion, the tears, the struggle, the victory or defeat and finally the learning process and self-discovery journey that it brings to us. That is what moves me today; the passion for what I do. The essence of life lies in our heart and our reasoning, not in our bodies.

Sensei, nowadays in our society karate is often referred and practiced as "sport" instead of as a "martial art", would you agree with this definition?

To properly answer the question we need to define what is a "martial art" and what is a "combat sport". What I see today is people trying to "separate" karate by pointing out the differences between these two universal concepts instead of understanding that both 'perceptions' [Martial Art and Sport] of the same activity fit perfectly in the universal 'idea' or 'concept' of what is karate or karate-do. To begin with to understand where these 'differences' come from we need to comprehend that the terms 'martial art' and 'sport' have different meanings depending if a country is located in Europe, America, Asia, Africa, etc. The definition of 'martial art' and 'sport' is not the same everywhere.

What we should do to correct this is to look for the elements that bring together these two concepts and stop focusing on what makes them different. All martial arts and all combat sports are practiced with two arms and two legs.

To me, what separates a martial art from a sport is exactly the same thing that separates one religion from another, one human being from another, one country from another, thus…fear, ignorance and personal interests. That simple. Follow the path of the "money" in karate and you will see where the "differences" begin. For some karate is a regulated way of fighting and controlling others. For others, karate is a civilized way of competing and testing yourself against others. For me, karate or karate-do (it doesn't really make a difference to me) is a vehicle to improve as a human being.

Why can't karate be a traditional martial art and a great sportive activity for our society at the same time? Is there any 'specific' way – Asian or Western – of describing universal values that excludes the other? Are the principles of respect, morality, ethics, honesty, etc. owned only by either the Asian cultures or the Western cultures? What are we talking about here…to finally get together in 'unity' or to keep separating and distancing one from each other more and more?

Stop and think for yourself just for a second, and you will see how that 'manipulation' is happening so we are 'against' each other [divide and conquer] instead of working together for the good of karate.

The 5th WUKO World Karate Championship in 1980 represented a turning point in the history of karate. That year you took the Spanish National Team to the gold medal and also many other competitors from the Spanish squad. How do you see the evolution of the modern competition since 1980?

The 1980 world championship represented a turning point in karate history for many reasons. From a competitive point of view, that championship meant the transition from the "Ippon-Shobu" to the "Sanbon-Shobu". We went from an old concept to a new concept of competing. The "Ippon-Shobu" allowed the transition from the very traditional karate [with no competition] to what we can call a "first-competition-stage as a combat sport". This format was kept in the first four World Championships; Tokyo 1970, Paris 1972, Long Beach 1975 and Tokyo 1977. In 1980 the change occurred.

From a technical and tactical perspective, the physical movements changed and the strategies changed to fit the new format. We went from a more static way of fighting to a more dynamic and mobile approach. The rules changed and karate escaped from the hands of the Japanese masters and teachers and ended up in the hands of the Western politicians [who for their own personal interest] re-named the very healthy competitive aspect of karate-do as "Sport Karate". See? Now we have two different 'karate'! There was no reason to separate it, but 'karate-dollar' always speaks louder than words. And this goes both ways…the traditional [budo] and the modern [sport]. One stayed with the "Japanese-based" format and the other went to an "all-countries-are-equal" format [similar to the Olympic Games worldwide approach]. Obviously many changes happened that caused these two groups to separate more and more from each other. It had [and has] to do with politics, interests, power and money and nothing with the art and the sport of karate as a tool for human beings to develop and progress in unity in their lives and within our society.

Oliva

"To me, what separates a martial art from a sport is exactly the same thing that separates one religion from another, one human being from another, one country from another, thus...fear, ignorance and personal interests. That simple."

Sensei, what are the main differences in the two most recognized methods of competition in the world of karate; the "traditional" Japanese of the more JKA-based method and the "modern" or more Westerner approach that we can call WKF-based style? *(Please note these two ways used here to describe two kumite competition formats, rules and regulations (JKA/WKF) and are simply descriptive to "represent" a philosophy or approach to sport karate and its format of competition...and not necessarily representative of any "ryu", style or branch of karate, i.e. Shotokan, Shito Ryu, etc.)*

Something very important should be understood before I can move forward and dissect the more intrinsic aspects of the question in my answer. A martial art, a sport and the element of competition – as they are understood and regulated by our society – are three different things and putting them in the same basket as if they were 'one', is a terrible mistake. Please allow me to elaborate on this.

On one side we have the Martial Art that as an "art of war" focused on efficiency in combat, a life or death encounter.

Karate Masters

"Why karate can't be a traditional martial art and a great sportive activity for our society at the same time?"

On the other side of the coin, we have the sportive aspect (attention: not necessarily 'competition' per se here), that as "an art of health" focused on the well-being of those who practiced it.

And last, we have the "competition". This element of competition is driven by the 'Olympic spirit' and a "professionalism" that – based on all the politics - has a very doubtful reputation to say the least. The main objective is to win (no-matter-what), accumulate trophies, medals, pride, glory, money, gifts, fame, etc. These things bring the attention of the big companies and eventually the 'big money'. The presence of the 'big money' in the Olympics basically 'swallow' the athlete into its powerful machinery and the individual becomes simply an "object" of marketing to sell a brand and/or a product.

This very unusual social and cultural situation involving the Art, the Sport and the Competition, brings us to an interesting 'scenario' where we have what we can call "traditional karate" (JKA Type) on one side and a "modern karate" (WKF Type) on the other. Both of them fight desperately to 'gain' the favors and attention of the practitioners spread all around the world. What is very interesting is that – regardless of what they preach – both of them use the "Competition" element as a "selling tool" to spread their principles and philosophies and memberships. This is the great irony of this dilemma. The "traditional" side claims to be based on budo values (call it as you please) and the "modern" side presents a more current, active and up to date [to the times] proposal for our modern society.

What is interesting is that neither one of them can exist and live without the other. Both ideologies are doomed to have to 'respect' each other. They may not share the same principles but they have to respect each other because basically both sets of values are positive and good.

Then, we need to have a deeper look at what each side represents in reality and 'why' they represent what they represent.

From the perspective of WKF the competition is an 'open practice' to all the countries around the world where the rules are changing and modified to better serve the modern concepts. Karate is not a "Japanese thing'...like 'football (soccer) is not a British sport anymore'. The origin is not important anymore. The country of origin does not 'own' or 'control' (!) the sportive activity anymore. This new and modern approach makes the karate walk away, little by little, from its roots in Japan; farther and farther away from the Japanese system of values that are intrinsic to all the art of budo. The danger here is that karate can eventually reach a point where it may become 'only' a sport with simply a competition approach to shoot for and thus becoming totally disengaged of its roots. As we know, the IOC offered WKF to try to enter in the Olympic Games but the kata division was not going to be included. This is a clear example of what I just said. A dangerous separation between kumite and kata, both key elements in what karate is.

The idea is to find a set of rules that make the matches very attractive, easy to understand for the spectators and with a lot of action. What is the true goal for these changes? Simply, to bring the big 'sponsoring money' to the sport and to the Olympic Games.

The JKA Type of competition that we agreed to call it [here for the sake of the explanation] "traditional" is 'closed' to few countries that agree to have Japan as 'leader'. Japan tells how to compete, how to judge and how to train. The main representatives in other countries follow their Japanese teachers and sensei. Everything is dictated from Japan. Obviously there are politics here too as I mentioned in the Olympic Games. Its type of competition tries to maintain and preserve a clean and pure art. It has a set of fixed rules and regulations, obviously dictated from Japan and rooted in the past. Following the rules set in kendo and judo, the powerful "ippon" concludes the match. This type of competition rewards a powerful, clean, well-delivered technique with a strong 'martial' spirit. Therefore, the type of technical movements that actually score a point must be solid, very standardized and even elegantly static.

When you train, teach and coach international and elite competitors, which are the principles ["common core elements"] that apply to both sides of this "coin" (JKA/WKF)?

I was a competitor in both "styles" and "methods" and I am an international Coach training and coaching national teams and world champions in both competition styles. For me, both competition styles are very exciting and I enjoy them very much because I don't see them as opposites. In order to be successful in any of them you have to have an understanding of the main elements that compose each style of competition. We need to know and understand the rules and regulations of each and also have a very precise knowledge of the different "interpretations" of the rules of each competition style, because sometimes the referees make decisions based on personal appreciation, based on the nationality, reputation and rank of the competitor. Not everything is scored based on the physical technique.

In the traditional JKA style of competition, the most important thing is to have a solid base technique. In this style the proper and clean technique is recognized and awarded. It is an example of a kind of technical excellence that only comes from many years of hard kihon and kata training. It is a "Japanese" approach to training and competition that reflects that. As an example of this...in the JKA you can see kumite champions that are also kata champions! This is the reason why. Kata and kumite are very close together because the excellence in kumite is based on a clean and perfect technique that comes from a very solid kihon, and kihon is the base for kata training. Everything makes sense. Full circle.

In WKF competition the important thing is to have a full and deep understanding of the tactical elements of the match and the competition, including all the collateral aspects. The technical element has to be organized in a functional and intelligent format so it can be applied specifically depending on the type of opponent, referees, etc that we face during the event. Unlike the JKA style of competition, the kumite competitors of the WKF are not very sound in kata competition, and some of them - as we all know - don't even train or know kata at all! Some of them are world-class elite athletes in kumite but they can't perform a kata.

These are the facts and either we like them or not, we should understand what is going on to maximize our possibilities when we enter in a competition. I am not judging any of them but explaining them so the readers and athletes can understand the fundamental differences and how these differences may affect a match in the competition.

After 40 years of experience teaching and coaching, the "common core" elements are the same for both styles of competition and they are the base of my training and coaching system. When I see a competitor, I don't see a Shotokan guy, a shito-ryu guy, a goju or wado-ryu guy, I don't see a Japanese athlete, a white guy or a black guy...I see an "athlete"; a "competitor"; a "karateka" and I analyze their mobility, awareness, timing,

"Stop and think for yourself just for a second, and you will see the 'manipulation' that is happening today so we are 'against' each other [divide and conquer] instead of working together for the good of karate."

cadence and tempo, their rhythm and distance judgment during the match, etc . These are the "common core" elements.

The technique without tactic is almost a useless tool. And tactic without a technique is simply…nothing, because it can win a match without a physical movement. The key or "secret" is to know how to combine both elements properly; giving them the importance and relevance that each one of them has. And this is exactly what I do when I teach, train and coach grassroots or elite competitors for the JKA style or the WKF style. World champions in both methods are developed on a base that comprises technique and tactic together, working in unity. They learn the fundaments in the Dojo or school and they develop them through state, national and international competition under the supervision of elite coaches.

Karate Masters

Sensei, what are the differences – if any – between a reverse punch and front kick "JKA style" and a reverse punch and front kick "WKF style"?

Let me say that, "a correct technique is a correct technique regardless where the karateka is competing (JKA or WKF). Period". This is the way it has always been and the way it will always will be, although sometimes when the referees and competitor's level is not good enough and the interest of "higher powers" are more important than the technical movements of the athletes, the problems arise.

Today the main difference between a JKA technique and a WKF technique is not in the execution of the movement but in the "perception" of that movement according to the rules. The traditional JKA style acknowledges a strong offensive action that scores first and clean, awarding it with an "Ippon". The WKF rules require 8 points to finish the match. Based on this concept, the way that coaches and competitors plan the matches has to be different. The technique is no different, the perception of it and how the rules award the points... is. In the JKA style and spirit of the offensiveness in the attacking action is paramount. The technique must be straight, clean and hard. Your mind is on the "offensive" and you want to make it that way to finish the match. Under WKF rules because of the rules of 8 points, the concept of "not giving the opponent a chance to score" is more important. You want the opponent to make mistakes that you will capitalize on to move ahead in the score. In this case and unlike the JKA kumite, we are talking of a hardcore "Defensive Approach" from the very first moment. In short, when you compete in a JKA style tournament, a hardcore offensive, well, directed attack with kime and zanshin may be enough to win a match. This is very true in the classical "Shobu-Ippon" category. In WKF, because of the way the match and the rules are set, you need to know how to use and maximize other "defensive maneuvers" because the match will keep going until someone scores 8 points.

In short, the "overall concept" of how the rules are set, determines how the competitor will use the offensive and defensive elements that I teach. Obviously when I coach one competitor in JKA style kumite we have already done the homework and the same applies for a WKF competitor that may train and compete under my guidance.

What are the elements of you teaching and coaching a program that applies to both styles of kumite (JKA or WKF)?

My coaching method and training system is based on the premise that all Human Beings, therefore the athletes or karateka, are composed on three parts: the body, the mind and the spirit. Only when these three aspects of the competitor are working together in unity, the karateka can give their 100%.

The Technique is the body language and is based on physical and technical gestures, stances, guards, footwork, controls, points of contact, sweeps, attacks, defenses, etc.

The Tactic is the language of the mind and is based on psycho-tactic acts, perceptions, observations, studies, analysis, synthesis, space, time, anticipation, rules, referees, scores, penalties, communications, etc.

The Emotic is the language of the soul (spirit) and is based on sensitive-emotive impulses, emotions, intensities, rhythms, cadences, tempos, intuition, inspiration, confidence, passion, etc.

"The technique without tactic is almost a useless tool. And tactic without a technique is simply...nothing."

In order to try to explain a long subject here within a short answer, I would say "the Technique dictates the forms, the Tactic adjust the forms to the rules/regulations and opponents, and the Emotic aspect brings credibility and the 'martial' element to the Techniques and Tactics."

This universal principle or concept – which it is the spine of my coaching method - is true for any type of kumite, traditional JKA style or modern WKF style and it is also applicable to any other martial arts like kendo or jiu-jitsu or combat sports like Boxing or Wrestling.

What are the differences that you see between a competitor of the "JKA styles and a competitor of the "WKF style"?

If we look at the heart of the matter...there should be none. Why? Because the experience shows, that "the individual is what is really important and not the style" of competition that you are in. If the competitor has a solid Technical and Tactical base with the understanding of the Emotic component ["Common Core" elements], he or she will be successful in any kind of competition style. If we look at the history of sport karate we

Karate Masters

"The 'Technique' is the body language and is based on physical and technical gestures, stances, guards, footwork, controls, points of contact, sweeps, attacks, defenses, etc."

will see many excellent competitors that were and are successful in the JKA style and the WKF style of competition.

I am going to explain some of the fundamental details that are necessary for a technique to be recognized in both 'styles' of competition. These elements are common for both types of competition and are interchangeable to say the least. If you "have" them, you can compete in both styles with guarantees.

• Explosiveness in the initial movement in order to "fire" the chosen technique once the body position and the distance are correct.

• Speed in the 'approach' and 'delivery' [from the "set point"] of the limb used to try to score (hand or foot).

• Accuracy and control in the moment of "engagement", thus once the 'delivery tool' (hand or foot) has reached the target.

• Automatism, coordination and a systematic method of recovering and recoiling the attacking limb back to the point of origin or to any position that the circumstances require for the follow-up movement.

• Firm balance and solidness at the final moment of the delivery phase in order to keep the right form and the overall body 'readiness' to follow-up with another technique [defensive or offensive] if necessary.

Of course, the execution phase is based on two previous and important phases called "observation" and "preparation", which allows the competitor to 'clear the technical mechanism' from all possible defensive interferences coming from the opponent's actions.

It is important to remember that once the attacking action has been completed, it will connect with another offensive or defensive maneuver [depending on the circumstances] or the competitor will revert back to the 'safety zone" [long distance] where he or she will be able to perform an analysis and assessment of the previous engagement and an observation of the new situation in order to proceed accordingly.

And last but not least, I would like to mention the important aspects of the correct defensive maneuvers more likely known as "blocking actions" in the sportive terminology. Unfortunately, these elements are not really supported and acknowledged in the current rules of any competition format either traditional JKA style or modern WKF.

- Perception of the 'set-point' on the preparation-of-the-attack by the opponent. This ability to detect that 'trigger' point should be perfectly timed and recognized.

- Reception of the attacking action. This movement is usually a circular or semi-circular action that absorbs or re-directs the attack.

- Neutralization of the striking power at the moment of impact. This is done by either re-directing the force of the attack or by blocking the action with our forearms, elbows, knees, etc.

- Obstruction of the recovery or recoiling phase of the opponent's attacking limb by grabbing, unbalancing or other forms of altering the opponent's structure in the recovery phase of his/her technique.

- Altering or 'breaking' the final phase of the opponent's attack with the intention of replacing it with our own counterattack [in time] or with a solid blocking action to fully nullify it.

All these different elements, phases and sub-phases of the technical aspect should be combined properly depending on the demands of the match and the level of expertise of the competitors.

Which are the most important elements for elite competition?

We have to understand that the 'elite competitor' is nothing more than a regular karateka but with an excellent base and fundamentals. The basics and fundamentals are paramount to become an elite competitor. The first three areas are: a) solid physic-technical base; b) solid psycho-tactic base and c) solid senso-emotic base.

These three areas are developed into three working 'nucleus':

- Physical Elements; resistance, strength, power, speed, flexibility, overall body limberness, general body coordination, balance, etc.

- Psychological Elements; character, maturity, intelligence, memory, willpower, concentration, adaptability, etc.

- Eidetic Elements; senso-perception, motivation, feelings, emotions, fear, mood, etc.

In short and using a simpler description to be able to compete at a high level around the world you need; 1. youth and experience; 2. excellent knowledge of the competition rules and the individual 'specificities' [likes and dislikes] of the referees; 3. experienced and knowledgeable coaches willing to teach and share with passion and love; 4. financial means and a solid sportive infrastructure matching the goals pursued and 5. strong personality, ambition, determination, motivation and commitment.

What is a 'coach' for you and what are the differences between a 'coach' and a 'sensei'?

All these questions are directly related to the point of view of the person's background. This background can be understood as cultural, sportive or martial art. To begin with I would like to say that for some karateka, the concepts of "coach", "sensei" and "trainer" are the same, because in many circumstances they do similar things but in other "environments" they play very different roles, all depending on if we approach its definition from an Eastern or Western perspective. On top of that, we need to remember that depending on the country you are in [different cultures], they use different terms to describe their trainers in sports and teachers in martial arts. The words mean different things and are used in different ways.

We all know that the 'sensei' is very well respected in Japan and the 'coach' is highly regarded in the U.S. in professional sports, Colleges, Universities, etc. Due to the modern interest in all kind of sports, the role of the 'coach' is becoming more prominent and visible in our society. The role of the 'sensei' is being 'left alone' for those who conceive the karate only as a traditional 'martial art' or budo.

Let's analyze important factors here to better understand the reality of it. Both, the coach and the sensei have one thing in common; they 'teach' and 'educate'. The 'education or teaching' of the athletes in sports and karateka in karate is based on common denominators described as 'Universal Values': respect, honesty, love, humbleness, dedication, understanding, tolerance, generosity, freedom, friendship, forgiveness, courage, etc.

All these values we reach through what is called "mastery". Mastery is defined as "the harmonious fusion of wisdom, spirituality and perfection". When we speak about these three important elements we are talking about the 'language of the heart' and not simply punching and kicking – what we can describe as the "language of the body".

Unfortunately, with the emphasis of the sport the role of the "coach" and "sensei" have taken a path moving away from teaching and sharing these important 'values' and have been focusing on the physical aspects only. They are not 'coaches' anymore... they are trainers. They are not "sensei" anymore...they are instructors. This is a big difference.

Another important factor is that nowadays we are seeing more "coaches" and "sensei" but less real "masters". Why is that? The answer is that 'teaching values" as a good master does, has fallen into a commercial trap. We look for the amount of students and medals and not for the real quality and the important values in our teachings. To reach 'mastery' is a slow process that takes many years of hard work and dedication. To become a 'coach' or a 'sensei", unfortunately, can be achieved and awarded at a weekend seminar simply by paying the required amount of money. That simple.

"The 'Tactic' is the language of the mind and is based on psycho-tactic acts, perceptions, observations, studies, analysis, synthesis, rules, referees, scores, penalties, etc."

What is a 'master' then?

To answer this I will refer to a quote: "Who knows and does not teach, does not know. Who teaches but does not know, does not teach. Master is the one who knows and teaches."

In our modern society a 'great sensei' is that one who has many students and a 'great coach' is the one who produces many champions. Interestingly, the 'master' does not have a lot of students and/or champions. Why? Because 'mastery" does not go well with big numbers. A 'master' is that one who is capable to lead to 'mastery' the number of the people he relates to and gets in touch with. A good King is not the one

Karate Masters

"Karate will always have the world championships, the European championships, etc. Karate will always be karate no matter what."

who has a lot of followers in his country but the one who makes it possible that everybody lives like a 'king' under his supervision.

What does the value of "respect" mean to you?

Respect is not an Eastern or Western value. It is not something traditional or modern. It is a "Universal Value" that does not change depending on the time or place where we found ourselves. The respect is originated in the concept of 'love'; love for what we do, love for whom we are doing what we are doing, etc. I remember when I got married in 1977, my father told me: "respect each other and the love will be there". And that is true for martial arts, sports and for any endeavor in life. Love for what you do brings respect.

If karate ever gets into the Olympic Games, how do you see that affecting the art/sport?

The Olympic Games are directed by very specific interests based on money and power. Because of the structure the IOC wants for karate, the art and sport will be even more fragmented than it is today. For obvious reasons the IOC do not want kata, too many complications. This will lead to an even deeper separation of kumite and kata and even the kumite will have to be 'adapted' from what it is now to what the IOC wants. The IOC dictated how judo and tae kwon do had to be presented and displayed at the Olympic Games. Judo changed the color of the judogi for television purposes. I am not sure that the karate people will be able to 'control' any of that once karate is accepted and gets in.

Be it as it may, karate will always be karate and kumite and kata will always be kumite and kata. Karate will always have the world championships, the European championships, the Pan-American championships, etc. Karate will always be karate no matter what.

Finally Sensei, what differences do you see in yourself from that first world championship as a Coach in 1980 to this day?

Many, but I will try to make this answer short [laughs]. At that time I had my school (dojo) and I was dedicated solely to the Spanish National Team. Today I train in 75 countries, travel all year long, and coach over 25 national teams directly with their national Federation coordination. In 1980, I was focused on training elite athletes and today I train national coaches and international coaches so they can get better themselves so they can improve and make the athletes of their respective countries better and more competitive in the international arena. I train,

"It is important that we open our hearts and look for unity amongst us".

educate, develop and form international coaches. In 1980 the competition was 'everything' to me. Today the competition is one 'part' of the whole concept of karate. In 1980, I was in the initial phase of 'coaching' others...today I try to help others to find their own 'mastery'. In 1980, I was concerned about what people said about me. Today I don't care. Therefore, I live better. In 1980, I had a position at the [Spanish] National Federation, today I am free as a bird. And last but not least, in 1980 I was a Coach highly admired by the results achieved by his world champion team and competitors. Today, I am a loved and recognized international "Karate Coach" around the world.

To finish I would like to mention that it is important that we open and expand our minds and our approaches and perspectives of things. Tolerance, respect and love are what make any country and therefore, mankind solid and strong. It is important that we open our hearts and look for unity amongst us, instead of focusing on the differences, because under the sky we are all one single family. O

TOSHIHIRO OSHIRO

EDUCATING THE MASSES

TOSHIHIRO OSHIRO FIRST EXPERIENCED THE MARTIAL ARTS DURING GRADE SCHOOL IN OKINAWA. AT THE AGE OF SIXTEEN HE STARTED HIS FORMAL TRAINING IN MATSUBAYASHI SHORIN-RYU KARATE UNDER THE TUTELAGE OF SENSEI MASAO SHIMA AND CHOKEI KISHABA AT THEIR DOJO IN NAHA CITY. HE ALSO SPENT A NUMBER OF YEARS PRACTICING AT THE MATSUBAYASHI HEADQUARTERS DOJO OF SENSEI NAGAMINE. SENSEI OSHIRO HAS STUDIED THE YAMANNI-RYU STYLE OF 'BO' UNDER MASTER CHOGI KISHABA FOR MANY YEARS, AND HAS BECOME THE DRIVING FORCE FOR PUBLISHING THIS WEAPONS STYLE IN THE MARTIAL ARTS WORLD OUTSIDE OF OKINAWA. SENSEI OSHIRO IS THE CHIEF INSTRUCTOR FOR THE RYUKYU BUJUTSU KENKYU DOYUKAI IN THE UNITED STATES.

Where were you born and how did you start in karate training?

I was born May 1st, 1949 in Haneji, Okinawa, Japan. And I started training at age sixteen. I actually started when I was 8 because at elementary school I learnt a little of karate and bo from a senpai. Obviously this was not dojo training...more a kid approach to learn some martial arts. I have trained also in judo and kendo as well, but karate and kobjutsu have always been my root.

How it was the training then and who were your teachers?

Well, it was a traditional way of learning karate. Okinawa was a very diffcutl place after WWII and the 'normal' training was not 'normal' at all. Shima Masao Sensei was my main teacher but I also learnt from other sensei. For instance, Shima Sensei, Nagamine Sensei, Kushi Sensei, Yamaguchi sensei, and Nakamura Sensei taught shared their knowledge with me too. Nakamura Sensei, especially, taught me "Chinto" kata in a very special way...by special I mean with a very deep approach to it.

Did you also meet Kishaba Chokei sensei?

Yes, I was brown belt at that time. Please remember that the training was not like today and the ranking system was also very different. We used to

Karate Masters

"It is important to have an open mind and understand why other styles are doing things differently."

train day and night, seven days a week. Shima sensei's dojo was jointly started by Shima, Taba, and Kishaba senseis. Then Taba and Kishaba Senseis went to Japan and Shima Sensei kept the school. When I made brown belt, Kishaba Sensei came back. That's when he started teaching us. But Shima sensei was my main karate sensei. My karate technique came from him. From Kishaba Sensei I can say that I gained a lot of deep knowledge and improved my technique.

When did you hear of Yamanni-ryu for the first time?
The first time I heard that name, it was from Kishaba Sensei. I was just a young kid and didn't know about it, other teachers and advanced practitioners knew about the style! The bo is very important in the history of Okinawa but there were not so many instructors teaching. Bojutsu is not as popular as karate, and the teachers didn't make a lot of effort to make their art known to the public. Therefore it was very hard to really find someone good to learn from

How were you accepeted to train under Kishaba Sensei?
I was recommended by his brother. Kishaba sensei taught me a lot of kata, techniques, and history but technically I had to research for myself and do a lot of self-training. The foundation and 99% of my knowledge and technique came from Kishaba sensei but I had to practice a lot on my own.

When did you come to the United States and what exactly did you teach at that time?
In 1978. I came because one of my karate sempai, who owned a dojo in California, had passed away. They needed a replacement instructor. I was not teaching kobudo or bojutsu because that was something I was doing

for myself so I strictly taught shorin karate. Eventually Someone asked me to do a bojutsu demonstration and the interest grew. That is how I started to teach the art of Yamanni-ryu.

Do you use Bo training to improve your karate training?
Yes. The old teachers used to do that too, I think. They would watch other styles or talk and practice with other instructors to add some new technique or maybe to just check their own practice By comparing the two arts, it is possible to see how karate used to be in the old times. I am very interested in this. Nagamine Sensei talked about the difference between "koshi" and "gamaku", your sides vs. your lower back, in making power and focus. It wasn't until I had studied bo that I realized exactly what he was trying to teach.

You always mention to analyze and study other styles, why?
It is important to have an open mind and understand why other styles are doing things differently. They have solid reasons and those reaossn may be good for us to know. Follow your teacher and understand your body but keep and open mind about your training.

We would like to discuss some of your concerns about training...
Some classical martial artists have taken issue with the way karate is being practiced today. From a strict 'bujutsu' perspective, it is possible to see certain aspects which appear troubling. Some traditonalists from the other arts have even gone as far as saying that karate appears to be a second rate martial art. This sertiment is even shared by certain karate instructors. To better understand their reaction, we must first look at traditional karate as it was practiced long ago in Okinawa and contrast that with the karate of today. A good dividing line would be to examine the karate that was widely practiced before and after Itosu Anko brought karate into the public school system in Okinawa.

Karate was modified to fit the public school physical education program in 1901 when it was first introduced as part of the school curriculum at Shuri's Jinjo elementary school. In 1905 Itosu Anko created the 5 Pinan katas to further facilitate this process. In the early 1920', Gichin Funakoshi brought karate to mainland Japan and was soon followed by other karate greats such as Choki Motobu and Kenwa Mabuni. But by the time karate crossed over to the mainland it had already been fully transformed into a physical education/sport type of regimen.

Karate Masters

When the mainland martial arts experts saw this Okinawan art for the first time, they reacted with a certain degree of skepticism. They felt it wasn't a first class martial art. But they were reacting to the version adapted for P.E. and not the original karate that was practiced before the modifications made by Itosu Anko.

What influenced the change and what would make it first class?

One must first look at the 'Zeitgeist' of the time. This was during the Taisho era (1912 - 1926). It was a time of great change in Japanese history. The Meiji restoration had just ended. Japan began modernizing and looked to Britain, Russia, France and the USA as role models for their financial, military and educational systems. The samurai warrior class was forbidden to carry the sword and was no longer allowed to wear the top-notch. Japan's current political system was established in 1885. Nationalism grew side by side with the industrialization of Japan. This had a direct affect on the martial arts. The leaders of the country were interested in creating a society of young people who were physically and 'morally' strong. The ideals of Budo were brought to the forefront during this time. The martial arts were viewed as a means of strengthening the body and spirit of the Japanese youth. Jujitsu, under the influence of Jigoro Kano, became Judo. Kendo was derived from various schools of kenjutsu. The 'revised' karate fit the bill perfectly. Of all the different types of martial arts, karate was the easiest to convert into a more sport like activity. Sport in and of itself is not a bad thing. This is the very reason karate is so widespread today.

We need to make a distinction between martial arts, military training and modern day karate. The older traditional karate of Okinawa was first a martial art for self-defense. Modern karate, which spread around the world, evolved as it was taught to the masses. Without modern karate it is unlikely that karate would have become so popular. Modern sports karate as we practice today is only maybe 20 years old. This type of karate is different from what your Sensei may have learned and taught originally.

The method in which the older traditional martial arts is taught is not suited for modern day military training. Traditional martial arts are based more on a one on one transmission of instruction and are not something that can be taught simultaneously to a large group of people. Also, in the military, it is important for the unit or battalion to move as a whole. When each soldier moves in a haphazard way the unit or battalion will not have strength. The military has strength in unity.

"Nagamine Sensei talked about the difference between "koshi" and "gamaku", your sides vs. your lower back, in making power and focus."

The karate of today is geared towards group instruction in a Physical Education type of format. Because of this it was easy for karate to spread all over the world. As karate traveled across the globe, people who encountered this art began questioning the effectiveness of kata. Does it really work? What are these movements for? What are the applications? To understand kata one needs to take kata back to its original form before it was turned into a PE type of training. In other words, one has to look at the kata that was done nearly 100 years ago, before karate departed from Okinawa.

Is it possible to bring the old ways back?

Take it back to where it used to be? That would be difficult and perhaps not really necessary. If you teach people the original meaning and movement of a kata, they can then integrate that into their training and come to a new level of understanding. Through this process of combining the old and the new, something greater can be created and modern sports karate can thus become enriched. This synthesis is achieved by looking to the older traditional karate of Okinawa.

Today the bunkai (application) of a typical practitioner is mostly for show. The real intent of the movement is not present. If one integrates the original ideas into current format then things like 'heighten awareness of their seichusen' and 'understanding embusen' will come into play and this

"We need to make a distinction between martial arts, military training and modern day karate."

will add flavor to the new development. We can improve the new by combining it with the old for a better understanding. We can respond to the people today who say "the kata does not work" and show them that it really does.

What is "seichusen"?

A simplified way of explaining it is 'line of attack' or 'line of defense'. 'Seichu' in Japanese means 'exact middle'. 'Sen' means 'line'. It is the path that the opponent's attack has to traverse in order to reach you. By the same token, it is the path that your attack must travel in order to reach your opponent. By defending your seichusen and attacking through his seichusen you can conquer your opponent. Seichusen also has to do with body posture. If you stand in heisoku or heikodachi relative to your opponent then you are presenting a large surface area for your opponent to attack. Instead of squarely facing your opponent, if you shift your body position so that you are now in a hanmi position (45 degrees relative to the front), the body now has less surface area exposed to the opponent. In other words you just made your seichusen narrower, thus making it easier for you to defend your seichusen.

Can you speak about Embusen, balance, and movement?

When people say embusen, they immediate think of the performance line of the kata. Embusen is more than the performance line. People also think that the kata must start and end at a precise location on the embusen. There is must more to embusen than that. Integrating embusen in true fashion with the movement of the kata is actually the soul of the kata. The act of moving along the embusen is an art in itself and that is what is important. Right now you are asking a technical question. Moving along the embusen takes a lot of skill, in fact, it is a major skill. The way people originally moved their body along the embusen is totally different than the movement that is taken for granted today.

For instance, one needs to go forward without raising one's heel or leaping forward without kicking off the ground. Imagine stepping backwards on a straight line. If you raise your back heel as you step back, there is a slight delay in the backwards movement of your torso. In Japanese we say that 'your body remains in place'. If you need to move back it is because an attack is coming and you are either trying to avoid it or draw it in. So the instant you start to move back, your entire body has to move immediately as one unit. There cannot be a time lag. Raising the heel causes a lag. When you move forward in the kata, if you raise the heel of your front foot that is going to be the new back foot during transition, you cannot move forward with your entire body weight. If you kick off the ground as you go forward, again there is a delay in the movement of the torso. Learning to move with the entire body is an acquired skill.

On balance - people talk a lot about the importance of maintaining balance. But the balance that most people think about and the balance we talk about in martial arts is totally different. In martial arts when we talk about balance, it is that moment in time when you are about to lose your balance. In martial arts, balance is actually the beginning of imbalance.

If we want to move from point a to point b and we are standing 'balanced' with our weight 50/50, then in order for us to move forward we have to first overcome inertia. If on the other hand, we are standing in such a way that our center of gravity is shifted slightly forward of center, then we will be able to move forward easier because we will have less inertia to overcome. In other words, going from point a to point b from a point of imbalance or leaning forward means less inertia to overcome. The end result is that you move forward more 'naturally' and smoothly with less energy expended and a minimal amount of telegraphing of movement.

Some people focus too much on 'moving the feet' but using your legs to move is slow. By feeling your center of gravity and developing an awareness of its position, you will be able to move your body much more quickly and efficiently. We call it 'moving from the center'.

Can we talk about sport karate?

Karate has attained world wide acceptance and popularity because of sports karate. If we had maintained karate as a true martial art, it would never have spread the way it did. If people begin integrating martial arts principals into their karate, it will further enhance their karate.

Karate Masters

What would you like to see karate become as a whole?

The bottom line is this - I want to see everyone have a greater appreciation of what karate is really about in terms of techniques. If karate has hit a technical plateau, then getting to the next level is not so much an issue of coming up with new ideas but researching old ideas and integrating them with the present.

When you think about it, only a relatively small percentage of students actually compete. The rest of the students train for the dojo. The majority can greatly benefit by learning how to move, how to use their body. And for the minority that compete, winning is important for them. And the question that needs to be asked is 'why does a given kata win today in competition?'. It wins because the judges believe it is a winning kata. If we can influence the thinking of the judges then the outcome will change. The competitor is no dummy so he will naturally adjust to the criteria set forth by the judges. So the challenge is to reeducate the judges, to help them understand and see the subtleties of movement. Can we influence their thinking to change what they think about and what we do in training? When someone judges kata and does not understand why one should move in a certain way, the properly educated competitors lose - and you feel sorry for competitors. We need to reeducate those that are teaching. Being on the Technical Committee Chairman for Kobudo (weapons) I feel that it is my responsibility to find a way to educate the officials. In the final analysis, it is the officials who decide what is' quality in kata'. The question that remains to be answered is how to best do this.

Karate comes from Okinawa. You cannot view karate in isolation but must see it in its cultural context. Unless you can understand the culture of Okinawa, you cannot develop a full appreciation for the art and it will become difficult to understand. For example, weapons have strong influence from China. In goju ryu you can clearly see the strong Chinese influence. Shuri-te, on the other hand, has some influences from China but the way that you move your body is identical to the body movement of the traditional Japanese arts of the mainland. The problem is that the karate that came to Japan was not the original Shuri-te but a version modified for PE. So the mainland martial arts were not impressed and thought, 'ok I guess that's karate', but that's not real karate. If you really want to understand what is true Shuri-te karate technique and kata, instead of going to China, go to mainland Japan and study traditional martial arts. The same core elements of Japanese martial arts are found in karate, jujitsu, kenjutsu, and the other arts. From my personal experience with Yamani-ryu bo, movement in that style of bo share similarities with the art of the spear when you thrust the bo and with naginata or kenjutsu when you swing the bo.

When you see the photos of the traditional Okinawan masters you can see the stance of the traditional martial arts from Japan. So the roots of shuri-te are found in mainland Japan.

What thoughts on the term budo?
Let's speak first of bujitsu. Budo is a set of ideals. Bujitsu is more the technical end and the part which we are concerned with here. Budo is an ideal that we should aspire to. The method of karate, the technical aspect, lies in the realm of bujitsu and not in the ideals of budo. Because the word budo is thrown around so casually, people really don't get it and don't have the respect for it because the word has become so commonplace. Learning just bujitsu itself is a formidable task. Learning bujitsu with your body takes years of training and discipline and that type of discipline and perseverance are the components of budo. Still, budo is something we ought to aspire to in our study of bujutsu.

"CAPTION"

Reeducation seems to be needed but when and how?
Reeducate teachers, this is the task at hand. We need to create awareness and peak the interest and curiosity of the instructors and the practitioners. We need to have more seminars. At the recent referee course we stressed what to look for during competition. For example I contrasted the difference between striking the bo with just the arm versus striking the bo using the entire body. I showed the difference between carrying a wide versus narrow seichusen. By demonstrating the finer points of kobudo, I am hoping to influence their thinking about not only kobudo but about

Karate Masters

"Traditional martial arts are based more on a one on one transmission of instruction and are not something that can be taught simultaneously to a large group of people."

karate in general. The principles of kobudo directly relate to karate. They are one and the same.

Can you explain or give an example as to how techniques have changed?

There is a distinct difference in the way a gedan barai (down block) is performed today. The way you use you arm is different. You can strike with your bone; your vital areas are covered as you keep you elbows in tight; your lats are tight as well as your arm pit and the elbow faces back. These details are difficult to convey to groups of 50 or more, so perhaps they may have been left out in an effort to teach the masses.

Another point, "Use your hip", this term has a different meaning as the Japanese hip region is different from the American hip. A person, by pre-loading and turning their body as they move along the line, will be protecting their vital areas and at the same time will be moving quickly. Using your hip means using your back, throwing your shoulder forward, relaxing, using what I call the "floating body" and being ready to move. Your stance is not a static but dynamic. There is a difference in real speed and perceived speed. This is the old fashioned way.

I think it is important to 'feel' the techniques. The pair is different upon impact - the type of damage and feeling is different in the traditional method. In modern karate, the energy is released into the target and the energy bounces back. Modern karate has concerns for safety so this is a good thing but the old way also takes safety into consideration. With the traditional punch our hands are relaxed until impact and then we focus kime and send energy through to our opponent. In the modern punch, they are decelerating instead of accelerating upon impact because they are over tightening their muscles. As they hit the surface, the technique has started deceleration. Another way of saying this is that in modern karate the punch is stopped instead of released. One needs to learn to release the energy. This is very apparent in the makiwara training of today. They are holding back their energy.

The purpose of kata is to teach you how to use your technique, how to move and how to release energy. Kumite teaches us distance and timing. That's the purpose of one versus the other. When you learn both then your karate comes alive.

In modern karate we step and punch. In reality, the foot plant of the step and the impact of the punch must be simultaneous, occurring in one motion so the energy will go with the technique. If you step first and then punch, some of the energy dissipates into the floor and not into the target. You must learn to strike with the body. Kata and kumite should be the same. You can not learn this from a video tape. You have to get hit to understand and the instructor has to feel that you can do the technique.

People's curiosity has to be peaked when they attend Oshiro seminars. There is so much to teach but in many ways it is different from the way many have learned. Don't push off with your feet. Bring your center of gravity forward. You never get stuck - it flows from one to the other. Too many are obsessed about stance. What is the proper stance? The stance is the finished product. It's the in between movements that are important. You are not supposed to show what you are doing. His arm is like a whip and there are no excessive movements.

Thanks to modern karate this art has gained terrific popularity and spread around the world. To understand the meaning we will need to do some re-education. That's why you cannot learn by yourself. It needs to be shown. We can take what we have now and reintegrate the meaning from before. Real karate is a first class art. O

TOMASZ PIOTRKOWICZ

BUDO INHERITANCE

SENSEI PIOTRKOWICZ BEGAN HIS MARTIAL ARTS JOURNEY IN JU-JUTSU TRAINING IN 1970 AND KARATE AT THE AGE OF 15 IN 1972, AS ONE OF THE YOUNGEST PRACTITIONERS IN POLAND. DURING HIS STUDIES AT THE WARSAW UNIVERSITY, HE CO-FOUNDED THE "AZS KARATE" SECTION WHEN HE WAS TRAINING SHOTOKAN KARATE AND THE KOREAN ART OF KYOKSUL.

IN 1980, HE FINISHED THE NATIONAL KARATE INSTRUCTOR'S COURSE ORGANIZED FOR THE FIRST TIME IN POLAND AND HELD TRAININGS AT THE WARSAW UNIVERSITY AS WELL. IN 1981, HE WAS A REFEREE AT THE 1ST CHAMPIONSHIPS OF THE POLISH KARATE FEDERATION. IN THE COURSE OF HIS SECOND STUDIES AT SGGW, HE ALSO FOUNDED AN "AZS KARATE" SECTION THERE. HE HAS TRAINED MANY WARSAW INSTRUCTORS FROM DIFFERENT STYLES AND ALMOST A HUNDRED OWNERS OF BLACK BELTS IN POLAND AND OTHER COUNTRIES. HE TAUGHT KARATE IN GERMANY AS A DKV (GERMAN KARATE ASSOCIATION) EXAMINER AND ALSO IN LITHUANIA AND IN THE CZECH REPUBLIC. HIS PERSONAL TRAINING CONTINUED UNDER OTHER LEGENDARY MASTERS LIKE HIDEO OCHI, TSUGUO SAKUMOTO, TAKEMASA OKUYAMA AND FUMIO DEMURA. HE MET SOKE KUBOTA AFTER TWENTY YEARS OF TRAINING KARATE, WITH 3RD DAN IN THE SHOTOKAN STYLE (AWARDED TO HIM BY MASTER HIDEO OCHI) AND DECIDED TO OCCUPY HIMSELF WITH THE GOSOKU-RYU STYLE. HE WAS THE PRESIDENT OF THE "POLISH KARATE ASSOCIATION" AND NOW HE IS THE PRESIDENT OF THE "EUROPEAN BUDO ASSOCIATION". SHIHAN PIOTRKOWICZ IS ALSO WELL KNOWN EXPERT OF KOBUDO, TANTO-JUTSU AND KENJUTSU. HE INTRODUCED IN POLAND JAPANESE SWORDSMANSHIP BATTODO AND SPORTS CHANBARA. MASTER PIOTRKOWICZ AUTHORED SEVERAL MARTIAL ARTS BOOKS AND INSTRUCTIONAL VIDEO SERIES.

How long have you been practicing karate?

I started training Japanese martial arts as a youngster, in 1970. Please remember that it was the dull reality of communist Poland – one could not travel to any western European country, not talking about Japan. Therefore, Japanese martial arts were known to few. People sometimes talked about "the karate strike" – done with the edge of the hand – but that was all that was known back then about karate. I started my training with jiu-jitsu. I

Karate Masters

"I was not a typical sports person at school. I was more of a thinker type who had a lot of friends – extraordinary sportsmen."

lived in quite a dangerous area of Warsaw. In communist Poland, no district could be labeled as safe or unsafe. The same neighborhood could be inhabited by white-collar and blue-collar workers, as well as pathological families. Being a son of an engineer, who worked in a big industrial plant, I often met young hooligans, or even criminals. I had to learn how to defend myself and make them respect me. It was the main reason for my trainings. Besides, in this monotonous reality, Japanese martial arts seemed very exotic and I had been fascinated with Japan for a long time. After two years of training I took up karate, which I considered to be more effective, and it turned into a lifelong passion. Back then, I was one of the first karateka in Poland.

How many styles have you trained in and who were your teachers?

I trained jiu-jitsu only with my friends, who were also engaged in other sports: wrestling, judo and bodybuilding. We used old Polish and German books for reference. I especially liked all sorts of joint locks.

In case of karate, at first we were taught by Italian instructors. Later, a Japanese karate master from JKA, Hideo Ochi, became my teacher. He lives nearby, in Germany. Naturally, the style was Shotokan. Thanks to Shotokan I mastered solid basics of karate and I can "cleanly" execute basic techniques, which has a direct effect on mastering kata. During my studies at the University of Warsaw I met a North Korean student, a master of the Kyoksul. I trained this military martial art with him, without interrupting karate trainings – me and my two friends held karate classes for other students. Trainings with Kim taught me how to use my techniques more effectively in a real fight. The Kyoksul style was more practical – it was focused on close quarter combat and aimed against taekwondo. Poland was even visited by a general from the socialist Korea – the head of the style. He offered to organize grading examinations but I refused, willing to remain faithful to karate. Later, I had the honor and pleasure to train many times with such Shotokan karate fames as Hirokazu Kanazawa,

Keigo Abe or Hidetaka Nishiyama. I also trained Ryuei ryu under the guidance of master Tsuguo Sakumoto. It was during his six month stay in Germany, during which I was, in turn, teaching Shotokan karate. I was fascinated with master Sakumoto's dynamics and effectiveness during short-range fights. After the fall of communism in Europe in 1989, I had the opportunity to train with numerous eminent Japanese masters, both in their homeland and in other countries. I will name just a few of them: Takayuki Kubota (Gosoku-ryu), Fumio Demura (Shito-ryu and kobudo), Takemasa Okuyama (Shotokan and Gosoku-ryu), Morio Higaonna (Goju-ryu). After many years of training karate, I started to get interested with weaponry and by the end of last millennium I fell in love with the samurai sword. In each martial art I had different Japanese teachers.

In case of kobudo, I started my education with master Demura, but I eventually managed to take lessons from all the greatest living kobudo masters in Okinawa: Tetsuhiro Hokama, Jyosei Yogi, Seisho Itokazu, Hiroshi Akamine, Sonoko Higa and sword master Hisao Hamamoto.

I learned the basics of Japanese fencing – battodo and iaido – during classes with the greatest students of Taizaburo Nakamura, with whom I corresponded, but unfortunately could not meet personally before his death. They are masters: Toshishiro Obata, Seiji Ueki, Mitsuo Hataya, Mitsuhiro Saruta, Shimeo Sato and Kunio Suzuki. In the last couple of years I had the pleasure to train with master Kosen Tabuchi, an expert on the short sword (kodachi); master Yoji Yamanaka, who mastered the long sword (katana); and master Kinji Nakagawa, who mastered fighting with two swords (nito).

I learn chanbara – soft weapon fighting – from its creator, master Tetsundo Tanabe, his son Kenichi Tanabe and the president of the International Sports Chanbara Association, Kenichi Hosokawa.

I have also been taught the basics of jukendo and tankendo by the vice-president of the federation in its headquarters – Budokan in Tokio. I have participated in trainings and exhibitions of yabusume, kyudo and various schools of jiu-jitsu, held in Japan. I have visited the Shaolin temple in China, where I was taught by the main instructor – a monk. I have also been to Kodokan, the mecca of judo, and to Okinawa, the birthplace of karate, where I participated in a special course held by holders of the 10th dan degree. From each of those visits I brought back many training materials and even more reflections. Okinawa allowed me to go back to the basics of karate and analyze the differences between the traditional karate of Okinawa and the Japanese schools. Shaolin proved to be an even more distant travel both in space and... time, as it was the source for Okinawan karate and kobudo. I was very impressed at the sight of hundreds of young people training at the same pace at the temple and in the neighboring martial arts schools. Even though the monastery itself has become a sort of a Disneyland for martial arts enthusiasts, its inner temple still has the spirit of Bodhidarma's students. In my opinion, adepts of jukendo possess the greatest fighting spirit. Even though jukendo's range of techniques is vastly limited, kime and focus of its students is very impressive and perfectly conveys the concept of "ikken hissatsu".

I am also a qualified instructor of the Polish Boxing Association, a teacher of self-defense, an instructor of knife fighting and a MMA couch.

How were your beginnings in the art of karate and your early days in karate competition?

Since I was one of the first karateka in Poland I sparred more often with students of other arts than karate. These were friendly confrontations with friends of mine who trained judo, jiu-jitsu, taekwon-do, boxing or kung-fu. That is how we learned to use specific techniques and apply them in the right situations resulting from spontaneous and not prearranged fights. It exposed to me differences between fighting arts and training methods. It helped me a lot as from the very beginning of my martial art journey I knew what are the gaps in karate training. However, it was in self-defense where the effectiveness of karate was most apparent to me. A number of times I didn't let a hooligan hit me because I "clocked" him with a punch or a kick. Even if he did not fall, he was scared to attack me again. The incident which brought me the biggest fame "on the block" was when I hit, partly by mistake, a local muscleman in his solar plexus. He was my older friend who used to wrestle with us for fun, often two or three people at the same time. After the strike, he fell as if struck by lightning. When he finally came to his senses, he asked me: "what was that?", to which I replied "a karate punch". I was short, but quite strong. Unfortunately, in self-defense I had a problem – as every cultural man, I had an inner inhibition against hitting a person, for instance in the face. I had to be really furious to do it. Karate taught me to defend myself spontaneously or to strike pre-emptively without any emotions, and thus more effectively. It also increased my composure.

Speaking of fighting, decent technique allowed me on one occasion to save Kim – the kyoksul instructor I have already talked about. We attended a student karate camp together. Unfortunately, another "instructor" was also present there. He was sent from the embassy of socialist Korea and he observed us all the time, especially Kim. Kim had a Polish girlfriend and he had to put a lot of effort into hiding from the spy. We could not even chat casually at a campfire. I asked Kim to pair me with this "instructor" for kumite during training. The spy had to go back to Warsaw to x-ray his ribs after my spinning back kick and he never came back. We were students back then and the world was different.

Regarding karate sparring, we used to do it in slow motion, but in a continuous manner. It was much safer that way, as we had no protective gear. It also taught us to use a variety of techniques and to hit effectively by outmaneuvering the opponent and using one's position to their advantage, instead of simply relying on sudden acceleration.

"Gosoku-ryu is a style which combines karate of Okinawa with modern Japanese and global ways of training."

Since the very beginning I was interested more in teaching karate than in competing. It's enough to say that I was one of the people who organized the first courses for judges and instructors, and during the first official Polish karate championships I was already a judge, not a contestant. Such is the fate of pioneers.

Nevertheless, there is a modest chapter in my martial art career which includes taking part in competitions and gaining a few medals, almost exclusively from international events.

Were you a 'natural' at karate – did the movements come easily to you?

I was not a typical sports person at school. I was more of a thinker type (top student), who had a lot of friends – extraordinary sportsmen. By playing and practicing with them, I started to display quite a good level in a couple of sports myself. Karate practice has always been giving me a lot of joy. From the very beginning I had little problem with learning individual techniques and kata. I was quite strong, fast and flexible – even before I started training karate I could do the split or 50 push-ups in a row. My agility was slightly worse, but it improved after my jiu-jitsu trainings. Karate vastly improved my coordination. I approached each technique

Karate Masters

"I am a biologist by education so I try to be rational. Sport karate was a good way to promote this art and to obtain money from sponsors and local authorities."

with the "I'm going to do it" attitude. Later, I practiced to do a given technique better than others. Those practices provided me with a lot of enjoyment. I simply love training karate.

What can you tell us about Soke Kubota?

I think the story of how I met him will explain everything. I learned about master Kubota from Italian instructors at the beginning of 1980s. They showed me pictures from seminars which the master had held in Italy. I quickly obtained one of Kubota's books and made it my goal to meet him personally. Back then I was the president of the all-Polish Student Karate Federation, but going to the USA and visiting the master was beyond my reach. It was possible for me to go to Italy, but unfortunately the martial law in Poland and its aftermath forced my dream to be delayed by ten years. We met in Italy at the beginning of the 1990s. I will never forget this meeting. We arrived in Turin to attend the Champions' Tournament, where Soke Kubota had been invited as the guest of honor. There were seven of us and the car we arrived in was not even a van. In the USA, even single people used bigger cars. Kubota asked us about the distance we had covered and upon hearing that it had been a thousand miles during which we had passed a few national borders, he only gave us a nod.

My students took part in the tournament, with good results. I also participated and won a bronze medal in kata. As an aside I can tell you that members of many different teams thought that Italian judges had been unfair to me and the medal should have been of a different color. Then, all of a sudden, Soke Kubota invited me to do an exhibition with him. I had never practiced with him before and still he was able to present, in an impressive fashion, the effectiveness of karate and his weapons – the kubotan and kubotai – in self-defense. Nothing was staged, I attacked and the master defended himself. The next day the master supervised a number of classes. It was then when, having already trained karate for twenty years and holding the 3 dan degree, I realized that my adventure with exploring the art was only getting started.

The seminars concluded with a master rank exam. Without any prior preparation I entered the 4th dan exam (others tried to obtain lower ranks). I knew neither the requirements used in Italy, nor those preferred by master Kubota. The exam featured some elements of kihon and kumite. Luckily, the Italian did not fight as roughly as we had done in Poland – I had lost one of my molars during my 3rd dan exam, whereas my opponent's face had shown signs of a serious beating. Later, master Kubota asked me to present all the master kata I knew. He did not know that back then I could already do nearly fifty kata from different styles, so around the tenth one he told me to stop and… promoted me to the 4th dan grade. Later, in the evening, we went to Venice to visit it on our way back to Poland. I was so filled with excitement that when we stopped at a roadside hotel I could not fall asleep the whole night. As a result, the next day I was walking around beautiful Venice in hot, sunny weather feeling dazed and sluggish. I'm glad it wasn't the first time I have visited this city.

What attracted you to the world of karate kumite competition?

For quite a long time I wavered between karate-do and sport. There was a time when I almost decided to train Shotokai, which is completely devoid of sport, but it was filled too much with mysticism. I am a biologist by education so I try to be rational. Sport karate was a good way to promote this art and to obtain money from sponsors and local authorities. Unfortunately, unclear rules, tendentious decisions of judges and phony behavior of contestants constitute major downsides of the sport aspect. Therefore, although I promote sport karate, I still have ambivalent attitude towards it. In my competitions, the contestants have for over 10 years been using special helmets with a plastic face mask. Such solution allows to avoid face injuries, which are a curse of sport karate, and makes judging easier. A contestant still has to control their punches aimed at the head, but they can make contact with the mask, which makes a characteristic sound leaving no doubt whether there was a hit or not. I named this sport karate rules "safe contact karate".

What do you think are the most important characteristics of Gosoku Ryu?

To answer this question I must explain a bit about my background. For the first twenty years I identified my karate as Shotokan , later I promoted the name of Gosoku-ryu style. Right now I prefer to talk about karate, without labels. In the spirit of Gichin Funakoshi who said that there is only one karate. My perspective is broader as except Shotokan and Gosoku-ryu I learned also from top Wado-ryu, Goju-ryu, Shito-ryu and Shorin-ryu masters, not to mention other martial arts.

One the most important characteristics of Gosoku-ryu are elements of jiu-jitsu and aikido added to sparring. What master Kubota presented already in the 60s-70s – adding a sweep and juji-gatame after a gyaku-tsuki counter – seems natural nowadays, in the era of MMA, but back then most karate practitioners thought that one reverse punch was enough to resolve a fight. Engaging in ground fighting was considered a stupidity. But not for masters like Kubota, who practiced Judo and Aikido, or Okuyama who knew Judo and Sumo before he started in karate.

Master Kubota devised very interesting kata, which include techniques from various styles. I always supplemented my repertoire of Shotokan katas with forms from different styles. I was the first teacher stemming from Shotokan in Europe who incorporated Sanchin and Tensho to regular training of the advanced students. I even included it as compulsory kata for brown belts. In some of the Gosoku-ryu katas there are sequences of movements resembling Shotokan kata mixed with parts resembling Goju kata. That's why I enjoyed practicing them so much, as I already trained according to this concept, but separating it into two different katas.

One the biggest turning points in my karate was shedding the symmetrical pattern of movement and linear offense and defense (without moving sideways) for which I give credit to both master Takayuki Kubota and Takemasa Okuyama. Other characteristics of Gosoku-ryu are offensive and defensive foot sweeps, quick position changes, more left-handed punches, innovative footwork as well as training focused on faster striking speed and following through after each attack.

Karate is nowadays often referred to as a sport... would you agree with this definition or is a martial art?
For me, karate is a martial art. Karate is a way of self-development, of physical and intellectual progress. The sport aspect is just one part of karate – just like self-defense or teaching the military and police. To my mind, karate is a certain way of life, just like sailing or skiing. It is certainly more than just a sport.

However, each person should take from karate what they find useful and we shouldn't judge people who only want to practice kata as a form of fitness exercise, or who only want to fight and compete in kumite tournaments.

Do you think Kobudo training is beneficial for a Karate practitioner?

Kobudo is a separate martial art. Still, t is worth to differentiate between Ryukyu kobudo, which shares its roots with karate, and Nihon kobudo, which originated from Japanese islands and was associated with the samurai. Actually, there are so many Japanese schools specializing, for instance, in bo-jutsu (long staff fighting) and they are so different from each other that we cannot really talk about one, common origin. Staff fighting also used to be popular in Europe, China and India. Fighting with weapons is a different matter from karate, which is a martial art of bare hands. When weaponry is involved, one hit is usually enough to end a fight. It is also out of the question to accept a hit and counter with one's own knockout technique. The distance is also different – a lot longer than in bare-knuckle fighting. Finally, we can use a weapon to target arms or even hands of an attacker. My favorite weapon happens to be rokushaku bo – a staff measuring six shaku in length (one shaku is more or less equivalent to one foot). A few years ago I received the 6th dan degree in bo-jutsu from Japanese masters. As for short weapons, I am especially fond of kama – you can use it to cut through mats, almost like with a samurai sword. You must be really advanced to even try it. Two sharpened kama are dangerous weapon to train with and I have at least one scar on my arm thanks to it.

"For me, karate is a martial art. Karate is a way of self-development, of physical and intellectual progress."

However, if a karateka wants to learn how to defend against an armed opponent, they have to know how to use the weapon they want to defend themselves against. Otherwise, successful defense is hardly possible. A number of karate kata contain techniques of defense against attacks made with staff, for instance Jitte, Jion or Meikyo. In Okinawa, karate masters practiced kobudo for a very simple reason – when attacked by a trained samurai armed with two swords, you have bigger chances of winning a national lottery than defending yourself just with your hands.

Karate Masters

"Fighting with weapons is a different matter from karate, which is a martial art of bare hands."

When teaching the art of karate – what is the most important element for you; self-defense or sport?

I teach all aspects of karate, but it is the student who has to decide whether they will commit to sport or train karate only for themselves. Naturally, I adjust my trainings to requirements of a target group – for instance, a dozen or so years ago I taught Marines guarding the U.S. embassy. They didn't need sport karate and neither do the police or security officers. Teaching Marines was easy and very rewarding. Who can be a better student than young, fit, confident and disciplined men who can concentrate and face any challenge with a smile on their face? Years later I watched documentary about Marines boot camp and for a moment I regretted that I didn't push them more. On second thought I understood that I made the training in the right way. I don't like to show authority by shouting or bullying my students. In addition they wanted to learn more technical aspects of hand to hand fighting and not to have small copy of boot camp. Good teacher knows not only the strong points of his students but also their weaker side and knows how to address it.

Currently, sport karate taught in a playful manner, and with the protection of helmets, is a great way to make karate trainings more attractive for little kids. Self-defense and sport are not mutually exclusive. Martial arts contain many aspects and that is what makes them so versatile. Each combat sport includes the element of self-defense.

Kihon, Kata and Kumite, what's the proper ratio in training?

The ratio between those three basic components of karate practice changes with a student's level of advancement. At the beginning, kihon is the dominant element, whereas kumite appears scarcely. With advanced students, traditional kihon can successfully be substituted by offensive and defensive combinations performed in free stances, as well as by kata bunkai. In the Warsaw Karate Centre, we use protective helmets and gloves, which allow for a quick transition to kumite, a real fight, instead of just punching the air, which is a common cause of injuries for karate practitioners. Japanese karate featured too many exercises without contact and too few exercises with equipment such as punching bags or mitts held by a trainer. Traditional Okinawan training with makiwara was too static; many techniques were done while standing in place. Kata is a great way to train individually and develop mentality, muscles, rhythm, focus and precision of movement. It greatly improves motor coordination. As for kumite, it teaches timing and proper assessment of distance from the opponent. It is here where we put techniques learned in kihon into practice. Kumite and kata constitute the essence of "the way of empty hands", but without kihon one can achieve perfection neither in kumite nor in kata.

"I teach all aspects of karate, but it is the student who has to decide whether they will commit to sport or train karate only for themselves."

What is it that keeps you motivated after all these years?

We have a saying in Poland: "old love does not rust". Many years ago, my hobby became my profession and now I draw satisfaction not from my own progress in karate, but from my students'. I feel especially happy when one of my students achieves success in everyday life, or... when they come back to the club with their children so "the Old Shihan" can teach them karate as well as discipline, focus and control over their bodies and emotions.

I am proud to say that my students include eminent members of our society: university professors, doctors, lawyers, famous actors, generals and businessmen. I have a firm belief that their successes were aided by what they have learned in the Warsaw Karate Center.

Karate Masters

How important is competition in the evolution of a karate practitioner?

Karate is a martial art so it is necessary at some point to check one's skills against a real opponent. Sport competitions are a safe way for such confrontations. There are people who are afraid of all confrontation, they simply avoid it. Sport karate can help them break those fears. Just like obtaining subsequent ranks, competing and potential sport successes can too serve as an objective indicator of one's progress in the art of karate. Sport karate should be present during an adept's youth. A mature karateka can either continue to compete or focus on new challenges.

What really means "Ikken Hissatsu" and how it applies when used in sport Karate?

This phrase is usually translated as "to kill with one blow". All Japanese martial arts strive for one successful attack which will cause the defeat of the enemy. Master Nishiyama popularized the expression "a finishing blow" and that is what I consider the best explanation of the phrase "ikken hissatsu". In kendo or battodo it will be "a finishing cut", in judo "a finishing throw" (armlock or a choke), in karate "a finishing blow" (a punch or a kick).

Depending on the level of danger, we should use defense of necessity acceptable within law. Nowadays we shouldn't even talk about killing. An effective technique is the one which allows me to defend myself, or to score a point (and possibly win) in a sport fight.

How do you see the art of Karate evolve in the future?

Obviously, karate is constantly developing, but it is also, to a certain extent, unchanging and timeless. Certainly the future will bring new, more effective training methods. I also think that karate techniques will be more unified – they will break free from hermetic styles and schools of karate. Sport karate needs a breakthrough in judging – the application of electronic devices, similar to what is gradually being introduced to taekwondo, would allow for more just verdicts clear to the audience, as can be observed in Olympic fencing. We are also bound to see protective gear of next generation, which will make the fighters safer. One thing I am absolutely sure of is that the era of grand masters who create karate styles, modern samurai, is about to end. It is time for a new generation.

What advise would you do to those who want to focus on becoming a Karate teacher?

A karate teacher has to really like this martial art and possess patience, which is necessary to teach other people, especially children. Each instructor has to remember that the goal of his classes is not to prove that he is the best of the whole group, but to convey his knowledge to his students and teach them karate. A teacher shouldn't also just train together with his students or try to beat them in confrontations. An instructor's duty is to correct mistakes, ensure proper execution, but also praise students and boost their self-confidence.

A teacher has to think thoroughly through each aspect of the technique they are about to teach. Therefore, they have to be very advanced in their karate. I often meet students who were taught by a technically poor teacher. Eliminating their bad habits is a lot harder than teaching somebody for the first time.

"A mature karateka can either continue to compete or focus on new challenges."

A karate teacher must not forget that they are not an expert in everything. They know karate, and perhaps a few other subjects, but in many other fields they possess knowledge of a dilettante. There are no people who mastered everything, save for James Bond perhaps. Seriously though – "errare humanum est."

What advice would you give to students on the question of supplementary training?

The focus of karate trainings should be, first of all, karate techniques. Strength and conditioning exercises can be done outside the dojo. Actually, proper karate training includes everyday gymnastics, developing one's body and mind, correcting own mistakes, as well as caring for proper nutrition and a healthy lifestyle. Like I said, karate is more than just training, it is a way of life.

It is worth to get acquainted with the newest trends regarding proper nutrition or muscle training. Your way of karate should be open for new solutions.

In my youth, I liked to play handball, badminton, ping-pong and tennis. Later, I also added skiing. Each of those sports helped me develop my martial arts skills. Regarding strength training, when I was younger I regularly

Karate Masters

"Karate is a martial art so it is necessary at some point to check one's skills against a real opponent. Sport competitions are a safe way for such confrontations."

trained with kettlebells. From what I can see, this piece of equipment is gaining popularity again. It is a wonderful way to develop muscles and dynamic strength. Currently, I have returned to my passion from when I was still a student – isometric exercises. They allow to maintain a very high level of strength in your muscles and joints.

What advice would you give to an instructor who is struggling with his or her won development?

They have to divide their main goal into smaller ones and systematically strive to accomplish them. Consistency is mandatory if you want to achieve something. However, one must not get discouraged by failures. Life does not consist solely of successes. You have to learn from your mistakes to win on next occasion. That's what life wisdom is about.

I also advise to think outside the box. Leave fixed patterns and look at everything as if you looked at it the first time. Think "like a white belt" again, be open to new learning. It also means that you should abandon all the preconceptions, because most of the time they just limit us. Perfect example of it happened many years ago when I was practicing advanced tameshigiri (test cutting). One of my beginner students saw me performing advanced cutting pattern called mizu gaeshi (returning water) in which you cut off a piece of mat by raising diagonal cut and immediately after you cut this small piece horizontally while it is still in the air. I did it so fast that he had to ask me what I actually did. When it was his turn to cut he replicated it almost flawlessly to my astonishment. It was far above his level back then, but he succeeded because he didn't know it was difficult. In my opinion lack of limiting preconceptions is what others call "beginners' luck".

What are the most important points in your teaching methods today?

I follow the rule of doctors – first of all, do not harm. I try to implement in my trainings the latest achievements of science, especially biomechanics and sports medicine. I also constantly introduce new training equipment. As far as fighting is concerned, I focus on its feasibility, but with care given to the safety of my students. I often watch old recordings of masters with whom I used to train and I try to search for some old, forgotten training elements which could be successfully used today. I consult my training methods with my sons and other instructors and I try to make it possible for people training in the Warsaw Karate Center to meet many different instructors and training methods. For example, ately in our trainings we've been using exercises with the thick rope, such as the team tug of war. In kids karate training I integrated elements of soft weapon fighting based on sports chanbara. It teaches kids, who are too young to free spar in karate fashion, basic and universal fighting skills like correct timing or "feeling" the distance to the opponent.

Do you think that Olympics will be positive or negative for Karate?

The question is whether karate has a chance to become an Olympic sport. With so many different karate organizations which deal in sport and with such inaccurate rules I highly doubt that.

On the one hand, I would like karate to become an Olympic sport. Both of my sons Kuba and Michael and a few of my students have their whole walls covered in medals they obtained in competitions. The title of the Olympic champion is the highest achievement in the world of sport. However, on the other hand, karate could possibly lose its features of a martial art, just like it happened with judo. Simply put, my attitude towards karate at the Olympics is ambivalent.

What are your views on the fact that kata won't be incorporated in the Olympics?

Such decision puzzles me, because kata constitute a very original idea in sport karate. Especially team kata and bunkai elements – it is a very spectacular event.

Besides, many sports feature technical events, and that's exactly what sport kata is.

For laymen, karate, taekwondo and wushu fights all look the same, but all three sports want to be part of the Olympics. Taekwondo has already achieved this status owing to the support of the Korean government. Wushu is extensively promoted by China. Japan is already responsible for bringing judo into the Olympic games and I don't think it cares about karate. After all, karate has been popular around the globe for many years now. Kata, an element so focused on in karate, could become an event which would differentiate karate from other disciplines I mentioned.

Please tell us about your experience and training in Battodo and Chanbara?

I don't even know when exactly I started to concentrate on the samurai sword. From the very beginning I trained samurai fencing very intensively together with my sons. My wife Theresa eventually joined us saying that either she will go crazy hearing about it all the time, or... she will practice with us. In 2001 I founded the Samurai Juku (Samurai School), which is a separate club. Thanks to fantastic teachers and experience gained from other Japanese martial arts, it took just a few years to achieve mastery. Already in 2005 I achieved the 5th dan rank in Toyama-ryu battodo, whereas my sons Kuba and Michael achieved the 1st dan. Currently, we have no equal in tameshigiri (the art of cutting with the sword) in the whole Europe. I regularly host tameshigiri and kata competitions as well as give dozens of demonstrations annually.

I wrote two books about samurai fencing and there are many video clips on youtube which feature me and my sons performing tameshigiri. I use knife (tanto) in one of those videos, which has been watched by tens of thousands of people from Japan and Korea. I know no better melee weapon than the samurai sword. By using it I also refer to the tradition of Polish nobility and their mastery of using the sabre. The sabre was as important for a Polish member of nobility as the katana was for a Japanese samurai.

Similarly to battodo, I also brought sports chanbara – soft weapon fighting – to Poland. It is the only martial art in which you can attack with full speed and force without the risk of injuring your opponent. It is great fun, which teaches how to fight at a longer distance. I encourage every martial artist to try it. I managed to train many wonderful competitors, who gain medals in European and World Championships of sport chanbara.

I think that fascination with weaponry comes with age, when we realize that using a weapon is more about precision and skill than physical attributes, which constitute such an important factor in hand-to-hand fighting such as karate or judo.

What is your opinion about the format "Shobu Ippon" division in Karate competition?

A fight until a single point is scored is a traditional understanding of karate competition. The one who successfully hits, wins. However, competition is not a real battle, it is a sport game. Therefore, I prefer "sambon shobu" – a fight until 3 points have been scored. I even agree with increasing the score limit over 3. It is easy to make an unjust judgment, which can eliminate a better contestant, during single score fights. The goal of a sport competition is to highlight the best athletes, not the most lucky ones. A number of old Japanese masters talked to me about sport competitions in the following way: "remember, that the silver medal goes to the one who would die last in a battle". There is some truth to it, but such approach shows a lack of understanding of the idea behind sport.

What karate can offer to the individual in these troubled times we are living in?

Training karate is a great way to actively rest and isolate from all problems of everyday life. We use our muscles less and less; cars, elevators and other pieces of equipment successfully eliminate physical effort, which is necessary for our health. Karate offers a very versatile way of performing gymnastic exercises, all of which are performed for both sides of the body. Karate gives self-defense skills which boost confidence in many situations, not necessarily associated with danger. It also teaches how to develop one's personality and overcome small obstacles to achieve a greater goal. It teaches how to be consistent, work in a group, listen and carry out commands and how to focus on specific actions.

Finally, what advise would you like to give to all Karate practitioners?

I would like to wish them perseverance on their way of karate and to find their own, individual path instead of blindly copying someone else. We have to be authentic in what we do. O

"A karate teacher has to really like this martial art and possess patience, which is necessary to teach other people, especially children."

AKIRA SAITO

BEING PRESENT

Sensei Akira Saito initiated karate with Wagner Piconez Angeloni for Shotokan style. Later, he traveled to Japan and started his training on the Goju-ryu style with Hanshi Konomoto Takashi – 9th Dan, at the Shizuoka Goju-ryu Honbu Dojo (Japan Karate-do Goju-kai Association), in the city of Sagara, Province of Shizuoka. He received the authorization to use the name "Shizuoka Goju-kan" in Brasil as a subsidiary. Back in Brazil, he continued his training with Hanshi 8th Dan Watanabe Ryuzo, representative of IKGA (International Karate-do Goju-kai Association) in South America until his death. Sensei Saito affiliated with the WKF (World Karate Federation) in Japan, when I lived there, by the JKF (Japan Karate Federation) and in Brazil by CBK (Brazilian Karate Confederation).

Based on tradition, but open to new forms and training ideas, Sensei Saito has evolved to the highest levels of skill and understanding. The way he explains the philosophy and technical foundation of karate, using common sense and keen logic, is refreshing and soothing in these days when martial arts in general are leading us to more combative and violent approaches. Sensei Akira Saito is a living example of how the past and the future can work together.

How many styles - karate or other Martial Arts methods - have you trained in and who were your teachers?

I've trained judo when I was a child for five years with Paulo Takahashi Sensei, nowadays I also practice Kendo and Iaido from the Shinto-ryu style with Marcelo Haafeld Sensei, where I am Shodan and Bojutsu Ryozen Chikubushima-ryu with Luis Kobayashi Sensei. In parallel I practice Shibu-do and Kenbujutsu, Shoko-ryu style with Kato Shoetsu Sensei, being graduated 4th Dan. I train all these arts at the Fukushima Kenjin Association in Brazil, province from where my grandparents come from.

Karate Masters

"I believe that the differences between the styles are in the characteristics of its origins."

Would you tell us some interesting stories of your early days in karate?

The stories from the beginning of my training are familiar to all apprentices, difficulties with motor coordination, enjoyed training more due to the physical practice, rather than the philosophic side and liked to fight (laughs). But an interesting fact happened when I was living in Japan and in order to start my training at my Master's Dojo, since I was the first Brazilian to practice there, I needed to find a "Hoshonin", a kind of surety whom would be responsible for my acts, in case I did not use the karate according to the standards of that Dojo and with the Karate philosophy. I think I left a good impression and gained my Sensei's trust, because after my graduation, no other Brazilian needed a "Hoshonin" in order to practice in the Dojo.

Were you a 'natural' at karate – did the movements come easily to you?

Truthfully, I always liked martial arts, especially when a child, enjoyed the movies. Seeing the kicks, made me want to try to copy them. I take myself as an endeveavoured person, not skilled, the hits are not easy for me, especially if studied deeply. I believe I still need to practice a lot in order to have my movements and strikes close to what I judge perfect.

Please, explain for us the main points of Goju Ryu and its differences with other styles like Shotokan or Shito Ryu?

I believe that the differences between the styles are in the characteristics of its origins. The techniques are similar, but its concepts are sometimes different. I see an important point in Goju-ryu the effort on strength concentration, stiffen the muscles to support and absorb impact from the hits applied when practicing the kata Sanchin, the flexibility of the circular movements applied in the kata Tensho and the Ibuki, the correct respiration, performing the "Tanden" and the energy flow, characteristics of the Naha-Te, that are worked differently than the styles that come from the

Shuri, like the Shotokan-ryu, as an example. The "maai" is also different, in the Goju-ryu style, the strikes are closer, emphasizing the short distance, while the Shotokan-ryu the emphasis are in long distances and its movements lean to be more straight and less circular. The Shito-ryu style, aggregate a bit of the techniques from each school, adopting the circular movement techniques from the Goju-ryu and the straight moves from Shotokan-ryu. In the Goju-ryu style techniques, the circular movement causes the end of the each defense, the forearm to remain "glued" to the attack, permitting to grab the opponent to hit, kick or knock him down for the finisher.

"The Karate-do is a martial art, cannot be simplified to only a Sport, even though the sports have its benefits."

Tell us a little about Gogen Yamaguchi.

Master Yamaguchi Gogen was born in January 20th, 1909, in the province of Miyazaki. Master Yamaguchi Gogen studied in the Ritsumeikan University, where he met and initiated his training with Master Miyagi Chojun. In 1937 received the name "Gogen" from Master Miyagi and the authorization of promoting the karate-do Goju-ryu all around Japan. In 1950 founded JKGA (Japan Karate-do Goju-kai Association) and by 1951 received from Master Miyagi the 10° Dan graduation, being considered one of the biggest Masters of Karate-do in all Japan. In 1964 managed to reunite the Masters of the present styles in Japan, initiating the creation and foundation of what is known today as Japanese Karate-do Federation. In 1969 Master Yamaguchi Gogen creates the IKCA (International Karate-do Goju-kai Association), entity that regulates the Goju-ryu style from the Yamaguchi family all around the world, nominating in each country and continent a representative. Master Yamaguchi Gogen died in May 20th, 1989, at eighty years old, leaving his legacy to his son Yamaguchi Goshi.

Karate Masters

What do you think are the most important characteristics of the Goju style?

I believe that the most important facts in the Goju-ryu style is the Ibuki, the correct breathing, the energy concentration applied and the connection between Heaven, Earth and Man (Tenchijin), concept used for example, when we do the kata Sanchin. Also, as a characteristic, being a style that comes from Naha, its members callous training, fingers and joint are very present. In the philosophical part, I think that an important point is the application of the rigid GO concept and flexible JU, in the day to day life, human character preparation. It is like the steel of the Japanese katana, if it is only rigid, it will break with the impact, on the other hand, if it is only flexible, it will not stand the hits, the same happens with our day to day like, we need always to seek the balance.

Karate is nowadays often referred to as a sport... would you agree with this definition or is a martial art?

The Karate-do is a martial art, cannot be simplified to only a Sport, even though the sports have its benefits. The sportsmanship and competition part of the karate have its value, because it is through the sports competition that it is motivated the practice among the children, for example. I see no harm in competition. I do not see with good eyes teachers that instruct their students to only practice for competition. That would be wrong. The Karate-do is a noble martial art, for personal and moral aggrandizement, of a search of spiritual elevation, the competition, in this case, is only a small fraction of the real meaning of the karate. At our Dojo, we teach Karate-do Goju-ryu at the traditional form and we have various champions in the competitions. In the competitions, there are rules, which need to be understood, respected and also an strategy to win with those rules. Specific training, physical, techniques and strategy is also needed, but nothing changes the concept of martial arts. Sport limits you to a range of age, while karate, as Martial Art, thinks that we can practice it until our last breath.

What are the most important qualities for a student to become proficient in karate?

It is necessary that the student be perseverant, a lot of willpower, discipline, humbleness and above all determination to win. Not only winning his adversaries, but winning oneself. Winning your problems, your weakness, your fears. The person that wins oneself each day, will achieve, for sure, your goals.

When teaching the art of karate – what is the most important element; self-defense or sport?

I learned with my Sensei that everything within the karate has to have the "Imi", in other words, meaning. Sports could have its meaning, but it is not the reality of all practitioners. Now, on the personal defense, the essential, since all the movements of the art are based on defend and counter-attack, if the practitioner does not learn the real meaning of the movements he is doing, will only be doing physical exercise, just a movement.

"Reaching the perfection and understanding of the katas, is the main point."

Kihon, Kata and Kumite, what's the proper ratio in training?

In my opinion, it is essential to practice a lot of Kihon and Kata, before accomplishing properly the strikes in the Kumite. In the Kumite, the kit being performed without the correct technique and application, could lead to a risk of lesion to the trainee and his partner. I don't know if there is a way to measure the exact training proportion, but I believe it would be about 50% dedicated to the physical invigoration exercises and techniques refining through the Kihon, 40% dedicated to the study of the techniques, some of them secret, within the Katas and 10% dedicated to the specific practice of the Kumites. Of course, all of this, being trained in the traditional Karate. If it is directed to the competition, it would be necessary a bigger percentage in the specific area.

How has your personal expression karate has developed over the years and what is it that keeps you motivated after all these years?

I believe that the changes happened mainly in my point of view. Fact that has influence due to the age and maturity. When we are young, we practice karate in a more physical manner, much more emotional than rational. When we get older and more mature, we begin to understand the techniques and that all the training was developed not only to build a strong body, but also the spirit, mind and energy. This brings harmony and balance and capabilities to train till the end of life. What motivates me every day is the fact that when we practice, we seek perfection, not only a perfect technique, but also the perfection of the spirit.

Karate Masters

"It is necessary that the student be perseverant, a lot of willpower, discipline, humbleness and above all determination to win."

How important is competition in the evolution of a karate practitioner?

I believe that not all practitioner needs to dedicate to competition. But in the competition, there are positive facts that can be used by the practitioner, mainly in children cases. In the competition it is possible to teach to win, going through obstacles which are needed for the human being development. Winning the fear before the competition, the physiological fact, the fear of losing to the opponent. Learn the value of competition, learn to win and lose, learn with the failure and convert it into motivation to reach your success.

What really means Ikken Hissatsu and how it applies when used in Karate?

The term "Kill with a strike or fist" arouse, in my opinion, due to the fact that in an unarmed combat versus an armed opponent, were your life is at risk, the training must be so intense that in this situation, you can kill the opponent, with only a hit. In the Japanese martial arts there is a concept of "Ichi Geki Hisatsu", "kill with one attack", which is normally used in the Kendo and Iaido, and I believe the concept is the same. Nowadays the concept could not only be used in the technique itself, but in our day to day life. If we think that everything we do, we have only one chance of making it right, do it well done and not postponing.

How do you see the art of Karate evolve in the future?

I see the evolution of the karate, mainly in the scientific field. Lots of the traditional exercises, today, not used exclusively in karate, has scientific answers, in the physiological and biomechanics sphere, seeking a better performance and efficiency. I believe that new discoveries and also the evolution of technology will bring a lot of benefits to the karate training. Of course that all of this should be added, never substituted. The karate-do is the evolution of human beings, the more we evolve in science and physics, more we evolve and learn with Karate-do. I see karate-do as an art of infinite evolution, because, we are the tools.

Do you feel that you still have further to go in your studies?

Yes, I believe I'm only in the beginning of my journey. Karate-do is an art very rich and we can learn something new. It is necessary to be training intensively and vigorously, to maintain your mind always humble and open to new discoveries.

What advice would you give to students on the question of supplementary training?

I always motivate my students to seek for supplementary training. The accumulation of knowledge enables you to a better understanding of the techniques and concepts. I do believe that all knowledge should be added and not substituted.

What advice would you give to an instructor who is struggling with his or her won development?

The recommendation I also tell them is that to maintain yourself humble, it is necessary an intense and vigorous practice, your personal limits will always tell you who you really are. The instructor needs to know that the only thing is has above the other practitioners is the responsibility and nothing more. We are in a constant progress, the experience of life and maturity will always give us a different point of view. There is a long path and we should always learn with it.

Have been times when you felt fear in your training?

Yes, I have felt fear lots of times. We should not banish fear from our feelings, but yet, should learn to control it, not being ashamed of feeling it, but facing it courageously.

Karate Masters

"Karate-do is a noble martial art, for personal and moral aggrandizement, of a search of spiritual elevation."

Do you think that Olympics will be positive for the art of karate-do?

I think there are lots of motives and reasons to think that Karate in the Olympics will bring benefits. One of them, for sure, will be the mass media exposure and a bigger publicizing of the sport. But I also think that this could lead a certain number of practitioners to dedicate themselves only and exclusively to competition, and that is bad. Mainly now with the present rules which they want to establish a sport karate, with no distinguish from the styles. The styles are the origins and its concepts, the traditional and martial part of the karate-do and it cannot be turned into just a sport.

What are your views on kata bunkai?

I see bunkai kata as a way, not the only one, to apply the techniques comprehended in the kata (lots of times hidden – "kakushi"). It is important for the traditional techniques of the karate-do within the kata be learned and transmitted in its original structure. Differently from the Bunkais shown in the competitions from WKF by the kata team manner, where lots of times we see the techniques (lots of them not even from the karate) being used with more emphasis in the esthetics, like a TV show. This has a value, only in the sports sphere, a way to please the audience.

Goju Ryu doesn't have a large number of kata, does this make a difference compared to other styles whose number of kata are higher?

Reaching the perfection and understanding of the katas, is the main point. In the competition point of view, yes, is does make a difference due to the used system of simple elimination, where, in an official competition, the athlete usually needs at least seven katas, being two of them mandatory. Demanding in some cases, that the athlete use katas from other styles in order to compensate the requirements in a competition.

How do you like to train yourself?

When I was younger I liked to train the combat part of the karate. Today I see the karate-do in a more complete form/angle and all the training is important. I always liked the physical exercise, the fortification of the body. The human body needs to be exercised every day, for that reason, today, besides the karate-do, I also practice kendo, Iaido, Bojutsu, Shibu Kenbujutsu and long distance race. When we are young we mainly think in the physical sphere and conquests, principally in the competitions case. More mature, we begin to comprehend better the values of the Japanese Martial Arts and with that, we change our goals.

"Learn the value of competition, learn to win and lose, learn with the failure and convert it into motivation to reach your success."

Shotokan, Shito Ryu, Goju, Ryu etc...How do you think the different styles affect the art of Karate?

I think that the styles are different from one another on their techniques and origin concepts, not from its philosophy. The Budo, if practiced in the correct form, shows exactly that the martial arts assist to a spiritual evolution of the human being, above all.

Do you think Kobudo training is beneficial for a Karate practitioner?

If the intention of the practitioner is the deep study of the traditional techniques of the karate-do, yes. Like the Goju-ryu, for example, which is originated in Naha, where they had lots of arts of combat with weapons (some of them existing till today). Lots of techniques were originated from these arts and some other techniques founded to combat them. I imagine that it is hard for a karate practitioner that does not have knowledge of the Kobudo, to understand and apply these defense techniques in its essence, as the name itself suggests, "karate-do" (way of the empty hands) was the art that in those days, did not use weapons against your armed opponent.

Karate Masters

"I believe that the most important point to teach today is the importance of the moral values, citizenship, of how reaching your goals with your own sacrifice and maintain the culture and traditions."

What is your opinion about the "Shobu Ippon" division in Karate competition?

I noticed that today, the karate competitions have become more dynamics and more alike the sports. A price paid to get an "Olympics Status" and have support from the mass media and tv. I do not see today, in this context, the same space for the "Shobu Ippon" as a competition sports.

What are the most important points in your teaching methods today?

I believe that the most important point to teach today is the importance of the moral values, citizenship, of how reaching your goals with your own sacrifice and maintain the culture and traditions. Another important is the good understanding between the traditional education and all the evolution of an Era. All the scientific evolution comes to benefit us and with that, add a lot of new possibilities of exercising. The competition cannot be considered the Art of the Karate-do, but part of it, and yet, nowadays its practice is very important, mainly for kids, since it is a way of stimulating the practice, in a playful way of experimenting the combat and a way to learn to loose and win.

The accumulation of knowledge enables you to a better understanding of the techniques and concepts."

What karate can offer to the individual in these troubled times we are living in?

The karate-do can offer more than just the physical benefits, a way of relieving the stress, a way of helping to succeed obstacles and daily problems, a way of self-understanding, cultural enrichment, a way of learning and spiritual evolution, besides being a way to rescue moral values, today forgotten by a big portion of the society. Not mentioning also the preparation of the individual for a probable self-defense, if needed.

After so many years of training, what is it for you that is so appealing in this style of karate and why?

As much as I practice, more I feel attracted to the art. I face the practice of the Karate-do Goju-ryu, or any other art that I practice, as a new daily discovery. This motivates me a lot, since I always see new possibilities of growing and new targets to be reached. I always think of seeking perfection of the techniques and not only in learning new ones.

Finally, what advise would you like to give to all Karate practitioners?

My advice is to always practice, with emphasis, will force, with no excuses. Instead of giving various justifications for not training it's better to have just one good reason to train. O

YASUYOSHI SAITO

A LIFE VISION

SAITO SENSEI WAS BORN IN NORTHERN JAPAN AND TRAINED IN THE JKA SYSTEM WITH HIS SENSEI, THE LEGENDARY KARATE MASTER HIROSHI SHOJI. WHEN SAITO SENSEI LEFT JAPAN, HE INITIALLY TAUGHT IN FRANCE, SOUTH AMERICA AND THE CARIBBEAN. IN GUADELOUPE, FRENCH WEST INDIES HE WAS CHIEF INSTRUCTOR OF THE "BUDOKAN FRENCH FEDERATION". IN 1971, SAITO SENSEI ARRIVED TO SOUTH FLORIDA WHERE, UNTIL 1992 HE WAS AN INSTRUCTOR OF THE "INTERNATIONAL SHOTOKAN KARATE FEDERATION", SOUTH ATLANTIC BRANCH. IN 1993, HE FOUNDED "JAPAN KARATE-DO INTERNATIONAL" WITH AFFLIATED MEMBERS IN ENGLAND, VENEZUELA, HAITI, PUERTO RICO AND CURACAO. TEACHING CLASS, TWO - THREE EACH DAY, SIX DAYS EACH WEEK ALONG WITH TRAVELING FOR TEACHING SEMINARS, SAITO SENSEI IS EXACTLY WHERE HE WANTS TO BE: IN A DOJO PASSING ON THE VALUES OF A LIFE DEDICATED TO KARATE. SENSEI OFTEN REMINDS HIS STUDENTS THAT ONE NEEDS MONEY, DEDICATION, TIME AND TRUST TO MAKE THE MOST OF ONE'S KARATE TRAINING.

How long have you been practicing Karate?

For over 50 years. I have taught karate for more than four decades internationally. I did only trained in JKA karate. Mr. Shoji was my main instructor. I was lucky to train with many top JKA karateka too but he was my main teacher. My focus is only karate-do, although I study many other professional sports and their athletes to see what really makes a worldclass competitor and athlete.

Would you tell us some interesting stories of your early days in Karate?

I remember being given the opportunity to teach abroad. This was a time when not many instructors, let alone, average Japanese people could travel abroad. I specifically remember the day, 14 December 1970. That was a day I remember as an exciting turning point in my life. I was given the opportunity to teach internationally and represent JKA in Guadalupe, French West Indies. This was a very exciting and proud time in my career. One other exciting memory was competing in the Olympic stadium in Tokyo representing Saitama prefecture in team kumite. Our team placed in

Karate Masters

"Karate-do and sport do not mix. Sport is for enjoyment. Karate is a way of life."

second position. That was 1968. Our team didn't win but it was good, exciting, competition.

Please, explain for us the main points of Shotokan and its differences with other styles like Goju Ryu or Shito Ryu.

Shotokan has around 100 varieties that are practiced. I can only talk about JKA Karate since its the only type I have practiced. This Karate was developed by the first generation Karate-ka of the JKA under the leadership of Master Nakayama. It is very dynamic, strong, fast, and big movements. We are very fortunate to have received such a high level Karate. This first generation of karateka competed in tournaments and were champions in their own right. Our texbooks reflect this. All the karateka demonstrating techniques in the textbooks were champions. The 'Best Karate' series of textbooks is a reflection of these Karateka's technical level and skill.

Please tell us a little about Masatoshi Nakayama Sensei.

He was at the highest level, all the way at the summit of a mountain and very far from everybody else. We are very lucky that he taught us Karate. He was the most senior of JKA, so I could not approach him, but later I had the honor to see him twice in Florida. During those times I was his personal assistant and translator. His teaching was very technical. I remember him always sweating during the sessions. He also loved to film things, such as Nature, with his video recorder on his trips. When I asked him questions, I recall that he always spoke to me in a very refined way and with great humility.

What do you think are the most important characteristics of the JKA style of Shotokan?

It develops the person. In addition, the early generation karateka developed competitions. They were very competitive. This is why each technique we practice is so effective. It passed the rigors and tests of competition. To further clarify, there is no JKA style. JKA simply means Japan Karate Association. The karateka who trained in the JKA were karate players who exhibited the epitome 'top-level' karate...their karate became synonymous with JKA, but still it is only an association, not a style of karate do.

Karate is nowadays often referred to as a sport. Do you agree with this definition?

Karate-do and sport do not mix. Sport is for enjoyment. Karate is a way of life. Most sports, unlike our art, are constantly evolving and improving. With respect to our Karate, I think that we must first focus on catching up to the level of the first generation of karateka. This has not happened, and we are not even close. Our goal for the future is to look back at the past and reach that level.

When teaching the art of Karate, what is the most important element; self-defense or sport?

Karate is karate. It is Budo. Budo is martial arts where we always have an opponent: Life or death is the result. It is no joking, no playing around - always serious. This is the principle of karate practice. Karate is working hard. I accept this. Nothing comes easily or naturally. I don't think of a person as being 'gifted' either. To achieve the level that we aspire to, one must be willing to accept the idea of 'sweating, injuries, and hard work'. This is what my seniors did. I think you should never say that you are 'natural' at anything. JKA Karate was never easy because the standards were so high. All around me were karateka who worked very hard.

Kihon, Kata and Kumite, what's the proper ratio in training?

Kihon 50%, Kata 25% and Kumite 25%. This is a basic formula for how one should train. This is my suggestion but the goal is great karate as a whole. Therefore, one should not separate any of the above mentioned. Kihon equals Kata equals Kumite equals Kata equals Kihon, and so on. All three are one idea. One contiguous entity, not three separate ones.

Karate Masters

How your personal expression of Karate has developed over the years, and what is it that keeps you motivated after all these years?

No change. Except that now I am older and I am adjusting to this fact. I enjoy meeting karateka from different countries and seeing how Karate is practiced worldwide. I greatly enjoy teaching Karate to so many different people.

How important is competition in the evolution of a Karate practitioner?

Karateka should compete at least once a year. To improve technically, you need to participate in competitions. This is why the JKA started and emphasized competitions. This is why the first generation reached such a high level. You test yourself in a broader arena than in your familiar dojo and you force your horizons to expand. You compare yourself to all the competitors and it helps you know where you stand…what are your strengths and weaknesses. It operates as a motivator. Now you train harder because the bar has been raised. It helps you visualize your goal until the next competition. We can give the example of genetics. When the gene pool is limited and becomes stagnant, reproduction suffers and genetic defects increase. Expanding the gene pool is a good thing because it produces stronger healthier specimens. Competition is a good thing in general, in life. When a market offers only one product and there is no competition, the supplier gets lazy and complacent. As soon as a competitor offers similar goods, both suppliers must work harder and improve the product.

What does "Ikken Hissatsu" really mean and how is this applied in Karate?

Again this is a Japanese Budo idea "One strike, one kill."

Do you feel that you still have further to go in your studies?

Yes, always. I must keep in good physical shape as age progresses. Everything becomes more difficult as we age. I must keep my technique the same. Learning never ends. One must keep the peak level and not let it drop. This is the challenge. It is like keeping boiling water at the same temperature. One must practice with more feeling.

What advice would you give to students on the question of supplementary training?

The elements of flexibility, muscle strength, stamina and stretching are extremely important. The muscles should be flexible like bamboo, not rigid like muscles from weight training. Basically there are 3 types of power that must be developed: External: This is simply to develop the muscles, and is easy to do. Second the internal power. This is more complicated in nature. This, you can achieve by sweating and exerting maximum effort during training. We must practice like sprinters instead of marathon runners. Eating good food is also vital.

And finally the mental power for which one must develop kiai, which is generated from the lower stomach area. Go out to the beach or a mountain, grab the earth with your feet and practice a strong kiai. This mental power does not need sweat. It is the result after achieving external and internal power. The kiai expresses this.

What advice would you give to an instructor who is struggling with his or her own development?

He or she should sometimes learn from another good instructor. As honest karateka, we should be willing to set aside ego or political ideologies so that we as sensei may continue to propagate strong karate and not let our own self-interests and ego diminish what our seniors worked so hard at creating. Perhaps we all need a second opinion from another great instructor to reevaluate ourselves and, how we approach teaching our classes!

"Karate is karate. It is Budo. Budo is martial arts where we always have an opponent: Life or death is the result."

Have there been times when you felt fear in your training?

No, I don't think along these lines. Getting injured in training is a reality, an integral part of Karate. One must not think about this. Karate is about facing yourself and facing reality. The quicker one accepts this as a reality, the more intense your attitude in training becomes. If you train with 100% life & death seriousness, you will not have time to be afraid. If you trust your instructor, then you accept all the aspects of training, including injuries.

Karate Masters

"Competition is a good thing in general, in life."

Do you think that the Olympics will be positive for the art of Karate-Do?

Possibly. However, before taking this step, a uniform international standard must be clearly established. We need to hold a major tournament where all karateka attend and compete. We need unity in order to work on establishing this standard. We are still very far from this. Also, we must give the right incentives for the competitors and judges to accomplish this. This will produce young karateka of an Olympic level.

What are your views on Kata bunkai?

Of course it's important. Kata is everything, and bunkai is part of Kata. Bunkai is application practice. Today in the tournament circle we see an artificial separation between Kata and bunkai, as if they were two separate independent aspects of Karate. It should never be this way. They should never be practiced separately. Bunkai is included in the proper practice of Kata. The essence of Kata is Kumite. This must be seriously understood, not just intellectually, but during actual practice.

There are only 15 original Shotokan kata although many more are practiced today in the style. How important is the number of katas practiced?

It is not how many Kata you know, it's the quality that counts. In the old days, the tradition was to spend an average of 3 years learning one Kata.

How do you like to train yourself?

I always move my body....every part of it. I work on keeping in shape and on flexibility. The more you sweat the better.

Shotokan, Shito-Ryu, Goju Ryu etc... How do you think the different styles affect the art of Karate?

Different styles basically emphasize different aspects of Karate.

Do you think Kobudo training is beneficial for a Karate practitioner?

Karate means "empty hand", both in offense and defense. We practice barefoot and barefisted. A weapon is an extension of the body. The idea is the same but also different. Because of this similarity, the benefits are also the same but the distance and range changes. As to the sharpness and lethality of weapons, Karate teaches you to make your hands and feet into a sharp lethal weapon. In Karate training we should not be thinking about weapons but about what we can do within our body limits. If I practiced Kobudo and held a weapon, then what do I need Karate for? Remember that the whole purpose of the development of Karate was precisely because weapons were forbidden. If they had not been forbidden, then Karate could have never created. JKA Karate is very strong, we do not need additional weapons. And since we forge our body into a weapon, we need nothing more.

What is your opinion about the "Shobu Ippon" division in Karate competition?

Ippon is a fundamental Japanese cultural idea found across-the-board in Budo. Budo is about life and death survival. Budo in essence is 'ippon shobu'. There is no second chance. Ippon means death for the opponent. It means the point of no return. This is why when you get an opportunity, an opening, then you must apply 100% and nothing less. The fight is over. If you fail then you don't return. If you succeed then the opponent cannot return. Therefore the training must reflect this same spirit. The right attitude must be applied to the training of Karate. Everything must be practiced giving 100%...not 90%. We have no second or third round in a fight. It should be a life or death practice. Would somebody be joking and talking during a deadly fight? We see this same Budo attitude in general Japanese culture, no second chances. This changes the way everybody takes on different tasks in Japan. It seems in western practice of karate, the focus is more sports oriented. We've seen multi-point competitions were it seems that 2 points, 6 points, maybe 10 points can be scored in a single match. This is where rules are critical. One must follow these rules so victory can be achieved through multiple chances. In Budo, ippon-shobu, there is no room for luck or winning by a technicality, you must clearly be superior to your opponent to achieve victory. You do not have a chance to overcome a poor start, you must be ready to win or lose, live or die in that moment.

Karate Masters

What are the most important points in your teaching methods today?

It is really not a method. One must understand the correct technique, which most people do not understand. Some say they understand it, but they mean mentally. They don't know how to actually apply it. We hear instructors say "great" to students, but what is the level of comparison? I never say "great" because there is no need to say this. 'Great' does not come from an instructor saying you are so. Great is very difficult to achieve. Not many practitioners achieve the level of "greatness". Also, many speak of philosophy. Again, I never speak of this. We should focus on training karate by forging our bodies and minds through honest and diligent daily practice first and foremost. Ideas and strength spring from this, not the other way around.

Practice slowly in the beginning, learn at slow pace, especially hand techniques. This is important to achieve the right muscle memory. Later apply power and speed. Once you get it right, never change it. During the learning stage you can practice in front of the mirror by yourself, you don't even need a gi. Practice it until you get the feeling and the rhythm. then practice it again and again. There are no shortcuts, no secret techniques.

With respect to being in shape, this is a completely different issue. Exercising for endurance, aerobic benefits and fitness is another aspect. This is unrelated to technique.

What the art of Karate offers to the individual in these troubled times we are living in?

I try to teach that Karate and Life are similar. Nothing is guaranteed to be fair in either, so don't expect this. One must accept the disappointments and the triumphs equally. Nobody can help you but yourself. Nobody can "give" you the skill, must earn it yourself by hard work. Always think of these four principles: Kiai: Karate means a strong Kiai and this equals strong spiritual development. This develops strong power and confidence. This is why it is important to practice with a strong kiai, with the correct attitude. Even if you have nothing in life, you can still have a strong kiai. Nobody can take this away.

Trust: Trust is important in Karate. You must learn to trust. Today's society needs to teach people to trust each other.

Humility: Karate also teaches the correct humility which is power.

There is nothing new in life. Just as life did not change, neither did Karate.

Stress: Karate teaches you to deal with reality, how to deal with disappointments, how to prevent false illusions. It teaches the correct rhythm of life. Our life and attitude in the Dojo is that if you cannot do something, just keep practicing. Don't think too much, just keep practicing and always positive.

After so many years of training, what is it for you that is so appealing in this style of Karate and why?

There are so many benefits. Good health. I enjoyed meeting so many people from different cultures. Karate accepts all cultures equally. In the Dojo we learn to have social harmony. Everybody is the same. I also enjoy the traveling and watching everybody practicing the same way. Karate is unique in that it needs nothing. No special place, no special equipment. One can practice anywhere, anytime, at any age and you don't need anyone...you can self-train. We are very lucky that our senior instructors gave us a great heritage, despite all the difficulties.

"The elements of flexibility, muscle strength, stamina and stretching are extremely important."

Basic and advanced technique, what is the difference Sensei?

There is no such thing in our method. It's all the same What you start in the beginning it is already the "advanced technique". This is why you must learn it right in the beginning and not change it later. The first step is developing the correct muscles. Then comes the right technique. You need a good Sensei to teach this. If the correct muscles are not ready to perform, then you will have a defective technique from the beginning and consequently develop the bad habits at this early stage. Without the correct muscles as the base there can be no improvement. I am always amazed at how many people keep practicing so many years with the same old bad habits. Since there is no difference in the technical aspect of the technique, "advanced practice" means improving speed, power, rhythm, distance and experience. 'Advanced' means that when you get older your muscles are natural, spontaneous, that you can still keep your skill and performance high. We see the same with other sports.

We can learn something from golf training. Before a student learns how to get out of a sand trap, he should learn how not to fall in one. In Karate, before one learns to fight one should learn how not to get drawn into a fight. (by developing awareness, confidence....) Before learning how to

Karate Masters

"It is not how many Kata you know, it's the quality that counts."

defend against a grab, one should learn how not to allow the opponent to grab you (by movement and distance training....) Then comes the actual defense training, integrating defense and attack into one.

What's your idea of repeating the techniques over and over? Do you think this is an effective way of training?

Yes, it is very important. Like in all other sports, there is a correct way to develop technique and long sets of many repetitions are important for skill development. During repetition training in the beginning one must do it slowly, to allow for muscle memory. One needs a good instructor to ensure this so that it pays off eventually.

Most people do not understand correct technique. This is why it is better to do it slowly and correctly in the beginning. People misunderstand the need for repetition and mistake it for getting into shape. Some students want to learn less repetition and instead learn a larger variety of techniques, thinking this is advanced training. They don't understand the nature of repetition.

Sensei, please explain the concept of "kime".

Kime is perfection. Not just karate, in all things. Kime means great. It means speed, power, balance, technique, distance, rhythm, focus, etc...

Do you think that Karate and its main technical leaders (sensei) can learn from other sports like Golf, Soccer, etc...?

Yes. We don't need to practice to learn from them. All sports and arts have the same concept: to seek the pinnacle of perfection and greatness. I like to look at Gymnastics which is very dynamic, and at ice skating or figure skating which is very graceful.

How do you remember Sensei Shoji?

I don't remember him correcting me too much, so I assume he must have thought I was okay. He was very strict. I visited his house several times. He showed me pictures of his Karate travels abroad. That's where I got my goal and dreamt of doing the same as he did. I was young and impressionable. I had trained about 6 years with him in Saitama Prefecture. I remember the endless repetitions of "Tekki Shodan".

Based on your traveling experience and teaching, what are the most important things that you see people should train to improve their karate?

Many instructors don't understand the difference between learning, and practicing Karate. In 'learning', in a 1-hour practice session, there should be 1-2 techniques. Start slowly and one must fully understand the correct technique. Your brain and muscles must be connected. At this stage, until you know the correct way, don't apply full speed or power. You need a good instructor with good eyes.

In 'practicing', you must find good role models to emulate. Models that are champions, in Kata, Kumite, etc... This gives you good ideas and helps you visualize. You should be thinking, "I want to practice this same way, I want to kick like him...." You need a good coach also. In 'practice' you apply full speed, power, rhythm, distance, endurance. Here you apply to 100% capacity. Imagination and spirit is important here and especially in Kata training. Watch the champions and emulate their way of performing it. That's the standard you should go by. Again, you need a good instructor with good eyes.

Sensei, what advise would you like to give to all Karate practitioners?

Dojo Kun is the 'minimum' that all karateka must have, that all people should have. It is just common sense in life. It is fundamental... the common goals of society. Many people quit training because they don't have these fundamental goals. Karate is not just about giving your best. Its win or die, its that simple. You need dedication and discipline.

Look at Olympic athletes, or great athletes in general. They exhibit the same concept. I have researched many top-level professionals and asked what is common to all of them, how did these people succeed?

You need to invest in the following: Time: Diligent training for many hours at a time. Daily practice Money: Monetary commitment for best supplies, facilities, instruction, etc. Trust: You need to look for the best instructor available and trust and do what that instructor requests. Commitment : You must 'want', desire to be great, to be a champion. You need to practice for winning. That is Karate-do. O

SADAAKI SAKAGAMI

IN THE NAME OF ITOSU

THE SAKAGAMI FAMILY TREE TRACES ITS ROOTS TO THE GREAT ANKHO ITOSU WHO WAS REGARDED AS ONE OF THE BEST KARATE MASTERS EVER PRODUCED IN OKINAWA. SADAAKI SAKAGAMI HAS FOLLOWED IN HIS FATHER'S FOOTSTEPS AND IS NOW KNOWN AS ONE OF THE MOST KNOWLEDGEABLE MEN OF KARATE AND THE SOKE OF THE "ITOSU RYU" STYLE. DESCRIBED AS AN UNSELFISH AND DEDICATED INSTRUCTOR, SOKE SAKAGAMI TRAVELS AROUND THE WORLD SHARING HIS KNOWLEDGE AND EXPERTISE. IT IS SOKE SAKAGAMI'S DESIRE TO PRESERVE AND SPREAD THE ORIGINAL ART DEVELOPED AND PASSED ONTO HIS FATHER BY THE GREAT KENWA MABUNI.

FOR SOKE SAKAGAMI, SPIRIT AND HEART ARE THE MOST IMPORTANT ATTRIBUTES IN KARATE TRANING. "IN ORDER TO BE THE BEST," HE SAYS FIRMLY, "YOU MUST HAVE THE WARRIOR'S HEART AND SPIRIT".

HE IS A KNOWLEDGEABLE AND FASCINATING MAN, FULL OF INTERESTING STORIES, AND BRIMMING WITH A POSITIVE ATTITUDE TOWARDS TEACHING AND LIFE. IN THE MODERN WORLD OF DISILLUSIONMENT, HE IS TRULY A UNIQUE INDIVIDUAL AND A TRUE KARATE MASTER.

How did your father, Ryusho Sakagami, become the successor of the Itosu Ryu style?

According to what I heard from my father Ryusho Sakagami, he was invited to his teacher Mater Kenwa Mabuni's house a few months before he passed away. At that time, Master Mabuni offered my father to be the successor of the Shito Ryu style.

But my father respectfully refused his offer because he had his own business and also he had never thought he would be able to live on karate at that time. So, my father told him: "I am not worthy to be the successor. Also, you have a son. So, please give him Shito Ryu Soke's title."

But Master Mabuni said, "If you don't be the successor, I will feel very bad and sorry for you. So, if you don't, please be the successor of my teacher, Itosu Sensei's orthodox lineage, using the name of "Itosu" instead of "Shito" to describe the style you will be teaching after my death".

Karate Masters

"Master Kenwa Mabuni was the founder of the Shito Ryu style. So, what my father learned from him was actually the complete Shito Ryu method."

How did your father start training Shito Ryu with Master Mabuni?

The reason my father started practicing Shito Ryu is that my father went to Kokushikan University in Tokyo to practice Kendo, and he met a classmate who was from Okinawa and was also a karate practitioner. My father started practicing karate when he was 12 or 13 years old in his hometown, Hyogo. He learned the art from a man from Okinawa.

Anyway, one day he was practicing karate's kata by himself at the University, and his friend from Okinawa surprisingly looked at it and he asked if it was karate or not. And my father replied to him by saying "Yes, it is Karate."

His friend also asked "Who did you learn it from?" My father replied to him that he learned the art from an Okinawan man in his hometown. The father of his friend was actually a karate teacher and he even owned a karate club in Okinawa. So, he asked my father to go to Okinawa to practice karate together. And while he was a University student, he often went to Okinawa to train.

After he graduated from the University, he wanted to keep training karate near his hometown in the Osaka area. So, he asked some Okinawan teachers if they could introduce him to a local karate teacher. They said that Master Kenwa Mabuni lived in Osaka [at that time] and he was a very good and reputable teacher. After the proper introduction, my father started training with Master Kenwa Mabuni.

Would you please define and explain the main characteristics of the Itosu Ryu style?

Master Kenwa Mabuni was the founder of the Shito Ryu style. So, what my father learned from him was actually the complete Shito Ryu method but before Master Mabuni passed away, he appointed my father to be the successor of Master Itosu's orthodox lineage, but what he was doing was actually Shito Ryu. Master Kenwa Mabuni knew he had to pass the Shito Ryu style to one of his sons and that is the reason why he named my father the leader and successor of the Itosu lineage. However, one day my father thought he had to distinguish the Itosu orthodox style from the Shito Ryu style, so he officially named it "Itosu Ryu".

Shito Ryu is based on Itosu Sensei's lineage and Higashionna Sensei's lineage. It was named after those two great masters' first kanji character, "shi" and "ito". So, we consider the Itosu Ryu style to be one of the roots of Shito Ryu and we keep cherishing the style although it is true we have the 'naha' elements and kata from the Higashionna lineage as well.

When did you start training in Kobudo?

The reason I started training Kobudo is because Master Shinken Taira started living at my father's house in 1957 or 1958 and was teaching Kobudo at my father's dojo. I directly learned Kobudo from Master Taira.

Karate was getting popular at that time, but Kobudo was not. I was wondering why we had to practice Kobudo at all. So my focus was relatively more on karate than Kobudo. However, since Master Taira and my father were living in the same place, I couldn't run away from Kobudo training. So, I trained and practiced Kobudo everyday. The sessions with Sensei Taira were very demanding and hard. With time I found practicing Sai strengthening the power of the wrist even for regular punching; training Bo is good for making sure distance is correct when facing an opponent. These discoveries made me practice Kobudo harder and harder so I could improve my karate at the same time.

Those practices in my young days became a part of my body, and they are a treasure for my martial arts' life today.

How did you actually feel when you became the successor of the Itosu style?

It was personally very shocking to me when my father passed away for obvious reasons. Then, a lot of my father's students, who were actually my 'sempai', senior students to me, told me that I should be the successor of the Itosu Ryu style. After thinking about it and getting the support from my 'sempai', I agreed and succeeded to be the successor of the style.

I received the huge responsibility to preserve the art which had been passed down for three generations: from Master Itosu, Master Mabuni, finally to my father Ryusho Sakagami, At the same time, I had strong feelings that it was my mission to promote the Itosu Ryu style to the world.

Karate Masters

Please tell us about the evolution and development of your personal training in the arts of Karate and Kobudo.

I directly learned karate from my father, so obviously I have huge influence from him.

However, there are a lot of styles in karate, for instance Shotokan, Goju Ryu and Wado Ryu, and I thought each style must have had wonderful techniques. So, I actually asked a lot of questions to many of the styles' instructors, regarding their techniques, and I especially asked about applications.

For instance, I went and asked other top instructors questions like; "In our style we have this kind of application, but how do you interpret this technique in your style?" This is how I studied the difference between the Itosu Ryu style and other styles.

I thought, "If I don't ask, I cannot develop Itosu Ryu itself. Learning other styles is also very important for having a full understanding of what my style, Itosu Ryu really is." This is how I accumulated my karate knowledge besides training under the guidance of my father.

How do you see the Itosu Ryu style around the world?

These days it is actually very difficult for any instructor to promote karate worldwide. Our karate organization is based on our karate techniques. However, not only the techniques but also humanity and communication skills are very important for international promotion. Also, there are cultural and economical differences in the world. Filling up the gap is a very difficult task these days. So, I always think spreading Itosu Ryu to the world is a very hard job because there are many other elements that affect the task.

What do you think about Budo and the sport aspect in Karate-do?

It is a very difficult issue. It is just like a diamond. If we look at a diamond, we can see a lot of glitters according to the angles. Karate is also same. According to the angle, there are a lot of aspects and facets. Some people consider it as Budo - the way of martial arts, but other people think it is sport. Budo is Japanese traditional martial arts which pursues the mental and physical ability through hard training. It is self-discipline. The idea of Budo is deeply related to Zen Buddhism. We have to have very hard training for that, and the final goal is developing ourselves.

But if you consider Karate-do as Budo, then the mental and spiritual aspects are very important, and it is a very difficult idea for regular people. I don't mean sports do not have a mental aspect, but the goal of sports is winning at a sportive competition, and that is the main purpose. Of course, any sports need hard training, but winning or losing is not so important in Budo training. Developing ourselves and especially our spirit is the focus of Budo training. That's the biggest difference between Budo and sports.

So, nowadays many people tend to forget about Budo's aspects, and they just focus on only winning tournaments. But I think Budo's aspects are very important in karate, and that's what I want to teach and pass onto my students and the followers of the Itosu method of karate.

We actually cannot say "This is the definition of the borderline for Budo or sport." Also, we cannot say, "Budo is better than sports" or "sport is better than Budo."

Furthermore, we have to teach both Budo and sport aspects to our students. So, now we - all karate instructors are in a difficult position. Actually I think not only Karate instructors, but also other martial arts instructors, such as Kendo and Judo, must have the same issue.

"I received the huge responsibility to preserve the art which had been passed down for three generations."

Real martial arts training has nothing to do with trophies and black belts. In fact we should learn the other way: think of losing your black belt or your trophy. Like the Zen master Sawaki Kodo said, "To gain is suffering; loss in enlightenment."

Can you elaborate on that Soke?

The main difference between the old time practitioners and today's is that old martial artists understood and looked at their training as a "loss." They gave up everything for their art and their practice. Today's practitioners only think of gain: "I want this, I want that." We want to practice martial arts but we want nice cars, a house, a lot of money, fame, etc…

It is important to not forget the spirit and determination of the great masters of the past.

Karate Masters

"We actually cannot say "This is the definition of the borderline for Budo or sport".

Please tell us about the traditional principle of "Shu-Ha-Ri."

The term "Shu-ha-Ri" came from Kendo. Actually, many Kendo words were introduced to the art of karate-do.

"Shu" means "Preserve." It means we firmly preserve what we learned from our teachers. We have to follow what our teacher taught us, and we have to practice it very hard.

"Ha" means "to add our own idea on what we learned from a teacher" and it is an idea for further personal study. "Ri" means "Being away from the idea of "Shu" and "Ha," and create our own style."

But there are a lot of people who do not understand the idea of "Shu" and try to do "Ha" and "Ri" right away instead of dedicating many years of practice to the concept of "Shu."

Many karate styles have this problem. There are a lot of groups and branches in any style now. I mean, many people make their own style by themselves simply to break away and be 'leaders'.

If anyone decides to make his own style, nobody can stop it. It is true that there is no such rule that we can't make our own style. That's why more and more styles and groups are created now without really bringing anything new. I let people judge that for themselves.

"Shu-Ha-Ri" is a concept of Budo, and it is actually for self-development. So, I believe the most important thing in Budo is that we have to preserve what we learned from our teacher...and later in life...follow and develop our own path.

What kind of message you would like to give to all karate practitioners?

I always ask this question to my students, "There are a lot of arts in Budo such as Judo, Kendo, and Karate-do, but why did you chose karate?" Some people simply say, "Because I like it," but I always ask them "Why do you like karate?"

They might reply; "Because it looks so cool!" and "Why do you think it is cool?"

They say; "fighting looks so cool!" But I finally tell them "I don't think it is the right answer," and I explain "Budo is for self- discipline, and we acquire it through hard training. If you just want to pursue the sport aspect, you will eventually quit karate-do."

Nowadays, most of the students are actually children. It is very difficult for them to understand what Budo means. It is very complex for them.

So, what I always do at first is "try to amuse children through karate training," and I let them understand "what is Budo" and little by little, taking time to do it.

How do you want everybody to remember the legacy of Itosu Ryu karate-do?

I think the most important element of a style is "Kata." The character of our Itosu Ryu style is preserving the art as much as possible, which has been passed down for three generations: from Master Itosu, Master Mabuni to Ryusho Sakagami. This is my mission, and I want everybody in the world to know what the Itosu Ryu style truly is.

Would you give us some final advice?

In Budo you learn "to do the most natural thing in the most natural way." But to find the most natural way and execute it in the more natural manner, it is not easy and that may be one of the biggest obstacles not only in our training but in our lives too.

Sometimes we seem to be unlucky in life and we start thinking negatively about training and about ourselves. Feeling sorry for yourself is self-defeat. We need to keep training and pushing forward because then the barriers will reveal themselves as teachings and a better understanding of things will come out of it. Just because the world is not going the way we want it is not a reason to surrender or to become negative about our lives.

Budo training is not about playing out our fantasies. It has to do with your own life and death. O

KENSEI TABA

AN OKINAWAN LEGEND

TABA SENSEI, LED HIS OWN ORGANIZATION, OKINAWA SHOGEN RYU KARATE-DO ASSOCIATION, AND WAS AT ONE TIME THE PRESIDENT OF THE WORLD MATSUBAYASHI RYU KARATE-DO ASSOCIATION AND THE RANKING STUDENT OF SHOSHIN NAGAMINE. IN THE SAME WAY SHOSHIN NAGAMINE SPREAD MATSUBAYASHI RYU TO THE WORLD, TABA SENSEI WISHES WERE TO SPREAD HIS STYLE OF KARATE.

KENSEI TABA WAS A MASTER AND ONE THAT TRULY DEMONSTRATED THE TRUE MEANING OF MARTIAL ARTS SHOWING RESPECT, KINDNESS, GENEROSITY, AND MOST OF ALL, HUMILITY. AFTER DEDICATING HIS WHOLE LIFE TO THE STUDY OF OKINAWA KARATEDO, IT IS WITH DEEP REGRET TO INFORM THE READER THAT BEFORE THIS PRINTING KENSEI TABA 10TH DAN PASSED AWAY IN 2012.

When and why did you first start your study of the Martial Arts?
On August 22, 1944, I was on a ship that was torpedoed by a U.S. Submarine. I watched many of my friends drown and since I was just a young boy, I could not save them. After being rescued by a Japanese warship and spending about a year on mainland Japan, I was returned home to Okinawa. In 1948 at age 13, I decided I wanted to become stronger so I would not be helpless again and I began studying Karate-Do.

Why did you start to study Matsubayashi Shorin Ryu?
When I decided to study Karate-Do, I went to many different schools and watched what was taught. I liked what I saw at the Nagamine dojo. I thought it was better than anything else I had seen. It was nice that the Nagamine dojo was very close to my home.

You studied under Hohan Soken and Chosen Chibana. Could you describe your memories and impressions?
Nagamine Sensei was a police officer and was moved to Nago and Motobu as part of police force. He was gone for a few years and that was when I began training with others. Hohan Soken Sensei had good tech-

Karate Masters

"Sensei Nagamine was like a father and I was like a son."

nique. He helped me a lot with my technique. We had a strong relationship. On his 90th birthday, he had 5 or 10 special dogi (training uniform) and obi (belt) made up and given to his top students. The obi was a shade of gold with a stripe of a different shade of gold running the length of it. I was one of the few to receive these gifts. I believe I showed you the obi. I still have it but have never worn it. Chibana Sensei taught good original Okinawa Karate-Do. That says it all. Another person that influenced my training during that time was one of the senior students of Nagamine Shoshin, Toguchi Seitoku. He was my "senpai" in Matsubayashi Ryu. He and I would train together outside of the dojo. It was very hard training. He was very good with the makiwara. After a few years of being away from Naha, Nagamine Shoshin returned and I resumed training under him directly. I did so until his death.

What was your relationship like with Shoshin Nagamine?

Nagamine was like a father and I was like a son. He taught me everything without holding back which is what I do with my students now. I only have a few direct students and we are family.

In 1991, he made his son, Takayoshi Nagamine, Soke. Were you surprised by this appointment?

No, I was not surprised. No one was. Takayoshi is the son of Nagamine Shoshin and it was only right that he become Soke. Soke is the inheritor of a system, not the person who is highest rank or the one in charge. In 1991, Nagamine Shoshin announced that his son was Soke but Nagamine Shoshin was still President and I was one of his Vice-Presidents. I had been promoted to "hachidan" (8th degree black belt) in 1975 and there were only three people senior to me in Matsubayashi Ryu. These people were Nagamine Shoshin, "judan" (10th degree black belt), Nakamura Seigi, "kudan" (9th degree black belt) and Takamura Seiko, "kudan" (9th degree black belt). A few years later, when Nagamine Shoshin was sick, he asked me to be the President of Matsubayashi Ryu. Nakamura Sensei was my good friend and senior and I urged that Nakamura Sensei be President. I was younger than Nakamura Sensei and he was also not in the best of health, so he and Nagamine Sensei both wanted me to be President. Takayoshi was still Soke.

"After a few years of being away from Naha, Nagamine Shoshin returned and I resumed training under him directly. I did so until his death."

You and the other senior students of Shoshin Nagamine continued to support Matsubayashi Ryu after the passing of Shoshin Nagamine. When did you decide to form your own style and organization?

When I was in Canada for a Matsubayashi Ryu seminar, a little while after the passing of Nagamine Shoshin, I saw people performing poor kata. They wanted it to be easy (soft). I did not feel that Matsubayashi Ryu was being performed well by people of all ranks. I never wanted to be President of Matsubayashi Ryu and did not think that I could change it, so I decided to leave.

What was the feedback from your peers?

Most of my peers approved. In fact, some of the seniors of Matsubayashi Ryu followed me. Two of the most senior Matsubayashi Ryu karate-ka, Tamaki Takeshi and Shiroma Seiei, helped form Shogen-Ryu. Several other seniors joined me.

Karate Masters

"My students know that I do not believe in limiting the knowledge I share with them and that I expect them to do the same."

Why did you decide on the name Shogen Ryu?

Nagamine Shoshin was my most influential teacher. I wanted to honor him so I kept the symbol for "Matsu" which is also read as "Sho." That is for his name, Shoshin. "Gen" means "root" and symbolizes my desire to get back to the realistic and effective root of Okinawa Karate-Do.

Shogen Ryu has spread to Canada, the United States, and Australia. While your organization is small, you have had good turnouts at your seminars. What does the future hold for Shogen Ryu?

I expect that Shogen Ryu will remain small. I have few direct students. Shogen Ryu will be passed in entirety to these few students and on through their students to keep Okinawa Karate-Do alive. My students know that I do not believe in limiting the knowledge I share with them and that I expect them to do the same. I tell them that they are to teach anyone who has an open mind and is willing to have a change of mind.

What is your goal with your organization?

I want to keep Okinawa Karate-Do alive. I do not want a large organization that is like a business. It is not about money. I want to find people that want to learn good, real Okinawa Karate-Do and teach them all I know. That will keep Okinawa Karate-Do alive. Shogen Ryu is also not about rank. People come to me wanting to join Shogen Ryu but when they find out that I am not handing out rank, they leave. People have to earn rank but not care about it. That is not easy to find in these times. That is why people have to train with me for a while before I will make them a full member. Even then, they are not guaranteed to have the same rank they came to me with, even if they are Matsubayashi Ryu.

"Nagamine Shoshin was my most influential teacher."

With the popularization of mixed martial arts, what are your views on mixed martial arts or sport karate in general?

Sport karate and MMA are sport with rules. Shogen Ryu is Budo. There are no rules. The two are completely different.

What do you think the future holds for traditional karate?

Unfortunately, many of the "traditional" styles are becoming more like sport karate. They are no longer real. I started Shogen Ryu because of this and have faith that it will be passed on through my students and their students. We have people from all over the world interested in learning true Okinawa Karate-Do. Shogen Ryu will grow slowly and strong like a tree. If a tree grows slowly, it grows a strong root. O

TED TABURA

THE SICKLE MAN

BORN AND RAISED IN HAWAII, SHIHAN TABURA BEGAN HIS MARTIAL ARTS TRAINING UNDER HIS COUSIN'S TUTELAGE IN A BACKYARD DOJO. A VERITABLE LEGEND IN HIS OWN TIME, SHIHAN TED TABURA BURST INTO THE MARTIAL ARTS WORLD AS ONE OF THE LEADING EXPONENTS IN OKINAWA TE.

IN THE COMPETITION FIELD, SHIHAN TABURA WAS DUBBED "THE SICKLE MAN" BY SIJO ADRIANO EMPERADO, FOUNDER OF KAJUKENBO, FOR HIS EXPERTISE IN THE USE OF THE JAPANESE KAMA (SICKLES). THAT NICKNAME STUCK WITH SHIHAN TABURA FOR MANY YEARS. HE PERSONALLY DIRECTED THE ANNUAL FESTIVAL OF THE KINGS KARATE CHAMPIONSHIP IN MAUI, HAWAII SINCE ITS ORIGINS UNTIL THE LAST EDITION.

HIS SIMPLE AND STRAIGHT-AHEAD APPROACH LED HIM TO MOVIES, WHERE HE WAS ABLE TO DISPLAY AN AMAZING AMOUNT OF KOBUDO TALENT AND SKILL. HE HELD A REPUTATION AS ONE OF THE MOST INNOVATIVE OKINAWNA TE KARATE INSTRUCTORS AROUND THE WORLD.

How long have you been practicing Martial Arts?

I have been practicing Martial Arts for more than 60 years. I studied several methods and systems from Okinawa Te to Kenpo, Lima Lama, Kajukenbo, etc. All of them have been very influential in my personal development as a Martial Artist. I can't say that one is better than the rest because the truth is I don't believe there is one "best" style in the Martial Arts. All styles have something that makes them different and unique. The practitioners have to look for these specific elements and see if they fit or not in what he or she s trying to accomplish. In the end, all styles will bring you to the same place but you have to dedicate your life to their study and analysis. Note that I am not saying only practice … but study and analyze.

What is the difference?

You can practice Karate all your life and have no understanding of what you do. You can be very good physically but have no clue of the inner meanings and principles of the art you practice. Mastery doesn't come

Karate Masters

"All styles have something that makes them different and unique."

from practice ... it comes from deep understanding. This is something that people misunderstand. Just because you have been training Martial Arts for 30 years doesn't mean you know what you are doing. I know this statement may hurt some, but it is true.

You are very straightforward ...

No reason not to be. Hopefully, after 30 years of someone training in Martial Arts, we hope the individual decides to go "deeper" into the principles and important concepts of the style he or she practices.

Do you have a particularly memorable training experience?

I have many. But I could not put one above the rest. I remember the first day that I trained ... I remember the day I got my black belt, the first competition, the fear, the butterflies in the stomach; all of them are memorable experiences that allowed me to grow. It is impossible to mention one and leave the others out.

How has your Martial Art style has developed over the years?

Styles always develop throughout the years ... but this is because the leaders of the style incorporate their own "flavor" and innovations. Therefore, the evolution of the style depends on the personal evolution of each of the leaders. At the end, the styles are changed or modified depending of the experiences of the master. The problem is that sometimes the personal evolution and development of the master or individual goes beyond the original boundaries of the style and then they have to "create" a new style based on their personal preferences. This is not good or bad ... it simply is the way it is.

Do you think is necessary these days to "create" a new style?

From a pure technical point of view, the answer is "no." There are already too many styles and if we think that the human body can only move in a certain limited ways, we can see what nonsense it is to create new styles. Now, if you keep in mind that sometimes the creation of a new method is because a certain person wants to "break away" from his teacher and feel comfortable missing different combat elements, then you start looking at it differently.

Do you think there is still a "pure" system or we are going to a more "mixed" approach?

I don't think "purity" has to do with the physical techniques. I think that what we should keep intact are the essential principles of each style. That is what makes them different and unique. The physical techniques change and the emphasis also varies, depending on the instructor. Unfortunately, we tend to think that if today we are not doing the same and exact movements that the founder did years ago, we are not "pure."

"You can practice Karate all your life and have no understanding of what you do."

How do you think a practitioner can increase his or her understanding of the spiritual aspects of the arts?

That is a personal process. The spirituality of the practitioners depends on one's own interests. Some Martial Artists simply want exercise and they are not interested in improving as human beings, just as fighters. Obviously, they won't look for any spiritual aspect in the Martial Arts. On the other hand, there are practitioners who want to go deeper and beyond the physical and try to find a spiritual growth using the arts of the warrior as a vehicle for it. At the end, it all depends of the individual and spirituality can be found in many ways. Some Martial Artists use religion to achieve that inner peace and balance. As long as you get what you are looking for, any path is right. To understand spiritual training you have to look at it from a "daily life" perspective and not from a Martial Arts point of view only.

Do you think it helps students physically to train with weapons?

Yes. When you use a weapon, your body has to develop a wider range in all the mechanics necessary to deliver the technique. This fact forces you to be more aware of how to use your body and at the same time how to transfer your body power into the weapon in your hands. You need to coordinate your body with the weapon and vice versa. This doesn't happen when you are training empty hand techniques. Your body is the weapon and it is easier to control your own body than to control your body and a weapon at the same time. Weapon training allows you to develop good body mechanics that you can use when you spar or train self-defense techniques. On the other hand, weaponry training teaches you how to understand those weapons so you can actually protect yourself against weapons in a real situation. Weaponry training is good and beneficial for all Martial Artists regardless of the empty hand style they practice. If you practice Escrima/Kali, you already have it there but if you train in Karate, it is always good to look for a supplementary weapon art that increases your knowledge and understanding as a well-rounded Martial Artist. In my dojo, we train with Japanese weapons; it gives us a sense of Budo ... but that is my personal preference.

Do you have to find a weaponry art that "matches" your empty hand style?
Not really. Karate people tend to train in Kobudo because it is "close" and the stances are similar. Kenpo, Kajukenbo, Lima Lama etc., tend to study Filipino arts like Escrima, Kali, or Arnis because it fits better in the body language of these systems, but there is no rule why a Karate practitioner can't train in Escrima or a Kenpo person in Okinawan Kobudo. It is up to the individual's preferences.

Who would you like to have trained with that you have not, and why?
I wish I had the opportunity of training under Aikido founder Morihei Ueshiba. His nonviolent approach to the Martial Arts is something that I have always admired. It is different from any other method and I believe his style is rooted on solid principles of peace and harmony. I personally am attracted to that and that is the reason why I think of Aikido as a "different" kind of Martial Art ... like a "higher level" method.

What keeps you motivated to train after all these years?
I think I am a student at heart. I love to learn and teach today with the same passion I did the first day I entered a dojo to learn the first basic punch or the first day I taught my first class. I love the Martial Arts and that is what kept me going all these years and what still pushes me today ... the love for the Arts. The sharing aspect of teaching others with care and love is something that still motivates me.

Martial Arts, although they can be practiced as sport and entertainment, are more than sport and entertainment activity for health purposes. They are a way of life because the philosophical aspects of the warrior's traditions. Martial Arts principles are very valuable for finding direction in life. Ethics, morality, discipline, etc., are important values that we need in our society and those can be found in the Martial Arts. There is a reason why traditional Martial Arts have stood the test of time.

Is it necessary to engage in street-fighting to achieve good self-defense skills?

No. It is necessary to the have right training in the dojo that prepares you for a real self-defense situation. Now, if the training in the school is competition oriented, then you may not be able to react properly when facing a real attack. Sport is good but the more you get involved in the sport, he more your mind tends to react in that direction. The key is to train a Martial Art for self-defense. That is the main idea. Then, do sport but don't think that because

"To understand spiritual training you have to look at it from a "daily life" perspective and not from a Martial Arts point of view only."

you're a champion you can protect yourself in the street. Also, we should learn from other sports. Look at football. They don't p ay games all the time when they practice, they do "training drills." These drills are very realistic and are composed of all the elements the players will need in a real game. Then, when they actually play the game, they have everything they physically need to deliver the play. Martial Arts are the same. We need to "drill" so we can efficiently face a real self-defense situation, but it is not necessary to go to bars and get into fights, let alone that this behavior is just the opposite of what a true Martial Artist should look for. And finally, let me say that the ability to defend yourself in the street has more to do with determination and proper mind-set than with the style or the level of technical skill you may have.

What's your opinion about mixing different Martial Arts styles?

Don't do it until you have developed a solid foundation in one system.

Karate Masters

"In my dojo, we train with Japanese weapons; it gives us a sense of Budo."

Don't go jumping from one style to another in the beginning of your Martial Arts training because you won't go too far. Now, after you have a certain level of skill and understanding in your style, let's say Karate, you may be interested in learning a supplementary method that improves your skills in a different area, for instance Jiu Jitsu or Judo. Or if you are a Judo/Jiu Jitsu practitioner, maybe you want to learn how to use your hand and feet to attack. The idea is to develop "elements" that make you improve as a Martial Artist.

What do you consider to be the most important qualities of a successful martial artist?

Dedication and a humble attitude. If you are not a dedicated martial artist, then it doesn't matter how much talent you may have. Talent is useless if you don't dedicate yourself to training as if you had no talent at all. Then, you have to be humble first to accept the fact that no matter how much you think you know, you don't know much, and no matter how many times you have been a champion, you are a champion thanks to those opponents you have defeated. And second, to recognize that all those who are less talented and know less than you still can teach you very valuable lessons if you listen to them. It is true that the reasons why people want to train in Martial Arts have changed but it is up to us, the teachers, to educate the students about what Martial Arts are and not what the student "wants them to be."

Do you think MMA events bring positive or negative aspects to the Martial Arts?

I think MMA is a contact sport with regulations and boundaries because it is a sport. It is harder and tougher than boxing and wrestling because it encompasses all ranges of combat. The physical conditioning of the fighters is excellent. But, the emphasis is in fighting, in destroying your opponent, hurting him. And at the end, that is not the right message of the true Martial Arts. There is another misconception that MMA has provoked in the masses; people tend to think that MMA is essentially the "best compilation of all Martial Arts styles," "all that you need to know to be effective." And this is far from the truth. MMA is a tough combat sport and that is only what it is. There is no philosophy, no spirituality or message behind it. Just a fighting business organized for fame and money. It is not good or bad. It is what it is.

Do you have any final advice to pass on?

Some people think that "traditional training" is opposed to "realistic training." And that is a wrong assumption. These people tend to think about Martial Arts with their head and not with their hearts and physical training. They try to intellectualize something that doesn't belong to the mind but to the body. A wise practitioner knows how to differentiate what it comes from his head (which is not real) and what it comes out from true experience (which is real). As the Zen master said: "Take off your head, put it by the side and train!" O

SHUNSUKE TAKAHASHI

UNDIVIDED PAST

IT WAS IN 1972, THAT TAKAHASHI SHIHAN DECIDED TO MOVE TO AUSTRALIA, BRINGING HIS WIFE AND CHILDREN, TO SETTLE IN BRISBANE FOR TWO YEARS, TEACHING KARATE AND ESTABLISHING A TECHNICAL AND ORGANIZATIONAL CORE OF MEMBERS TO ADVANCE THE AUSTRALIAN SHOTOKAN KARATE ASSOCIATION, LATER TO BECOME THE JAPAN KARATE ASSOCIATION OF AUSTRALIA, AND AS OF 2009, TO BECOME THE TRADITIONAL SHOTOKAN KARATE-DO FEDERATION OF AUSTRALIA, TSKFA, AS WE KNOW IT TODAY. IT WAS THAT YEAR SENSEI TAKAHASHI BROKE AWAY FROM JKA (AUSTRALIA) TO FORM THE TSKF AUSTRALIA (TRADITIONAL SHOTOKAN KARATE-DO FEDERATION).

IN THIS DAY AND AGE, A PERMANENT COMMITMENT OF MORE THAN FOUR DECADES TO ANYTHING, WHETHER IT BE A MARRIAGE, PARTNERSHIP, OR JOB, IS VERY RARE. OVER THIS PAST PERIOD OF 40 YEARS, SENSEI TAKAHASHI HAS BEEN RESPONSIBLE FOR THE EXPANSION OF TRADITIONAL STYLE SHOTOKAN KARATE IN AUSTRALIA. HE HAS ALSO ARRANGED MANY EXCHANGES BETWEEN JAPANESE AND AUSTRALIAN UNIVERSITIES, AND PRIVATELY FOR INDIVIDUAL JAPANESE STUDENTS TO ATTEND AUSTRALIAN HIGH SCHOOLS AND VICE VERSA. IT IS UNDER SHIHAN TAKAHASHI GUIDANCE, THAT ALL PRACTITIONERS ARE WELCOMED AND ACCEPTED IN H'S ORGANIZATION, SIMPLY THROUGH A MUTUAL LOVE OF KARATE.

How did you decided to train in karate ad how it was your first contact with the art?

I was 18 years old I entered Komazawa University I met an old friend from high school, who convinced me to join the karate club there. That was the first time I ever saw karate and I decided to start immediately. During my time at the University I was practicing karate all the time. Right there, the karate club at Komazawa University was very famous in Japan. The instructors then were Shihan Nishiyama, Shihan Shirai, Shihan Itaya, Shihan Ohishi and Shihan Mizuno. There were so many great instructors at my university that I wanted to take advantage of the situation and therefore I decided to dedicate my life to karate-do when I was a third-year student at Komazawa University.

Karate Masters

"I am still teaching karate as a full-time instructor, but my primary purpose is to introduce Japanese martial arts, karate-do, as one of the forms of Japanese cultures."

I think I was very fortunate of having these great karate teachers at my University.

What did you do right after graduation at Komazawa University and how you decided to go outside of Japan to teach?

After I graduated from university I did not have no doubts that what I had to do was to enter the JKA Instructor School. I was also asked to teach karate at Komazawa University for Physical Education. I accepted the offer and the position with only one condition: that my commitment to the JKA Instructor School had first priority.

I always had a desire to teach karate abroad, as other instructors did, but back then it was also the "unwritten law" that most graduates had to go abroad and spread karate. When Shihan Nakayama told me that an instructor was needed in Australia, don't forget that I had just graduated from the school, I decided without any doubt in my mind to go to there. I chose Brisbane as the main city because Mr. Mike Connolly, had established the Australian JKA and the karate club at Komazawa University belongs to the JKA, so it was a logical decision.

Today, I am still teaching karate as a full-time instructor, but my primary purpose is to introduce Japanese martial arts, karate-do, as one of the forms of Japanese cultures.

Sensei, you were the JKA representative in Australia for over three decades years. What goals did you set when you took that role?

In JKA karate, the fundamental approach to master karate is established in the three essential components: basic movements [kihon], kata and kumite. There are 25 kata. Kumite has the "ippon" rule, and the JKA had it first karate tournament in the world based on these rules that Shihan Nakayama developed based on other activities like Kendo, I believe. I think that all practitioners of karate should be open to the world and compete against anyone in the world. This will bring the level up.

I remember that in the beginning the people used to think that karate training was similar to the ones shown in the action movies. It has changed completely because practitioners of karate understand now that the three fundamentals pillars and encompasses the development of the human spirit as well.

Where do you see the art of karate going in the future?

Things are changing in our society and that is normal. Karate perception as a method of communication in our society has to change too. I think that the young practitioners of karate are hoping that karate will be an Olympic Games sport one day and are quite sure it will happen. This may be positive and also negative...it all depends on how the people responsible handle the situation. In karate there are four dominating styles, shotokan, shito ryu, goju ryu and wado ryu ; they will not be changed and will be passed on to the future in the right way and with their own philosophy and principles.

"In the beginning the people used to think that karate training was similar to the ones shown in the action movies."

Nevertheless, I believe that karate-do is only one regardless of how you do the technique. The spirit and the essence...it is the same for all of us.

Is it very different the way karate is practiced outside Japan when compared to the training in Japan?

There should be no difference between world karate-do and Japanese karate-do, as long as practitioners train and practice karate sincerely with the right heart.

The ways of thinking are due to the different nationalties, of course, different. And that may affect the perception of the art. Countries all over the world recognize have invited high-level karate instructors from Japan (whatever the style may be) and try to understand correct karate-do and Japanese culture. And that's the correct way to learn, develop and pass karate to the next generations.

What do you think that it is the most difficult aspect for the student to develop or achieve?

I should say the "naturalness" of the body. It is normal to become rigid and move like "karate" but after years of training the body should move differently. Yes, it is karate but it doesn't "look" hard or rigid. In both kata and kumite, this is an important. It is very hard to see karatekas moving with a true "naturalness" in their actions. Basically it is like the principle is "there" but the body doesn't look like the rigid mold we used to have in our beginnings. In short…your body is "expressing" a karate principle but your body doesn't necessarily has to "look" like the basic or primitive karate we know. Karate should be very relaxed and flexible art. You can see this principle in other great teachers…unfortunately some of them are not with us anymore.

What are your personal thoughts about karate?

During all these years of training, I had the opportunity of knowing and meeting a lot of people and some of them have become very close friends. All the people around me have been my teachers in other ways. They are what I like to call "my assets".

In karate training, when done seriously, you may get hurt, but at the same time you can develop certain areas of yourself due to that kind of training.

I think that through the serious training you learn how to have compassion for others, even though you may get hurt.

Any martial art is fine. I am not talking about karate now. The aim of all martial arts training is to seek perfection of character.

How much time and effort should a student be prepared to put into learning karate and what will they get out of it?

The most common reason why people become involved in karate is for health and fitness. I think instructors should train as frequently and hard as they can. The important thing is to continue training. Many people stop training. I think that if you continue training you will find other motivations for karate. You will find ways that will improve your karate without necessarily being karate. Recently, more people have started karate after

"Things are changing in our society and that is normal. Karate perception as a method of communication in our society has to change too."

watching a karate competition, since there are now more opportunities to watch tournaments. They begin the training because they want to win a competition. And that is good because it brings them to the art of karate. In that case they have to train very hard, depending on the size of the competition. You have to train more than others and you have to think about karate all the time — by that I mean how to improve your techniques, study the psychology of opponents and learn to control your own thoughts. That's why I think that competition is good because it forces you to improve and get better...always trying to improve.

From a traditional point of view, it is polite manners to train hard before you fight in competition because it shows respect for your opponents, it means that you take them seriously. Train hard and often. If you decide to train for karate without any kind of challenge like a competition, only your personal development as individual then constant training is paramount. In fact, nothing changes… it is important to continue training no matter what. It is easy to slack off and a true martial artist should make sure doesn't fall into this trap.

Karate Masters

"There should be no difference between world karate-do and Japanese karate-do."

So you are not against competition…
Sport competition has a big part in our society. It brings the excitement and attention of the young people and it is up to us – the instructors – to eventually teach them the traditional values of "do" and Budo. Karate is karate but we need to understand our modern society and see how we can use the art as a tool for the education and moral development of the individual. This is important for our society. Important principles are being lost in this modern times and karate can be used to teach these principles to the younger generations. Traditional karate is not about how we punch and kick or we do this or that movement in kata but about the kind of ethical and moral values that we preserve as budoka.

Sensei, what do you think is the deepest fear of any human being?
That's a tough question. As a budoka, I know that Samurai had to learn to be liberated from death, and they trained for that. Therefore, I should say that facing our own death may be the most difficult thing; knowing that all can be coming to an end. Everything we did, do, felt or feel. Western and Eastern religions deal with this topic differently but the

important point here is to find a way tat is meaningful to you and follow it. That it will be what gives meaning to your existence. For me personally, the key is to have a sense of direction, a mission, knowing that your life is here to accomplish something. That gives a 'meaning' for everything else.

What happens when we reach a point and we can't progress anymore?

The point when we "can't" progress anymore does not exit. I will explain. Sometimes we can get to a point where our technique doesn't seem to improve but that doesn't mean that we can't improve. The body has its limitations and when that occurs – depending of the level of the practitioner – we need to find ways to break that wall. The answer may be to change the way we train or change the way we do karate. It may be a "break through" in your life as karateka. You have to look into yourself and try to find the reason why things are not going and evolving in the same way and direction than before. It is about introspection. Then it comes the mental aspect of it…if you encure and keep training regardless of what you think…your are getting better at a different level. Special training like "gasshuku" is designed to train the mind through exhausting physical sessions. The body is a tool for reaching a higher mental level.

Sensei, any final words of advice?

Do your best, always. Only when you do your best you don't have to worry about future insecurities about who you are. You will be in peace with yourself no matter what the overcome may be. Like a Samurai…do your best in the fight…to live or die is not relevant…since you already have reached the goal of a full personal accomplishment by giving your best. O

TAKESHI TAMAKI

CYCLES OF SHADING

SENSEI TAMAKI TAKESHI, ONE OF THE SENIOR TEACHERS IN OKINAWA, NOW OVERSEES THE "SHOGEN RYU KARATEDO ASSOCIATION" THAT WAS FORMED BY OKINAWAN KARATE LEGEND KENSEI TABA WHO PASSED AWAY IN 2012. TAMAKI SENSEI IS ALSO ONE OF THE SENIOR INSTRUCTORS FROM THE NAGAMINE SHOSHIN KARATE DOJO IN NAHA, OKINAWA. SINCE TABA SENSEI'S PASSING, TAMAKI SENSEI HAS STEPPED UP TO OVERSEE THIS ORGANIZATION. AS THE SENIOR OF THE SHOGEN RYU KARATEDO ASSOCIATION AT 73 YEARS OF AGE, HE POSSESSES AN INCREDIBLE ABILITY TO DEMONSTRATE THE PHYSICAL TECHNIQUES OF SHORIN RYU KARATE AS WELL AS YAMANI BO THAT WAS TAUGHT TO HIM BY KISHABA CHOKEI SENSEI. HIS PERSONALITY IS ONE THAT HAS ALWAYS MADE HIM ONE OF THE FAVORITES IN MATSUBAYASHI SHORIN RYU. HIS DEMEANOR IS UNASSUMING WHILE CARRYING HIMSELF WITH A GREAT DEAL OF CONFIDENCE AND HUMILITY AND IN SOCIAL ENVIRONMENTS CARRIED HIMSELF WITH A GREAT DEAL OF CLASS AND LEADERSHIP. HE IS VERY APPROACHABLE AND WILLING TO SHARE HIS SKILL AND KNOWLEDGE OF THE MARTIAL ARTS. TAMAKI SENSEI WAS ALSO INSTRUMENTAL IN HELPING GRANDMASTER SHOSHIN NAGAMINE WITH HIS BOOK, "THE ESSENCE OF OKINAWAN KARATE", WHICH HELPED SPREAD OKINAWAN KARATE-DO THROUGHOUT THE WORLD.

I noticed you still possess a lot of speed and power at 73 years of age. What do you attribute to this?

Of course, my karate training being consistent. That is the secret. And to always keep moving. I take pride in my personal karate training and try to be an example. I had a good foundation at an early age. I started training at 15 years old; I started because I 'wanted to be stronger'.

I want to thank you for this opportunity. Not only for me but for having my students with me as well. Sensei, how did you get involved in the martial arts?

As a child, I wanted to become stronger, and I knew that the martial arts was a way to achieve that. I started training at the Grandmaster's first dojo. Sensei Nagamine's dojo was at Tomari in Naha. After World War II

Karate Masters

"The individuals who have made an impression and inspired me in the Nagamine Dojo were Kensei Taba, Chokei Kishaba and Masao Shima."

in 1953, he moved his dojo to Naha City. I have continued ever since.

What was your early training like?
Before "The Essence of Okinawan Karate-do" was published, training was different. There were variations in the way kata was performed. It was more of the old ways of doing the movements. When the book came out, it gave people around the world a guide to which to refer to. Master Nagamine designed this so people could follow along a lot easier using the book as a reference. Before the book, it was really more technical; the book made it more fundamental to help spread the art of Matsubayashi Shorin Ryu.

What do you remember from Shoshin Nagamine's teachings?
I trained with Grandmaster Shoshin Nagamine from when I was a young boy and I watched the Honbu dojo grow and produce a lot of good karateka. One of the most inspiring times for me personally was when the Grandmaster wrote his book, "Essence of Okinawan Karate". I along with other people supported him in his efforts to help spread Okinawan karatedo to the world. His karate-do teachings have influenced many people and his legacy with continue to live on. It is very exciting to think that I was part of that history.

Who are some of the students you have trained with in the Nagamine Dojo who have made an impression?
The individuals who have made an impression and inspired me in the Nagamine Dojo were Kensei Taba, Chokei Kishaba and Masao Shima. Also, in the dojo, was Ansei Ueshiro. All of these gentlemen have helped me in my growth in my continued study of karate-do.

Tamaki

What was your impression of Ansei Ueshiro?

Ansei impressed me very much with his physical skill and determination. The disability to his hands never limited him in his training. Everything that he demonstrated was always with 100 percent effort; he never held anything back.

What skills should a beginner focus on?

Number one would be to create a foundation first, especially with children. They will get bigger and stronger. If these fundamental skills (strong stances) are developed at any early age, they could stay with them for the rest of their lives. Also focus and concentration at this early age is very important in the mental development of the student.

How has martial arts personally helped you?

Karate has become my life and has kept me healthy. I have rarely ever been sick. The movement I have now at age 73 is because of the benefits martial arts gives a person. Some people my age have a hard time moving because of the lack of physical movement and exercise. Martial arts not only develops the physical, but also the mental attitude to keep going, but the spirit as well.

How has your journey changed from when you first started?

In the beginning, it was all physical skills to develop my body and make myself stronger. At my age now, I want to help spread karate-do to future generations. I want them to understand that there is no secret to karate, just hard work.

What are your thoughts on modern sport karate or mixed martial arts?

When there is a sport and it is rule-bound, it is totally different from real karate. Most people who compete in the sport, which is really a small part of it, do not have the longevity. The true meaning of martial arts is longevity…to continue training into the later years of your life. This is a true component in the martial arts. I also see a lot of misunderstandings---the essence of karate is kata. Many Westerners like to fight but they don't have kata. This is a missing element. Kata can teach you to fight but it can also give you longevity. This will give you keep you in the martial arts for life. O

PEMBA TAMANG

KARATE'S CLOUDS AND WAVES

Sensei Tamang has been involved in Karate since childhood, and was one of the first foreigners to graduate the original JKA Kenshu-sei - Instructors Training Course. In 1989, he became the first non-Japanese International Instructor.

The globalization and competitive development of Karate has had some positive affects on Karate, but unfortunately, the original principles of Karate are being lost. The "Nihon Shotokan Karate Federation" was established to follow the spirit of Grandmaster Gichin Funakoshi and his way of Karate in cultivating the mind, body and spirit. In this chaotic world, clear direction and strong leadership are needed to guide students to their goals. The NSKF, under the chief instructorship of Sensei Pemba Tamang, was founded for this reason. "Karate is one of the many paths to self-perfection, preservation and enlightenment. I love and respect Karate and have therefore devoted my life to its true path. For many years, I have followed this path with honesty, dedication and hard work," says Sensei Tamang.

After living in Tokyo for 25 years, he returned to the natural surroundings similar to those of where he was born (near the Himalayas). Only two and a half hours from Tokyo, surrounded by the beauty of nature, he was able to go deep into his Karate training and sharpen and understand more fully the techniques that were been bestowed to him by so many illustrious Sensei's that he studied under. "To me, the pursuit of good 'waza' (technique) brings satisfaction and great happiness," he says; "Concentrate your mind and body on the execution of these techniques. Sometimes we spend too much time philosophizing over techniques. Using the body and mind in practical training will answer our questions. 'Silence is golden' the old masters used to say. NSKF seeks to encourage karateka's from all over the world the value of this path, and along with the lessons of nature, show the simple, pure and dynamic way of Karate, and that of the Bushido spirit."

Karate Masters

"Observing kenshusei was much more comfortable than taking part. But of course, no satisfaction can come from just observing and later wishing you had done it."

Could you tell us how you went into karate, how you came to Japan and how you got acquainted with Japanese karate for the first time?

When I was young, I simply wished to be a strong man and joined a Karate club near my home in Darjeeling when I was ten years old. I trained at this dojo for eight years and not only obtained my black belt but became regarded as the best fighter. In such a small town this carried a lot of respect. However, I realized that the Karate I was being admired for wasn't the real 'way,' and didn't feel true to myself. The only place I felt I could truly find Karate was Japan, so I flew to Narita when I was 19 years old. I couldn't speak any Japanese and knew no one in Japan. I didn't know where to go when I arrived at Narita Airport, and I had no idea about which dojo to train in. I felt anxious and worried that I had made too bold a move by coming to Japan, but after I settled and did some research, I joined the JKA Hombu dojo in 1980.

What did you expect from Japanese dojo trainings and to what extent were these expectations realized?

I only had experience in my hometown dojo and back then there wasn't much video footage or 'youtube' to give you any idea of what to expect in a Japanese dojo, so I had no expectations, only that the training would be very high level. My first experience of training in a Japanese dojo was a complete surprise. I'd like to say, pleasant surprise, but it was very tough and frightening, luckily there wasn't much time to think and therefore worry about what was happening. We just trained and it was very satisfying.

What made you apply for kenshusei courses and what is it like to observe it from aside and to be kenshusei yourself?

Originally, I thought I would go back to my country after I gained my black belt; the admiration amongst the towns people would certainly have sat more comfortably, but like many of life's desires and goals, they keep changing. Through training hard everyday and being around so many talented karateka I began to realize that there were bigger dreams than just gaining a black belt.

Observing kenshusei was much more comfortable than taking part. But of course, no satisfaction can come from just observing and later wishing you had done it. Observing kenshusei and all the top instructors inspired me and showed me the true beauty and strength of Karate. I was hooked and had to do it.

I was very afraid to join and at 26 years old, I was seen as being quite old at that time. Usually students were recruited from universities, but Yahara and Asai Sensei acknowledged my application to take the course, so I took the exam under Nakayama Sensei and other JKA instructors.

Could you tell us about the Japanese senseis who influenced you greatly during the courses?

All the sensei's were a great influence on me and I learnt many things from each one. I also feel very lucky that my karate was influenced by Nakayama sensei. He taught us many great things, but he really showed me that having a small body wasn't a disability. That it can still be powerful, as well as quick. His karate was very dynamic, and he taught me how to use my hips. At the time, I was too young to understand, but now I understand what he was saying about hips. As a young man I wanted to kick and punch, I didn't realize the importance of the hips.

Why do you think there were no non-Japanese graduates before you? Did you feel any special attitude towards you other than towards Japanese kenshusei?

A foreigner coming to live in Japan is faced with many challenges and that's even before he or she steps into a dojo. The language itself is an ongoing battle that last many many years. Then there is the added distraction of earning a living and avoiding loneliness. Of course, many foreigners come to the dojo for regular training and they observe the condition of the kenshusei, not just how strong they are, but their bandages and bleeding knuckles, they may even see kenshusei being 'blooded' before a tournament, all of this may not make the course very appealing, especially if you've come to enjoy Japan as well, and not just karate.

Karate Masters

Once I entered the kenshusei course I felt no difference in attitude towards me. The sensei's were only interested in karate and developing your skill. They were hard on everyone. They were trying to develop not only physical strength but mental strength, which is essential in any fighting system. I saw many Japanese quit the course and had there been more foreigners, then maybe some foreigners would have also quit. I guess it would have been a bad thing for the first foreigner to enter the kenshusei course and then quit, so this was extra pressure for me.

Why do you think kenshusei courses raise so much interest all over the world? Is it due to unprecedented inflexibility or sometimes brutality? Or due to the fact that for many people in the US and Europe these courses symbolize a real world of Martial Arts? Looking back, what would you say was the most important that you learned during the courses?

I think it's a combination of all those things. All martial artists have heard stories of the samurai and these stories are often romanticized, especially in films. Their amazing skill, strength and discipline will always be admired. That kind of martial training is no longer necessary in this day and age, but the closest thing you can find to it is the kenshusei course. People are always interested in other people and how they choose to dedicate their lives, especially when they choose to spend many years of the life under tough and brutal conditions.

I learnt many important things during the course. Under those tough circumstances you learn so much about yourself. You train so hard sometimes that you start to imagine your breaking point. If you hit that breaking point then it's over. I learned that my breaking point could always be pushed further and further. In terms of karate I learned what is required to perfect techniques and reach a higher level. Watching senseis with amazing skills every day gave us something to imitate and aspire to. It's easy to think that something is missing in your technique, but sometimes there is too much in your technique. That little extra move you make that complicates and slows it down. Karate and the 'killing blow' philosophy requires you use your body and mind in the most efficient way to generate as much power and speed as possible. Efficiency often involves reduction. This is also important for the mind as well as the body. If you're in a kumite or street-fight situation and you think too much then this can be a big problem. Your mind must be free of any doubt or unnecessary thoughts to work efficiently.

What is your opinion regarding the meaning of kenshusei courses? Are the cruel living conditions really worth? Are these courses necessary for the organizations that intend to support high technical level of their instructors and are they possible solely within the frames of Japanese dojo? Or such hard training conditions can be organized in any country of the world in order to reach the same goal?

There are many programs around the world where you train hard as an athlete. Gymnasts, runners, soccer players, they all train very hard every day. Pushing yourself physically is a battle with your body, but most importantly a battle with your mind. We have all faced the resistance from within on those cold Sunday mornings when your bed seems so much more comfortable than the dojo. The kenshusei course isn't just about overcoming early mornings, but facing severe physical and mental challenges. It's these challenges in life that define us as a person.

"Kata practice is an essential element in learning Karate."

All organizations have to continue and evolve. It's important for an organization to maintain its standard and spirit. You can have beautiful dojo's and expensive dogi's but they will do little to maintain the standard and spirit. We need the next generation of instructors who can pass on the lessons from Nakayama, Shoji and Asai sensei. The kenshusei course is the breeding ground for this next generation, so it's important that training is similar to those early days.

I think a strong dojo can be set up anywhere in the world providing you have dedicated and strong instructors. However, culture is very important. The Japanese are fanatical about getting things perfect and they're willing to push themselves to extremes. Many Japanese people work very long hours in the office and most students give all their free time to their club activity and are not easily distracted. This is why the kenshusei course works so well in Japan. I'm not completely sure how it will work in other

Karate Masters

""Budo" to the Japanese is the "way" to achievement and master martial art in the spiritual way."

countries. However, I've seen lots of strong karateka from all over the world who haven't graduated from a kenshusei course.

After your graduation, a very important event in the karate world took place. JKA split into two independent camps. Could you tell us about your life during that period of time. How did the Japanese instructors' life changed in that period?

It was a big shock for me to find this sudden division amongst the sensei's who had trained so long and hard together. It was a frustrating and confusing period, though my life as an instructor continued the same way until everyone chose who to follow. Once we made our choice, the transition was quite quick and smooth. Not all relationships were damaged. I still have a good relationship with some of the other senseis and there is still much respect; after all, we were like brothers in arms.

Budo-karate is widely spoken nowadays. In those days, when you trained at hombu dojo JKA as kenshusei, was Budo-karate as widely spoken as now? Was the importance of karate as a martial art brought up? And what is "Budo" to the Japanese? Do the Japanese imply the same meaning to Budo-karate as foreigners do, that is fighting in the right way without having mercy either for one's self or for one's partner?

"Budo" to the Japanese is the "way" to achievement and master martial art in the spiritual way. In Japan, Budo exists in many arts, such as Sumo, Kendo, Judo, Karate-do, Kyu-do (Japanese archery), etc. They are all spiritual. The goal of Budo is accomplishment through serious and dedicated training. In Shotokan we have the Dojo-kun to remind us of this. I'm not really sure how Budo is viewed in other countries.

Karate always has been regarded as "ikken-hisatsu" art, that is "killing with one strike." However, people with experience in real combats know how difficult it is to overcome your adversary with one stroke, not mentioning of killing him. Could you comment on that?

This is our philosophy in Karate and because of this philosophy it allows us to set very high standards and goals for our techniques. Other Martial Arts rely on several techniques to win over their attacker. We aim to finish the fight with one technique; this is why we train so hard with each technique.

Sometimes, techniques can look very nice and impressive but they aren't developed with 'ikken-hisatsu' philosophy in mind. Sometimes more emphasis is put into speed and height. In karate we try to bring all the important elements together for one technique, Karate is an art so we are trying to produce a masterpiece. However, even the best artist can't produce a masterpiece every time, so of course we practice many combinations of techniques. We also need to be mindful of our skill; to deliver a killing blow over a silly argument on the street is not good for anyone's health. We need control both mentally and physically, this is the spirit of Karate-do.

Competitions play an important part in any karateka's life, but sun-dome (no contact) is very important for competitions. What could you say here? Was this principle used during your active performances in Japan?

As I said earlier, it's important to develop your karate skill with "ikken-hisatsu" in mind; this makes our karate very powerful and dangerous. Kumite is an important part of training as it allows us to test our skills in a controlled way. It's also very important for our mind. We cannot go into the street and fight people to test our skills, so tournaments allow us to develop important skills like overcoming fear, nervousness and hesitation. You can have very good technique but without confidence in your Karate then it could fail you in a life and death situation. Tournaments help us prepare for this in a safe way. However, even with strict rules and controlled contact people still get hurt. With this fear of getting hurt present at a tournament you can really pressure test your Karate. The higher the tournament the stronger the competitors and the closer these competitors are to achieving 'ikken-hisatsu', therefore the greater the risk of serious injury. Of course, I got injured and injured others during my competition days.

I would like to touch upon some technical details in our interview. My first question here is regarding kata and bunkai. Many students nowadays can't help asking why should they learn kata, if they can just learn kumite, and what do they need bunkai if it's so theoretical and can't be used in a real combat?

Bunkai is very important for understanding the kata more fully. However, I tend to spend more time practicing the actual Kata's rather than the application of the kata. Practicing bunkai is still very important, especially as there are lots of useful self-defense techniques to be found within each kata. Some of the bunkai is theoretical but a good sensei will be able to choose and adapt many of the techniques for today's self defense situations. Kata practice is an essential element in learning Karate. It helps us develop control, timing and of course kime, so in some respects practicing Kata regularly is part of the process to improving your kumite. If you practice kata correctly with good visualization and breathing it can become almost like meditation and help you reach a deeper and more meaningful understanding of karate.

Could you explain what kime is and its role in Shotokan. Is it solely muscle tension?

When you see good kime you are seeing sharpness and strength in each technique. It's important to keep the body relaxed so it can move quickly and without resistance from tensed up muscles. At the last moment, you exhale and tighten your muscles for impact. All your power from inside is expelled into the technique and this creates an explosive technique followed by a brief pause showing good finish. This is why good kime looks sharp. This is essential in Shotokan Karate and relates to the philosophy of "ikken hisatsu," as every technique you do is an attempt to deliver a killing blow. This is the reason why Shotokan looks so powerful when done with good kime.

Did karate change technically from the point when you started learning it and up to now? What would you say is the most important technical thing in mastering karate today?

I don't think Karate has changed since I began learning it in my home town or in Japan over 30 years ago. I continue to practice kihon, kata and kumite in the same way I was taught by the great sensei's of the old JKA. However, the way I teach Karate continues to change and develop as I must find ways to help my students understand not only the technique but how they must prepare their body for the technique to work with good kime. All students are different so I will always need different ways to get my point across.

For me, the most important technical thing is mastering the use of your hips. This is very important for generating power with all techniques, punches, blocks or kicks. In the centre of your hips in your lower belly is the 'chakra' or 'tanden' in Japanese. This is the centre of your power and energy. Being able to use your hips in an effective and efficient manner is essential to good kime and will make your Karate extremely powerful.

You are now the Chief Instructor of "Nihon Shotokan Karate-do Federation." Could you tell us the reason for creating this organization and what it is like now?

The NSKF was established in Hokkaido (Northern Japan) long before I became Chief Instructor. It was of course established to promote and develop traditional and strong Shotokan. It was a great honor for me as a non Japanese sensei to be made Chief Instructor of this organization. As an organization, it is still very young but it is growing at a nice pace. I am working hard to teach in many places in Japan and the rest of the world and as a result our organization is steadily growing. However, it is important for me to develop the quality of our karate and not the size of the organization. It's also important for me to spread the right philosophy of karate and human spirit. I feel the NSKF is helping me achieve this.

You could consider my next question rather abrupt, but I would ask you to answer it as understanding of such situations is very important to many people. You headed the organization after you had been member of the three strongest Japanese organizations (Nakayama's JKA, Asai's JKA, KWF). It is considered that when strong masters leave one strong organization in order to found one of their own, this does not benefit karate. As most of the organizations are similar in their ideas, their constant splitting and

"The kenshusei course isn't just about overcoming early mornings, but facing severe physical and mental challenges. It's these challenges in life that define us as a person."

Karate Masters

"Karate and the 'killing blow' philosophy requires you use your body and mind in the most efficient way to generate as much power and speed as possible. Efficiency often involves reduction."

decrease in members weakens karate, deprives it of competition within the organization, impairs possibilities of communication, exchange of experience and further development. What could you say in such case? How do you see your organization's development in accordance with its philosophy and concept? What could show that your organization is vitally important in karate world?

I feel the disappointment regarding the split and I'm sure it might give a negative image to the rest of the world who looked with admiration to the old JKA. Honestly, I wish the original JKA still existed and I was still able to develop students under this organization. But like many organizations, companies and religions, conflict and eventually separation happens, sometimes it's unavoidable. People have strong convictions and they believe they are doing the right thing at the time, but it doesn't always work out for the greater good. However it's important to make best of every situation, so the development of other organizations like the NSKF is about doing this. The most important thing is to follow the correct and true path in Karate. It doesn't matter what organization you belong to, just as long as it's true to the ways of Shotokan Karate.

As mentioned earlier, our organization is still developing, and has not yet developed widely. It's not so important to be a huge organization. Sometimes large organizations can neglect the grassroots. I think it's more important to develop the student. We should do only what is right for our students' progress and understanding in Karate. Our destination is to provide simple and effective Karate, and bring a great joy to the student's life.

I think Karate is one path to finding yourself and inner peace and to understand your life like any other Budo. This is especially important in today's world with many people living with such fear and confusion. I find salvation in loving Karate and devoting myself to perfecting it. This is a lifetime challenge. We want our students to have this love and feeling about Karate and I'm sure there are many students out there who want this kind of uncomplicated feeling about Karate, so as a result our organization will continue to grow.

What is the most important for you today in your trainings and communication with your disciples?

For me, I continue to place great importance in good kihon (basic) training. Simple and natural movement is very important. Karate must eventually feel natural and the only way to achieve this is through basic training. I treasure my disciples, some of them have been following me for a very long time, we are all loyal, honest, and deeply respectful of each other. I am grateful for the relationships I have built up through Karate.

Not many people understand why karate is a martial art. They say that music, painting, literature is an art, but not hand-to-hand combat. Is karate really an art?

Yes, Karate-do is an Art. Karate brings the physical and spiritual into harmony. Like other art, it is the pursuit of perfection and free expression. When done correctly, with minimal movement and without any wasted energy, Karate's movement is very beautiful. Karate is discipline and concentration. I have the same feeling when I'm painting, cooking and playing music. To concentrate your heart and energy with such deepness, dedication and focus allows the brain to reach a higher state of meditation. This is a beautiful thing. Karate is most definitely an art. Love Karate and devote yourself to the perfection of its techniques and you will discover many lessons to the mystery of life. The path is long and hard, but immensely rewarding.

Sensei, thank you very much for your time.

You are most welcome. It is a great opportunity to share my ideas with other martial artists and also to consider deeply my own thoughts and visions about Karate. O

GEORGE TAN

KARATE PILLARS

From day one, Sensei George Tan has been driven by the spirit of Budo in his Karate journey, a journey that started 40 years ago.

Shihan Tan is currently the president of "Asia Pacific Shito Ryu Karate Federation" as well as president of the "Traditional Shito Kai Karate-do Association." Awarded a 7th Dan in 1994 by the Japan Karate-do Federation, Sensei Tan went through the "Shihan" exam in 2006 in Japan and was officially recognized by WSKF (World Shito Kai Federation) with the "Shihan" status after passing the earlier Jokyo (2003) and Jun-Shihan (2004) exams.

Although no one can ever question Shihan George Tan's dedication to traditional teachings, his unwavering practical sense of Budo values set him apart from other karate instructors around the world. "I love the focus and the discipline that Karate provides," he says. "Karate allows me to be completely in the moment for myself, with myself."

How long have you been practicing martial arts?

I started training Shito Ryu Karate in the mid-1970s, almost 40 years ago. I was and am still with Shito Ryu. My first teacher was the late Shihan Naser and in Japan, I also trained under other Shito Ryu masters including Ken Sakio and Kenei Maburi Sensei. So, all along, Shito Ryu is the only style I have ever practiced.

From a physical point of view, I would consider myself talented for Karate. Karate was never physically difficult for me but of course this doesn't mean it has been "easy." Karate requires a lot of work and training but my body always has responded properly to the hard training.

In the early days, we were all extremely serious in our training. I trained seven days a week and since we had movie icons such as Bruce Lee, we all tried to be like him. I think many Martial Arts masters of my generation were attracted to the training by Bruce Lee. This is not bad if we come to understand that movies are not real Martial Arts. My early training sessions were

Karate Masters

"The most important point is to be serious in training. It is something very simple but very difficult."

"never ask questions, just do as you are told." We conditioned our bodies for kumite, had many injuries, and never complained about pain. We enjoyed the pain and when limbs were black and blue due to injuries, we were proud of it. Breaking bricks, boards, tiles, and blocks of ice were part of our way to show how strong we were. I did not come from a wealthy home so I cherished the training as I had to work hard to get the money to pay the training fees.

How has your personal expression karate developed over the years?

The "Do" or " Way" of karate is a lifelong process when it comes to learning. Karate is now so natural for me that sometimes I wonder whether I was a warrior in a past life. "Bunkai" or analysis from kata also comes so naturally to me that sometimes it surprises me. I have been asked so many kinds of questions that I almost instantly answer when it comes to kata application. I guess it could also be because of my experience in attending a lot of seminars and interacting with the Shito Ryu masters I had the opportunity of training under.

What are the most important points in your teaching methods today?

The most important point is to be serious in training. It is something very simple but very difficult. Discipline is the most important thing. Students come and go because they lose interest. It is common to have only one person out of one hundred achieve the black belt status. Most students drop out ... they find many excuses, tuition, homework, pain, no time, no money, school exams, parents object ... the list goes on and on. These people only need to find an excuse to stop training because they simply don't want to keep training.

Tan

"The "Do" or " Way" of karate is a lifelong process when it comes to learning."

What do you think has been lost from Okinawa to Japan in terms of Karate evolution?

I have trained in Okinawa and most people there keep their traditional values. Believe me that the Okinawans treat Karate very seriously and they make the modern Japanese Karate look like kindergarden stuff. It is because too much sports-karate in Japan currently spoils the value of true karate and Martial Art.

The normal objective of sports today is "win" and be rewarded. Although one also also to condition the body for sports, that is not Martial Arts. It is better to train in running because your opponent will never be able to catch you. In real karate, it is important to remember that the adversary is not defeated by the technique, but well before, right at the precise moment he has lost the initiative in the fight. It is exactly because the adversary is already defeated that it is possible to apply the technique on him to concretize and carry out his defeat.

Karate Masters

What are the most important qualities for a student to become proficient in karate?

I teach both the traditional and the sport aspect of it, but they all have to go through the normal traditional training procedures. Basics, or kihon, is the most important. If one's basics are weak, the foundation will be weak. It is like the foundation of a building; if it is weak, the building will collapse. There is no other way around it.

When teaching the art of karate, what is the most important aspect the student should be aware of?

Kihon and kata as kumite will come naturally. One should overcome the fear of pain. The principle of "shin-gi-tai" (heart, technique, and body) should be emphasized as "one" – otherwise it is incomplete. The art of karate-do allows us to be ourselves, humbly but firmly. Our internal weaknesses do not instantly disappear, but it takes time to change our perception of what karate is and begin to actually "see" what karate can provide to us. We still must persevere as progress in Karate-do is not measured by immediate result but over the long term.

What do you think is more important, the technique itself or the principle that the technique represents?

Practice of the physical techniques permits us to arrive at an understanding of the principle, but the proper understanding of the principle will help us to improve the physical technique. Therefore, both are extremely important. At the end, it is important to understand that karate is not simply a matter of technique. The physical techniques in and out of themselves are not what karate-do is all about. Techniques have no meaning whatsoever if we take them out of the context in which they have to be used. It is like the actual words and their meaning ... two different things.

What do you mean by that?

When you try to communicate a "feeling" or a "lesson" to somebody - in any field, the meaning of the words used matter less than the impact of their evocative power. But in order to fill words with strong and pure energy, you have to be more than a teacher; you have to be a "master." The words become a simple instrument to communicate a concept; that is why the entire act of a true karate master is based on the right choice of words, actions or symbols that truly represent and communicate the thought that he wants the student to grasp. In true Budo teaching, the student needs a very special kind of predisposition or receptivity to understand the hidden meaning of words and ideas, and find out what its real meaning is. This is the true way of teaching traditional Budo.

So, is there a chance that the student misinterprets the teacher's words ...?

Of course. That is the problem when we use words to communicate. Between the thinking of the master and that of the disciple, there is always an ambiguity of words that can be misinterpreted by the student and prevent him from actually fully understand what the master is trying to convey. That is why in all Budo arts, "feeling" is more important than "talking." The problem is that the student can train for 40 years and still not understand things. Then the teacher has to use words to clarify things.

"Practice of the physical techniques permits us to arrive at an understanding of the principle, but the proper understanding of the principle will help us to improve the physical technique."

How we can learn to "connect" kata with actual fighting?

Performing kata repeatedly to perfect the kata can give you the reflex as you are in an imaginary combat with your opponent. The directions you face from all over gives you a sense of facing several opponents from different angles. Imagine in sports kumite that you are only facing one opponent and he is always in front of you. Kata is very different but we need to know how to look at it and how to learn from it.

How do you think a practitioner can increase his/her understanding of the spiritual aspects of the art?

You become almost a spiritual leader and practitioner if you can answer all your students questions at ease. You need time and there is no short cut to it. To be a champion in sports Karate, you may need only five years, but the spiritual aspects of Martial Arts need many decades of training and study to understand. Please note I did say "study" and not only "training." Many people "train" Karate for 40 years but they do not "study" Karate.

Karate Masters

"As martial artists, we are not controlled by the flesh but by the spirit."

Is there anything lacking in the way Karate is taught today compared to how it was when you started training?

Unfortunately, Karate has been diluted to make it easier to understand. Students easily get their black belts so that they can retain the interest to carry on. In my early days, just being a brown belt commands a lot of respect from all ... more than what you see in black belts today. It took more than four years to obtain a black belt, but today students train less and expect to get their black belt in less than three years. The color of the belt is more important than the training. Students today look for the shortest and fastest way to obtain this status. And this is not right. Many teacher see how students show lack of interest because they are bored or maybe because they find that their limits has been reached. With these idea hanging over their training, the temptation of others are likely to occur example staying at home, watching a movie, computer games, hanging out with friends, etc.

Do you feel that you still have further to go in your studies?

Definitely. Learning never stops!

What advice would you give to students on the question of supplementary training?

Using light weights is very good for speed training. However, students are advised to do more in repetition rather than overstretch with force to avoid muscle tear. Running is good for stamina training. Yes, all these additional physical trainings are good for body conditioning ... but in no way can they substitute for the actual Karate training.

Have there been times when you felt fear in your training?

There were a few times when I have got hurt really bad during sparring and this affects your confidence, but you have to push through. Spirit is very important in Karate and all Budo arts. As martial artists, we are not controlled by the flesh but by the spirit. Only the spirit defends the body and frees the mind of the karate-ka.

Do you think that Olympics will be positive for the art of karate-do?
I have heard of Karate in the Olympics for more than two decades and it is still not a reality yet.

What are your views on kata bunkai?
Bunkai is the most important after one learns to perform the Kata. Without bunkai, it is just a dance. It is like you are singing but without the music. Understanding and performing the bunkai is very important for Karate training – especially in Shito Ryu because this style has more than 65 katas, which is the most amongst the four major styles of Karate in Japan.

What are your thoughts about doing thousands of repetitions of one single technique in training as in the old days? Is it a good training method?
Of course it is good, but it needs time. Today, most instructors teach the easy ways in order for their students to excel in training. Students like getting their belts upgraded fast. Never forget that the level of a karate-ka is not judged by the number of techniques one knows but by the manner in which one uses them. What is important is not the technique itself but the right attitude to apply it.

If you had only a one-hour class with a student, what would be the most important thing that you'd teach him/her?
It depends on the rank or the seniority of the student. If he/she is a beginner, correct kihon such as proper stances, how the defense blocks are done, etc. If he/she is a more senior student, I would concentrate on reviewing the katas and to perfect the performance. In Karate, it is important for the practitioner to understand that when we get to control the intent of the attacker, he/she loses all possibility of resistance. It is only then that we can apply any technique we wish. The technique we actually decided to use is of little importance because hopefully we have trained enough to be able to adapt to all circumstances. Basically, we should lead the adversary to a situation where the application of our technique becomes possible.

What can Karate offer to the individual in these troubled times we are living in?
Mentally, you have to be strong in Karate, and when in troubled times, a good workout will release the stress that is accumulated in your body. After

a strenuous workout, you should feel more relaxed. This is just from a physical point of view. As a philosophy, the art of Karate-do can help the practitioner look at life from a well-balanced inner center.

After so many years of training, what is so appealing to you in the Shito Ryu style of karate and why?

Shito Ryu is a fusion of Naha-te and Shuri-te, an excellent combination of power and speed. Shito Ryu has both and that makes it unique. In simple laymen's terms, power does not necessary means speed and likewise speed does not necessarily mean power.

How do you like to train yourself? Has this changed over the years?

My training at this age is to maintain my form and not let it slide too quickly. I enjoy kata as one can go on and on. Kumite movements are limited and I have been more careful at my age, as injuries take a longer time to heal.

Westerners generally are physically bigger than Okinawan/Japanese (Asian) practitioners; how do you think this has affected their karate?

The Europeans are very good in sports kumite. They move very fast. It is all in the training and basically for competition. Your body structure will depend on the events in which you can excel. For example, for kata division, tall persons don't look as good as short practitioners. However, for self-defense, it is generally known that big and tall ones' moves are much slower than the smaller-built ones. In terms of defense, the smaller, shorter moves can be deadly as they are taught to attack only the vital parts of the body.

Is your style of teaching the same as the traditional Karate-do method or do you have your own ideas?

Basically, we have the same principles of training as found in many Japanese dojo. Different instructors have their different ways of teaching but the essence is more or less the same. The only difference is whether you are teaching from your heart or your mind is concentrated on going to the dojo to collect training fees only and do it just like a business.

What advice would you give to an instructor who is struggling with his or her won development?

I would advise instructors to learn from different masters. That is the only way to improve. Of course, we have to be loyal to our own masters first. But other masters can identify your mistakes easily and you will learn more. If

"If you are trained in sports Karate only, do not expect to defend yourself on the streets".

you are Shotokan, go learn from Goju Ryu masters, too, and vice versa. If we are from Shito Ryu, learn from Shotokan and Goju masters ... each master and style has individual good points.

Finally, what advice would you like to give to all Karate practitioners and martial artists in general?

If you are trained in sports Karate only, do not expect to defend yourself on the streets. Be realistic and true to yourself. If anything happens to you on the streets, you should not blame Karate because you only study sport/competition Karate and not real Budo Karate. Budo karate is totally different. We are trained to protect and really defend ourselves, whereas in sports Karate, the ultimate goal is "winning a trophy." I am not against sports Karate as I have also represented my country in tournaments. It is fun and it is all about winning and losing. Lastly, I would advice teaching students first in Traditional Karate and later they can decide whether to excel in the sports areas, as not everyone can be a world champion. O

ALLEN TANZADEH

A WEALTH OF KNOWLEDGE

ALLEN TANZADEH (7TH DAN, RENSHI FROM ALL JAPAN KARATE FEDERATION SHITOKAI AS WELL AS WORLD SHITORYU KARATE FEDERATION) BEGAN HIS KARATE TRAINING IN 1972. EVER SINCE, HIS LIFETIME PASSION FOR KARATE ENABLED HIM TO DISTINGUISH HIMSELF IN NUMEROUS WAYS. AS A COMPETITOR, HE WAS A MEMBER OF THE IRANIAN NATIONAL TEAM FOR SEVERAL YEARS. AS A COACH, HE HAS BEEN NATIONAL TEAM COACH AND CHAIRMAN OF THE COACHING COMMITTEE IN IRAN. AS A TECHNICIAN, HE WAS A MEMBER OF TECHNICAL COMMITTEE IN ALL IRAN KARATE DO FEDERATION, AND CURRENTLY IS A TECHNICAL ADVISOR WITH ASIA PACIFIC SHITORYU KARATE DO FEDERATION (APSKF) AND SECRETARY GENERAL OF PAN-AMERICAN SHITORYU KARATE FEDERATION (PSKF). HE IS ALSO AN OFFICIAL EXAMINER OF THE WORLD SHITORYU KARATE DO FEDERATION, AS WELL AS THE MEMBER OF STANDING DIRECTORS OF WORLD SHITORYU KARATE FEDERATION.

MOST RECENTLY, RENSHI TANZADEH RECEIVED THE COVETED DISTINGUISHED SERVICE AWARD FROM THE WORLD SHITORYU KARATE DO FEDERATION AT THE 6TH WORLD SHITORYU KARATE DO FEDERATION (WSKF) WORLD CONGRESS IN CHINA IN 2009.

How long have you been practicing karate and who were/are your teachers?

I started practicing karate in 1972, at the age of 12 with Sensei Farhad Varasteh: the founder and the father of karate in Iran. At that time and for a while after that, he was the vice President of former WKF. The karate style that he introduced in Iran was based on Okinawan style that strongly emphasized on Kumite, which became foundation of Iranian karate.

Before studying and practicing other karate styles, I continuously practiced karate for 8 years under the instruction of Sensei Varasteh and, in 1977; I received my Black Belt Shodan. During those 8 years, I occasionally trained in Taekwondo. I was curious about this form of martial arts and wanted to try it. I also practiced Judo every now and then. Since martial arts in general were new to me, I was eager to try all of them, but karate remained the martial art that seriously attracted me and which I practiced and trained for in a constantly.

Karate Masters

"Karate is a martial art and has been popular in the last decades, and we owe this to sport karate."

How many styles have you trained in, and who were your teachers? Do you practice any other art in conjunction with karate?

After about 10 years practicing karate, I started studying other Japanese Karate Styles more in depth; more specifically, the four major Japanese karate styles that are Shitoryu, Shotokan, Gojuryu and Wadoryu. At that time I was the chairman of National Coaching Committee in Iran, Member of Technical committee and also the National team coach. Therefore knowing the 4 major Japanese styles of karate was extremely important and essential to me. However, I was more attracted to and more successful in Shotokan and Shitoryu. I was following the fundamentals of different associations, but specifically those of Shitokai in JKF and expanded my study in that particular association.

In 1986, I eagerly and seriously focused on Shitoryu. But at the same time, I carried on my study of other Japanese and Okinawan styles.

One of the reasons for which I then became more interested in Shitoryu was that this style contained all the aspects of Okinwawan karate such as Shurite, Nahate, Tomarite and also part of Crane fist (Kakkaku ken of Master Go Kenki) as well as Kobudo systems. I therefore decided to choose Shitoryu as my major style of karate training.

Were you a 'natural' at karate – did the movements come easily to you?

I am not sure if I can say that karate was natural to me or I was a natural at karate. But as far as I remember, and as everybody around me used to tell me, I was exceptionally talented in karate. My older brother used to practice karate when I was 11 years old, and I remember the time when he was practicing kata and kihon in our backyard. And by just watching him, I could exactly copy his movements without any mistake. Of course, did not perform them as well as someone who had learned them under the instructions of a sensei, but everyone around me was really surprised to see me performing the movements by just watching them. My brother discovered this talent in me and enrolled me in karate school. By the first time I put on my Gi to attended my karate class, I could already perform the first Heian kata, and everyone in the class was amazed that I could perform this kata without any instructions of a sensei.

I think the reason that I can understand the concept of movements and techniques and digesting and performing them properly is my talent in karate; as has been proven to me and others around me.

Did you train and study in Japan?

Yes, I lived in Japan for 3 years where I trained in Shitoryu, from 1990 to 1993. My training took place at dojos in the Tokyo and Saitama areas. In 1990, I received 4th Dan from Master Manzo Iwata. After that, I had training sessions every single evening, even on Saturdays and Sundays. During those years in Japan I trained with some great masters including Genzo Iwata Sensei, Sakanashi Sensei, and Yamazaki Sensei who was the first Japanese Sensei who officially introduced me to Shitoryu Association of JKF (Shitokai) in Japan. I also attended many seminars including the All Japan Shitokai Gassuku, where many great Shitokai masters such as the late Tsujikawa Sensei, the late Sakio Sensei, the late Hisatomi Sensei; as well as Murata Sensei the present WSKF and JKF Shitokai president, and Soke Kenei Mabuni instructed. Before traveling to Japan, I retired from competing. However, while in Japan, I decided to compete again. In 1992, I attended the 32nd All Japan Shitokai Championships and I placed 3rd in Open Kumite. Right after that I attended the 2nd All Saitamaken Championships and won Silver in the Open Kumite division. It was the same year that I attended in All Japan Shitokai Masters Clinic and I as a first non Japanese who could be able to passed the exam for the official Instructor License.

During my stay in Japan, I also practiced iaido and could manage to spend some time on learning this form of martial art. As it was new to me at that time and I found myself very much interested in it and I received the Shodan title in iaido before leaving Japan.

In my opinion, iaido is one of the most beautiful martial arts. In iaido, katas are basically performed with sword, and I was really amazed by the zanshin, focus, concentration and the beauty of movements that were applied in katas. In March 1993, I attended the 1st World Shitoryu Championships held in Tokyo. There, I won 3rd place in the Individual

Kata division, which was a great honor and achievement for me. After 3 years living in Japan, I left the country in April 1993 and traveled back to Japan in 2000, 2006, 2008, 2010 and 2013, to attend the Championships, Seminars, Congresses and the exams.

Please, explain for us the main points of Shito Kai and its differences with other styles like Shotokan, Wado Ryu or Goju Ryu?

Any style in karate, emphasis on a specific point, one on power, the other one on speed, another style on defense or counterattack and so on. One of the major and most important points that Shitoryu emphasizes on, is speed. In Shitoryu, we increase speed by shortening the distance and especially through shortening the path of blocking. You may have noticed that in Shitoryu, the techniques and stances are short. For example in shuto uke or gedan barai, the path of execution is shorter compared to the way they are done in Shotokan, Gojuryu or other styles. The reason why Shitoryu emphasizes on this matter is to reach the target faster. As we know, $V=D/T$ (speed equals the distance over the time). The founder of Shitoryu, Master Kenwa Mabuni, was completely aware of this physics formula and wanted to apply it to techniques. Distance is one of the major elements determining speed. So, the shorter the distance, the faster the speed. This fact is extremely important in Shitoryu.

Although it is an endless task, but Shitoryu practitioners strive to master a number of principles. To assist in this mastering, everything in Shitoryu is systematized and organized. This structured approach includes the four elements of martial arts and the main goals of training of Shitoryu (physical education, martial arts or Budo, and education of spirit and mind). Practitioners must also strive to apply the three main elements of Shitoryu (Sappou, Kappou and techniques of mentality), five principles of blocking (Uke no go gensoku: Rakka, Ryusui, Kusshin, Ten I, and Hangekei), the five principles of attaching (Seme no go gensoku: Hasshi, Suishin, Ju-nan, Karauke and Denko), the bunkai of katas and Oyo Kumite, and Kunshi no ken as the philosophy of the Shitoryu karate Do.

What can you tell us about the fonder Kenwa Mabuni and the evolution of the style in two different places like Osaka and Tokyo where the late Sensei Manzo Iwata lived? Do these two groups were different in training and development of the style?

Kenwa Mabuni, the founder of Shitoryu was a genius, and everybody is agreeable with this fact. The founder of Shotokan, Master Funakoshi and the founders of other styles always gave him this credit. Mabuni was not only famous as a genius, but also well known as a technical knowledgeable person in Okinawa and Mainland (Japan). Because of this, Master Mabuni had a special position in those days and was greatly respected. Often, he was being asked for technical advices. Some called him the encyclopedia of karate. If they needed to develop a special program, they certainly consulted with Master Mabuni.

Osaka and Tokyo were not and remain not so different. Since Master Manzo Iwata and Master Kenei Mabuni were both two of the senior students of Kenwa Mabuni, the two regions, Osaka and Tokyo developed in parallel and, in 1993; the World Shitoryu Federation was formally established by them. Master Iwata became its 1st president and Master Kenei rolled as the Soke (Governor) of the World Shitoryu Family.

"Karate is a lifetime study: it's a lifetime journey."

How do you see the different "branches" of the Shito Ryu style...Shito Kai, Hayashi-Ha, Kuniba-ha, Tahi-Ha, etc... and what makes Shito Kai different in comparison to these?

The masters and founders of most branches of the Shitoryu groups were in contact with Ryuso Kenwa Mabuni or were his students. They also had their personal ideas, which they gained from other styles or schools, and added them to their own school or to the syllabus of their own association, and modified them. The difference between Shitokai and others is that in Shitokai, pure Shitoryu is being practiced, exactly following the advices and instructions of Master Kenwa Mabuni.

Do you have any favorite technique?

I have always been using different techniques in kumite particularly in both guards (hidari kamae and migi kamae), but I can say that there are a few techniques that I have been using more than others. One of them is

Karate Masters

"Kihon in karate is divided into several groups and the whole point in practicing kihon is to get prepared for kata or kumite."

the sweeping of both legs (moro ashi barai). My other favorite technique is front leg jodan kick either mawashi or uramawashi.

The other technique that I have always used is counter attacking or doing Deashi with Zuki. But I have always been trying to use as many techniques as possible.

What are the most important points in your personal training these days?

Because of my responsibilities as the technical director of my organization, I have to travel a lot for seminars inside and outside of Canada. My goal has always been to transmit proper technical points of Shitoryu Technique, katas and principles. So, most of my personal trainings are the subjects of my seminars, which emphasize on karate in details, bunkai, main principles of training in kata, footwork and how to apply them to Kumite. And... I always try to stay in good shape, because I know that although my explanations are good enough to get the concept, I also would like to apply and perform these points in my seminars and in my classes, so that attendees and students would be able to learn more by watching and copying.

Are you against sport karate?

Absolutely not! Karate is a martial art and has been popular in the last decades, and we owe this to sport karate. The way sport karate is done, has led karate to be recognized in the world. For years now, we can see children as young as 3-4 year old in dojos, practicing karate. There are also summer camps for younger children teaching them karate. The sportive aspect of sport karate has promoted all this. This is a great thing.

We may think that sportive aspect of karate can take us away from the real or traditional karate, but as we can see, there are a lot of people who practice sport karate and traditional karate at the same time. The most important point is that as long as sportsmanship is considered, respected and applied in sport karate, as well as traditional karate, they can coexist at the same time. In other words, as long as the true spirit of Budo is applied in the training sessions and competitions, it's positive and beneficial.

What are the most important qualities for a student to become proficient in the Shito Kai method of karate?

Karate is a lifetime study: it's a lifetime journey. To be able to proceed in this long journey, just like to achieve any goal in life, we need to have love, while being patient and perseverant.

As a teacher of the art of karate – what is the most important element of your teachings?

There are many important elements in karate. I have students at different levels and with different motivations. Some of them are very young and interested in the sport aspect of karate. So I teach them the sportive elements of karate in their training sessions. Some are very much into traditional karate and are way more than those who would like to compete. But in general, I strongly emphasize on the proper form of karate techniques, correct posture, strength and speed to techniques and I also try to give them the concept of karate do and how to exactly apply katas and techniques in reality.

The word "Do" in Karate Do means "way". Do will never come to an end, the art of karate do is the way for a life time. So, the most important element to me is Budo or lifetime karate. However, as I mentioned, I train my younger students to be able to compete. Even when they get older, they become interested in Karate Do: and by all means, I train them Karate Do.

Kihon, Kata and Kumite: what's the proper ratio in training?

It depends on the season of training: whether it's competition season, a special occasions or regular training time.

In general, I recommend that in every regular training session, 30% kihon, 30% kata and 40% kumite and bunkai being practiced. But as I mentioned, it depends on the situations. For example, if more emphasis is supposed to be on kata, because of upcoming exams or championships, or during seasonal training, the ratio must then change to 10% kihon and 90% kata. The 10% kihon here must be practiced in order to improve kata. The same change in ratio can also be applied on Kumite when necessary.

Kihon in karate is divided into several groups and the whole point in practicing kihon is to get prepared for kata or kumite. So kihon trainings must be systematic. The combination of techniques in kihon must be determined very carefully, according to its goal. Kihon training is extremely useful for the improvement in kata and kumite.

How has your personal expression of karate developed over the years and what is it that keeps you motivated after all these years?
My personal expression of karate has developed over the years to "My Life Style". Karate, now, to me is how to communicate with others, how to think, how to deal with problems in life, how to help, how to improve and how to make changes, which are all the philosophy of karate. What keeps me motivated is to share my karate and what I have learned over the years, with people around the world. I would like to transfer my knowledge to others. I like to be useful in any way possible, using my life style which is karate.

Although knowledge is power, I think applying knowledge is real power and sharing the knowledge is a way to apply that knowledge.

How important is competition in the evolution of a karate practitioner?
Sport karat and competition can be done in a limited time of one's life which, is during youth. In general, competition is not necessarily applicable to all karate practitioners and I cannot say that it has a great effect on their evolution. There are a lot of karate practitioners who are not young enough to compete, but still have the motivation to continue practicing. But for those who are able to compete, the competition motivates them to train more. Competition also has a lot of positive points.

What really means "Ikken Hissatsu" and how it applies when used in Shito Kai Karate?
"Ikken Hissatsu" literally means "killing with one strike". The katana or sword is the symbol of Budo in Japan. I believe "Ikken Hissatsu" origins from Budo culture or symbol. But in karate we certainly do not want to kill with one Strike and do not want to think this way!

I think the concept of "Ikken Hissatsu" in karate would be to "knock out", as it has happened at times and as it's possible to knock out the opponent with one strike.

Having that said, I believe there's a mental statement in "Ikken Hissatsu" which is to encourage the students mentally, particularly while training in

"Since physical activities are greatly involved in karate training, using supplementary training can therefore be beneficial in the physical aspect of karate."

kata. As we know, kata is to combat different imaginary opponents, in different directions. When we finish with one direction, we should make sure that the opponent in that direction has been knocked out, and then start with another direction and so on.

How do you see the art of Shito Kai evolve in the future?

After the 1st World Shitoryu Championships in 1993, every year, more countries have been joining Shitoryu. In the Summer of 2013, the world Shitoryu federation was held in Japan. During this event, the number of participations was twice as much compared to 10 years prior to that, as about 1000 athletes participated. This shows that every year, the number of Shitoryu fans and participants increases in different countries and will increase in the future as well. I believe that one of the reasons behind this is the beauty of the technical aspect in Shitoryu.

Do you feel that you still have further to go in your studies?

Definitely, these studies will carry on. I am still studying every single day and improving my knowledge, using different articles, older books and

Karate Masters

"Bunkai in Shitoryu is one of the most important elements in practicing Shitoryu Karate."

new ideas. I try my best to use any available source to learn more and more about different methods of trainings, even basic techniques. I try to find out the best way to perform techniques, how others practice and perform them, and what their point of view about them would be. I want to understand the motivation of masters and pioneers in creating these techniques. So by studying every day, I will be able to have a more detailed and comprehensive view of these. This has a great effect on my personal practices: particularly when I train my students. I have noticed that by having more knowledge about karate, I can better transfer such knowledge to my students.

During all the years practicing karate, I have gathered more than 1000 books, magazines, articles and videos. I have studied a lot of them and I don't know how many more years I would need to read to finish all of them, considering that I keep on adding new ones! I will do my best to take advantages of all these sources.

What advice would you give to students on the question of supplementary training?

Since physical activities are greatly involved in karate training, using supplementary training can therefore be beneficial in the physical aspect of karate. Supplementary training can be done by elastic bands or weights to improve the strength and speed of the movements (techniques). Cardiovascular practices such as jogging and running are also very helpful.

We can also use sport science (physical education) or kinesiology to improve the physical aspect of karate and our techniques. For example, pushups on the knuckles have been done at the end of the training sessions for many years. But nowadays simple pushups have many variations these days and can be done in 20-25 different forms. These supplementary pushups are kind fun and also makes different muscles stronger, which helps in physical movements in karate. There are also plyometrics exercises that can be added to karate sessions in to give practitioners speed and give agility to their body and techniques.

Have been times when you felt fear in your training?

As far as I remember, I've never felt fear in my training. Perhaps because of my passion and love for this art, such a feeling never occurred to me.

Do you think that Olympics will be positive for the art of karate-do?

It will be absolutely positive in terms of more recognition for the art of karate. But I think traditional karate Do with its specifics and as an art will never go to Olympics. Nowadays, a lot of younger people are interested in sport karate and are involved in it. So a lot of countries are trying to get sport karate into the Olympics and if they succeed, it will still be useful for more recognition. Some people agree with the idea that karate do may disappear eventually because of Olympics but we should not mix sport karate and karate do. These are two different things. There are a lot of people involved in sport karate and, who at the same time practice traditional karate. Also, training in karate Do is still being done in a lot of dojos all around the world. So, I think by sport karate going to the Olympics, karate do will still survive. It will go on and will not get hurt nor will it disappear.

What are your views on kata bunkai? Is bunkai really important?

Bunkai in Shitoryu is one of the most important elements in practicing Shitoryu Karate. In Shitoryu, a kata does not exist without practicing Bunkai and applying Bunkai. In all katas, even in primary ones such as Heian, the application of Kata in the attack and Block techniques must be completely understood and practiced.

Bunkai is one of Shitoryu syllabuses component and is mandatory in the exams and tests.

How important is for a Shito Kai practitioner to know all the Kata of the style?

Although in Shitoryu, there are numerous katas from Shurite, Nahate, Tomarite and Hakkaku Ken systems. However, particularly in the beginner's level, it's not necessary or mandatory to train and practice all those katas. If we notice, there are some katas with 2 or 3 versions such as Naihanchi (Naihanchi Shodan, Nidan and Sandan). Even in Okiniwa, all masters and pioneers of karate emphasized mostly on the first (Naihanchi Shodan) version of the kata, because all the technical aspects of the kata are included in the first one. The 2nd or 3rd versions do not include much more than the first one. Therefore in some styles such as Wadoryu or other Okinwawan styles, only Naihanchi Shodan is being practiced. There are other katas the same as Naihanchi, where the first version is more important than the others like Itosu Rohai series. However, a master in Shitoryu, in high levels, must eventually know, be able to teach and perform all of the katas in this style.

I need to mention that right now in All Japan Karate Federation (JKF) and All Japan Shitokai, there are 4 designated katas as the mandatory Katas for the style of Shitoryu for those who want to upgrade their Instructor's level or to become a judge or examiner and… These 4 katas are the representatives of 4 major systems in Shitoryu, Bassai Dai represents Shurite, Seienchin represents Nahate, Nipaipo represents "Crane Fist" or "Hakkaku Ken" and Matsumora Rohai represents Tomarite.

How do you like to train yourself? Has this changed over the years?

I practice almost every day between 45 minutes to 2 hours. I try my best to practice everything in every session which is sometimes not possible because I need more time to practice katas, kumite and kihon. I have to say that the methods of trainings change with the age of trainers. The more we age, the less pressure should be applied during the training sessions. Obviously, the way I used to practice in a session when I was 30 years old was different from the way I did it at the age of 40 or now. This is an important point and must be taken under consideration. But I still enjoy every session of my trainings and try to practice bunkai, kihon and kumite and of course katas as much as possible and every time, I start with kihon and basics.

Do you recommend "Cross-Style" training in karate?

Knowing and doing cross-style training in karate is a good thing and it is an asset, but certainly not at the beginner's level. I recommend that everyone who practices any karate style, fist improve to a very high level in their own style and master that style. Then, they should start to get familiar with other styles and gradually, but seriously practice the main and basics of them. There are and there have been karatekas mastering different styles equally. So cross-style training is possible. If someone realizes in himself that he is able to do it, he should go ahead and do it. For those who are active in Sport karate, whether for training athletes or judging, and athletes themselves, cross-style training can be beneficial. By training cross-style, you should pay attention to details of not just the styles, but also paying attention and putting time on training for different moving and turning mechanism. For example some styles emphasize on heal rotations and

"Makiwara training is very important because it not only improves the strength in hands and knuckles, but also has a great effect in understanding, feeling and practicing Kime."

some other styles emphasize on rotations on toes. So it is necessary to understand all those mechanism, not just doing different katas from other styles.

What is your opinion of Makiwara Training?

In my opinion, Makiwara training is very important because it not only improves the strength in hands and knuckles, but also has a great effect in understanding, feeling and practicing Kime: which is the essence of karate techniques.

Makiwara training has also other important effects, which are the increase of confidence for the karateka and the improvement of concentration and focus. All these are in fact, included in Kime.

Therefore, makiwara training is extremely important. However, I must mention that, before starting makiwara training, the technique itself must first be fully understood and properly applied by karateka. The precision of the technique is of a very high importance and it's not just about punching and kicking on the makiwara pad.

Karate Masters

"Knowing and doing cross-style training in karate is a good thing and it is an asset, but certainly not at the beginner's level."

As I mentioned, makiwara training improves the strength of hands and knuckles and kime, therefore it is necessary for those who are interested in Tameshiwari to have a lot of makiwara training. Since the main goal of makiwara training is to improve kime, I recommend that in the beginning, karatekas start this training under the supervision of their instructors and, after a while, when they master the techniques, they can continue on their own.

You are working on a new book project. What can you tell us about it?

That's right. For many years, I have been thinking about publishing a book about Shitoryu karate. Fortunately, this project is becoming practicable, and I estimated that by mid 2014, this book will be published.

What I have in mind is to introduce Shitoryu in a comprehensive way, as much as possible. There are many points and details in Shitoryu karate that can hardly be found in other books.

There are already many useful books as "Shitoryu Kata Series" published by JKF Shitokai which, are great references for students and instructors. But I am willing to present Shitoryu from the very beginning, all kihons, fundamentals and technical aspects in details, using illustrations and computer graphics. My goal is to provide all the information that one would need to know about Shitoryu from the beginner up to Black Belt level.

Unfortunately, so far, there have not been a lot of books or publications about Shitoryu karate as opposed to other karate styles. This has been for such a long time another motivation for me to publish this book, and I hope that I will successfully achieve my goal.

Do you consider kata an important part of karate training?

Definitely yes! There are a lot of technical points including applications, blocking techniques that can be learned by practicing kata. Every single kata in karate includes a specific usage in terms of technical aspect and certain technical abilities. Therefore, practicing kata is extremely important in karate.

If we look at the history of karate, we can see that in the past, they used to teach the kumite strategies, by teaching kata. So, kata is a useful tool in learning self defense and kumite.

We can practice and learn a lot of basic movements in kata. As a matter of fact, kata consists of kihon and complex techniques including punches and blocks and counterattacks. It's important to know that we should not perform a kata just for the sake of performing it. What we should do is to understand and analyze all the movements in each kata and have enough knowledge of their application. By understanding what we are exactly doing and why, we can actually perform the kata and every single movement in a kata, in a more advanced, perfect and beautiful way. Therefore, I strongly recommend that while performing kata; it is important to understand the movements and their applications.

What are the main aspects of your teaching?

As we are aware, karate develops in different aspects. One of them is Budo or combat and self defense. The other aspect is health. Karate training can make us healthier and stronger. Other aspect would be sport. Another one is the mental aspect and is aimed at perfecting character.

I have always tried to teach all these aspects to my students. Nowadays, the students enter karate dojos willing to practice karate with different reasons and motivations in their minds. I have always tried to give the proper response to their motives. Some of them come only for the sport aspect of karate and would like to attend the tournaments. So, in my trainings, I emphasize on the ways of combat and sport karate more than other aspects.

Some come to my dojo to learn martial arts. I certainly consider that while training them.

But in General, although each individual starts karate for different reasons, I have always tried to teach them the moral and mental aspects of karate. Kenwa Mabuni has a famous saying: "kunshi no ken" which means

"Fist of a Nobleman" that means use your fist and power in the right way. So we can simply interpret that to: "power brings responsibility". By talking about kunshi no ken, I try to teach the development of character and spirit which is the essence of karate and this is extremely important to all of us with any motivation. I want my students to understand the real meaning of Kunshi no ken and apply them in their life.

Shotokan, Shitoryu, Gojuryu etc. How do you think the different branches/styles affect the complete art of Karate?

We are all happy and satisfied with the style of karate that we practice in. But we are all also aware that no style is perfect. Therefore it could be beneficial that masters and instructors study other styles too in order to be able to use one another's point of view. In the past decades, different styles have influenced each other and sometimes, some masters have even combined different styles. Some Shotokan masters have added Gojuryu and Shitoryu katas to their trainings and syllabuses. In general, I think that studying other styles can have a very positive effect on the art of karate.

Do you think Kobudo training is beneficial for a karate practitioner in general?

Kobudo and karate do were developed in Okinawa almost at the same time and parallel to each other. I am confident that to learn Kobudo, one must learn and know karate techniques first. In fact, we use karate blocks and strikes to be able to use those weapons. So, having karate training is very beneficial for those who practice Kobudo. However, Kobudo training is also, in a way, beneficial for karatekas, because you can apply karate techniques to use the weapons.

What is your opinion about the "Shobu Ippon" division in Karate competition?

Sport karate and its rules are going through a lot of changes and we all know that Shobu Ippon is still a part of Sport karate. Shobu Ippon in general is tougher than most resent regulated rules within WKF (World Karate Federation). Therefore, I don't mind it to be just a division.

In Sport Karate, techniques are limited and you can wrap it up with a Chudan geri or Jodan geri or Chudan zuki and Jodan uchi. Sport karate is expanding in the world and students start competitions at a very young age, like 12 year old in an international competition. So I think the high quality techniques of shobu ippon for these young athletes are not appropriate. Different rules and regulations can be tried, but eventually they have to come up with a logical conclusion. Perhaps in the future, we can achieve and observe something better and more advanced than shobu ippon.

What can karate offer to individuals in these troubled times we are living in?

We are all aware that people with depression and mental problems, in long term, will end up having physical problems as well. Their bodies will get damaged because of the damage in their souls. It's also true that if we have positive and healthy minds, the positivity and health will transfer and affect our bodies. Since there's a discipline in karate training, such as in blocks, in different forms of kata, stances, etc. the repetition of this physical discipline can have a direct reaction on mental health. So, in long term, a karateka will be able to deal better and easier with the troubled times we are living in.

During our karate training, for years we do blocks, counter attacks, we use different strategies in kumite and so on. All these have a very positive and constructive affect on one's mental state because one learns how to block or avoid problems, and how to use different strategies when dealing with problems and so on.

"Karate has gone through lots of changes during many years."

After so many years of training, what is so appealing for you in Shito Kai and why?

Different styles of karate overall pursue the same goal. But as I have already mentioned, Shitoryu includes Shuri, Naha, Tomari and Hakkaku Ken "Crane fist" systems: and that's why I look at it as a complete style. This advantage in Shitoryu gives me the motivation to study more and more, and it was through Shitoryu that I could more deeply understand and comprehend the concept behind the techniques and therefore found them more enjoyable.

The nature of the practices and trainings in Shitoryu gives me a better and particular appreciation of karate and practicing it. I have been able to get familiar with other karate styles through Shitoryu because of its nature: that has made me significantly detail oriented. So, with the studies that I

Karate Masters

"Kobudo and karate do were developed in Okinawa almost at the same time and parallel to each other."

have had through many years and am still pursuing, I could understand karate much better. The way Shitoryu looks at the technical aspects of this art is very realistic. In Shitoryu, katas and bunkai in particular are being noticed realistically; therefore all the movements are being done naturally.

Is Shitokai in constant evolution?

Shitokai and Shitoryu karate are not excluded from other karate styles and schools. Karate has gone through lots of changes during many years. This evolution will continue in the future too, and all these changes will bring better and more positive results. The same is with Shitokai. As master Mabuni, the founder of Shitoryu has said, karate do has never been perfect and will never be. This means that evolution in karate do makes it more and more perfect as the time goes on. For example, the way kata trainings were done in 40's or 50's was in many ways different from the way they are being done today. I am sure that there will be more changes and evolution in karate in the next years and decades, which will all be in a very positive way. I hope that I live long enough to see some of these changes that will occur in the future, in Shitoryu or any other styles.

Finally, what advice would you like to give to all Karate practitioners?

The most important advice is that karate must be accompanied with respect, discipline and good manners. Without respect, discipline and proper manners, karate would be nothing but throwing some kicks and punches: it would be nothing but fighting. In fact, understanding and training in any style in karate must become the life style of the individuals. So, applying respect, discipline and proper manners in karate is critical and extremely necessary as they are in our lives, in our communications and relationships with people, and also in different situations.

My other advice is that in your training sessions, be honest with yourself and others and take your training seriously. Try to pay attention to details in every single point that you learn. Try to feel and comprehend them. It's extremely important to do your best in every training session and take them seriously as well as enjoying them. This way, after every training session you will feel satisfied and joyful. If not so, then you have to consider that something should have gone wrong in that session. Think about it and figure out what the problem was. At the end of every training session, you should strongly feel that you have gained a benefit out of it, if not, find out why.

I would like to add here that an athlete, an instructor and a referee, all together make a triangle and are closely related to one another. My advice to athletes is to try and practice different ways of training in their sessions, use different samples that have already been used by masters and champions. Always respect your instructors and referees. Always trust them.

My advice to instructors is to keep updating their knowledge. Just like physicians, constantly study and improve your knowledge about new sport technologies, information and physical trainings in order to be able to adapt yourself to the evolutions happening in sports.

My advice to referees and judges, especially in Kata, because of their huge responsibility, is to choose the right athletes for the podium and to improve their knowledge about different styles and katas as much as possible, to be able to judge easier and more accurately to pick the right athlete. O

MASAHIKO TOKASHIKI

LIGHT ON THE DARKNESS

SENSEI MASAHIKO TOKASHIKI ORIGINALLY BEGAN HIS STUDY IN MATSUBAYASHI SHORIN RYU UNDER THE GUIDANCE OF GRANDMASTER SHOSHIN NAGAMINE. HE CURRENTLY HEADS THE TOKASHIKI KARATE DOJO WHICH IS THE HONBU DOJO IN OKINAWA FOR THE "SHOGEN RYU KARATEDO ASSOCIATION". THIS GROUP WAS FORMED BY OKINAWAN KARATE LEGEND KENSEI TABA WHO WAS ALSO TOKASHIKI'S SENSEI. TOKASHIKI SENSEI'S PASSION FOR TEACHING KARATE ALONG WITH HIS HIGH ENERGY LEVEL WAS DRIVEN BY HIS SENSE OF RESPONSIBILITY TO SENSEI TABA WHO PASSED AWAY IN JULY OF 2012. TOKASHIKI SENSEI HAS GREAT CONTROL AND COMMAND OVER HIS MOVEMENTS AND IS A WARM AND CARING INSTRUCTOR, PASSING ON HIS KNOWLEDGE TO THE NEXT GENERATION. HE IS A GREAT EXAMPLE OF AN OKINAWAN SENSEI LOOKING TO PRESERVE HIS ART.

Sensei, how did you get involved in Shorin Ryu Karate?
I first started training in Karate in my third year of high school. I was 16 years old at the time. A year before, I came across a Karate book on Bushi Matsumura. After I finished reading it, it sparked an interest. It was then I began my journey in the martial arts.

Who was your first sensei?
My first teacher was Grandmaster Shoshin Nagamine. This is where I began my studies in Matsubayashi Shorin Ryu Karate.

Did you have any other instructors who helped guide you in the Nagamine Dojo?
Yes, Seigi Nakamura as well as Kensei Taba Sensei who was my teacher until he passed away in 2012. They were a very big influence on my early training and why I still continue to train even today. Through Taba Sensei, I felt that there was something more in the interpretation from his katas. This had a big impact on me. He also gave me the opportunity to not only teach here in Okinawa, but also in Canada and the United States as well.

Karate Masters

"Developing a Japanese garden and Karate-do are similar in their aspect of putting your heart into some- thing which is important."

I was very moved by the method of his instruction. These memories are very special to me; I will continue to cherish them.

What is your mission in running your own dojo?

Besides running my dojo here in Naha, Okinawa, my mission is to help spread Okinawan Karate to the world. It is very important to me to spread the teaching of Okinawan Karate and what has been passed down to me. Karate is not a sport, but a way of life; it is very important for people to understand this.

Can you tell me about running the landscaping business while having a dojo?

I feel Japan is the heart and center of the world when it comes to gardening. We put our heart into its design. Developing a Japanese garden and Karatedo are similar in their aspect of putting your heart into something which is important. There is beauty in both.

What do you feel is the future of Shorin Ryu right now?

My dojo in Okinawa is open anytime for people to study and understand the technical aspect of Karate training. I want people to succeed and understand their own personal journey of karate...I want people to enjoy this journey.

How do you feel when Westerners come to visit your dojo?

Like I said, my dojo is open. I am for the improvement of the person who is coming to me. I understand the basics of Karate, and I want to bring that across in my teachings so there is an understanding when they leave Okinawa.

What misunderstandings do Westerners have in Okinawan martial arts?

That martial arts is mind and body. The internal heart is very important in how one approaches their task. The power we produce has to be generated the right way. The training has to be scientific and smart for the durability in the person studying Karate. It is important that people understand the principles and the basics. Once they achieve this, then these principles can be applied to their kata and bunkai.

"I believe keeping the spirit of the sensei who have taught me before alive."

What else consisted of your early training?

Besides the basics in kata, we did a lot of makiwara training.

Is there anything else you would like to share with the readers which you feel is important?

I believe keeping the spirit of the senseis who have taught me before alive. In passing that information onto the next generation of students for them to carry on, this will help keep traditional martial arts alive. We have to remember Karate comes from Okinawa and it important that people show an appreciation for this art which has been shared with the world. O

GARY TSUTSUI

THE SPIRIT WITHIN

SENSEI TSUTSUI HAS DEDICATED MORE THAN 50 YEARS OF HIS LIFE TO THE ART OF KARATE-DO. INTERESTED IN THE PHILOSOPHY AND PRINCIPLES OF THE ART OF 'EMPTY HAND' AT A VERY YOUNG AGE, GARY TSUTSUI IMMERSED HIMSELF IN THE NEVER-ENDING PATH OF BUDO. "EARLY IN MY TRAINING," HE REMEMBERS, "I HAD THE URGENCY TO KNOW AND FIND OUT THE TRUE SPIRIT OF KARATE-DO. THIS PERSONAL INTUITIVE PERCEPTION LED ME TO A LIFETIME OF QUESTIONING AND SEARCHING; OF STUMBLING AND FUMBLING TOWARD THE IDEALS OF BUDO."

A TRAGIC ACCIDENT BECAME A TURNING POINT IN SENSEI TSUTSUI'S LIFE BUT HIS TRUE "AWAKENING" SO TO SPEAK, WAS MUCH MORE GRADUAL, TAKING PLACE OVER A NUMBER OF YEARS, WITH MUCH CONSIDERATION AND CONTEMPLATION. "DEATH CAN BE A VERY POWERFUL MOTIVATOR SO I STARTED TO ASK MYSELF VERY SERIOUS QUESTIONS," HE SAYS. "I REALIZED THAT I DIDN'T WANT TO DIE WITH IDEAS AND THINGS BURIED INSIDE OF ME. AFTER ALL, IN BUDO IS THE IDEA OF DEATH THAT GIVES MEANING TO LIFE."

How long have you been practicing Martial Arts?
I started training when I was 18 so I have been practicing for almost half a century.

How many styles have you trained in and who were your teachers?
I define "training" as consistent and extended practice so I can claim training in only two ryu: Shotokan and Shindo Jinen-ryu. I started Japan Karate Association Shotokan training under Yutaka Yaguchi in 1965, continued the study of JKA Shotokan under Joseph Castillo to 1970 and finally Shindo Jinen Ryu under Kiyoshi Yamazaki from 1971 to 2008. I am currently independent and non-affiliated but maintain membership in the USA National Karate-do Federation.

Obviously, during all these years I had the opportunity of training in clinics and intensive seminars under the guidance of some other great masters like Morio Higaonna, Takeshi Uchiage Takayuki Kubota, Takehiro Konishi, Yasuhiro Konishi, Teruo Hayashi, Tetsuhiko Asai, Masatoshi

Karate Masters

"My challenge, even in my early years of training, has always been the same: seek perfection of character, right thinking, and right action."

Nakayama, Teruyuki Okazaki, Mikio Yahara and Toshihiro Oshiro just to mention a few. They all provided with a great deal of knowledge that tremendously helped to improve my understanding of what true karate-do is about.

Would you tell us some interesting stories of your early days in karate?

I have so many good memories that I really don't know where to start. My desire to start training was sparked when I saw a karate demonstration at the Denver Buddhist Temple in the winter of 1965. Mr. Yutaka Yaguchi had just arrived in the United States and was in his prime. He demonstrated such unbelievable skill and incredible power. I especially remember his roundhouse kick – connecting to the head in a downward arc. I was hooked.

In the late 60s, the Japan Karate Association of Colorado under the leadership of Sensei Joseph Castillo had a huge number of members that were Denver police officers – young, physically fit, big, athletic, aggressive and fanatical in the way they trained. In one sparring session, I remember getting pinned to the wall when I attempted to block a front snap kick.

At the same JKA dojo, we often had visiting schools for special sparring sessions. I was lucky enough to spar with Russell Peron – a Tae kwon do stylist and a highly skilled kicker with amazing jumping ability. Since then, I have had an enduring respect for Tae kwon do and all Martial Art systems.

In the early 70s, I began a long and productive association with Sensei Kiyoshi Yamazaki, a serious traditional Martial Artist, yet friendly and approachable – so many great memories of tough, demanding training and also so many untold moments of light-heartedness. One summer in the late 70s, a number of us used to train late into the night after the dojo was closed. After training we would then go to a Baskin-Robbins (also closed). The owners were an elderly couple and with their trust we got into a routine of helping them clean in preparation for the next day of business. And, we got ice cream.

Were you a 'natural' at karate – did the movements come easily to you?

I have been told by my colleagues I was a "natural" but you know I am not so sure. I have often thought a certain technique or combination of techniques was easy until I was instructed to make corrections. In all honesty, I have to admit I think now it's all difficult – kihon, kata, kumite. Some days, even the warm-ups are difficult.

How has your personal expression of karate developed over the years?

My challenge, even in my early years of training, has always been the same: seek perfection of character, right thinking, and right action. I try to be the person my dog thinks I am.

What are the most important points in your teaching methods today?

I try to be as critical and honest with myself as possible in analyzing whether I am communicating to my students traditional karate techniques and their proper execution.

Hopefully, I am also giving them a historical framework as well as insight into the traditions and customs of Japanese culture. And, finally, I like to think I am successfully motivating them to make the study of karate a lifelong pursuit and instilling in them the values and traditions of Japanese karate-do.

If you had only a 10-minute class with a student, what would be the most important thing that you would teach him/her?

Train everyday, be honest with yourself in assessing your accomplishments and failures in the study of karate-do, be humble, and do not give up. There are always challenges in life. All of us are faced with situations when the rug could be pulled out from beneath us at any level. We can't always see how things will turn out but we can always have the right spirit to face these situations.

Karate nowadays often is referred to as a sport. Would you agree with this definition or is it a Martial Art?

I agree and disagree. I choose first to view karate as a Martial Art and will continue to strive to provide the highest level of professional instruction in the art of karate, and to promote the history, philosophy, and techniques of traditional karate-do. That said, I also think there must be an acceptance and tolerance for its practice as a sport.

What are the most important qualities for a student to become proficient in karate?
The same qualities that guarantee success in any endeavor: thirst for knowledge, ability to recognize and capitalize on opportunity, no fear of failure, hard work, recognition that one's success is the result of multiple people, humility, and luck (a plethora of unforeseen occurrences can easily alter a person's life).

When teaching the art of karate, what is the most important element: self-defense or sport?
For me, it will always be self-defense.

Kihon, Kata and Kumite – what's the proper ratio in training?
Many answers here: 1) in the initial stages of training proper warm-up, kihon, kumite, and kata in equal proportion. 2) in a more matured (physically, mentally, spiritually) individual with more extensive training, the amount of time spent in these areas will fluctuate. Obviously, if one is an elite athlete, there will be naturally a focus on one's specialty (kumite and/or kata) but always with recognition that kihon training is indispensable. 3) If one has very little time and a very fragmented and inconsistent training schedule, I would recommend doing kata with minimal kumite and kihon.

Who would you like to have trained with that you have not?
Hidetaka Nishiyama. My unofficial survey indicates he was not liked by all and even hated by some, but all agree he was a great teacher.

How important is competition in the evolution of a karate practitioner?
I think competition is very important. Competition is a good testing ground for evaluating one's training. Obviously, as an instructor promoting perfection of character, I cannot justify taking students onto the streets to pick fights to test their skills. But I can encourage them to recognize the value of competition where one is forced to analyze and adapt to the fighting skills of different opponents and to test one's mental strength in a high-stress environment.

Modern day sport competition is to some degree a manifestation of musha-shugyo: "One Zen custom used by the classical warrior and adopted by the exponents of the classical budo forms is musha-shugyo, a kind of 'austere training' in warriorship."

Musha-shugyo requires the trainee to travel in monk-like fashion, living simply, and exposing himself to natural hardships in the course of travel. At the same time, this voluntary pattern of life involves him in training sessions in as many different dojos as he can enter.

Musha-shugyo is indispensable to the trainee at the jutsu level of skill and is a path of rugged endeavor that is a prerequisite for mastery of the do. Most of the founders and developers of the classical budo ryu engaged in musha-shugyo, and by testing and proving their techniques, as well as their own mastery, through this activity were able to formalize the component systems of their ryu."

How do you think a practitioner can increase his/her understanding of the spiritual aspects of the art?

Study Eastern religions and their influence on the Japanese Martial Arts. Make the training and philosophy a part of your daily life. Seek perfection of character.

"Train everyday, be honest with yourself in assessing your accomplishments and failures and do not give up."

Is there anything lacking in the way Martial Arts are taught today compared to how they were when you started training?

Two things in particular: 1) Today, I think protocol and etiquette are not viewed as critical elements in one's training and not as strictly enforced, and 2) with the increased focus on the possibility of karate becoming an Olympic sport and the omission of kata competition in the Pan American Games, kihon training and kata training do not receive the same attention as in the early days. I still firmly believe kihon and kata training will make one a better fighter.

Do you feel that you still have further to go in your studies?

Absolutely. The older I get, the more I know what I do not know. So, these days I often feel like a beginner.

Karate Masters

"I think competition is very important. Competition is a good testing ground for evaluating one's training."

What advice would you give to students on the question of supplementary training?

Just be careful in choosing what you are going to do for cross-training and how much time you are going to dedicate to the supplemental training. Remember that one's proficiency in any physical activity is based on concentrated repetition of movement in a specific activity. No reason to question whether running is beneficial but do you need to run 10 miles every day for your karate training? I don't think so. Weight training is essential but lifting too heavy weights will slow you down – lower weight and higher repetitions. One thing I would suggest is that one not use music for serious training. Listen to your body – learn to interpret your pain and fatigue to reach a higher performance level.

Why is it, in your opinion, that a lot of students start falling away after two to three years of training?

We live in a culture of instant gratification and, as a result, the necessity and demand of long-term investment (i.e., training daily for twenty, thirty, forty years) to achieve world-class success in any endeavor is not fully recognized and appreciated. May I suggest a book by Geoff Colvin titled "Talent Is Overrated" for further insight into what separates world-class performers from everyone else.

Have there been times when you felt fear in your training?

Yes. One time remains particularly vivid in memory. In the nine months prior to competing at the WUKO (now WKF) World Championships in Tokyo, Japan in 1978, I was in intensive training. My days started at 4 a..m. and ended late at night. The actual physical training probably distilled into about 6 or 7 hours – a lot of time spent eating and recuperating. One day, Yamazaki Sensei was pushing me in kata training. I performed the kata, he made a correction, and I immediately would perform the kata again. This process repeated itself for I do not remember how long. I came so close to quitting and telling him I could not do another kata. Fear of being labeled a quitter, as well fear of disappointing all my supporters and dishonoring my family name, motivated me to push past the pain and continue. I am so thankful I did not give up. The success of winning at the world championships was a critical time in my life. Also, I remain grateful to Yamazaki Sensei for knowing he could push me so hard.

Do you think that Olympics will be positive for the art of karate-do?
I think it will be great for business. It should spark new interest in karate and sustain it for years to follow. It also will present some problems for me in that I will not change how or what I teach, and I am certain the type of student coming into my dojo is going to be recognizably different from the students of years past. Hopefully, I can transform the thinking of those students interested in only sport karate into thinking about karate more as a Martial Art.

What are your views on kata bunkai?
The old masters who designed and implemented kata were visionaries. What a perfect way to transmit technical information – train the body and mind to memorize techniques, reinforce that knowledge with bunkai analysis, and hide secret techniques within the structure of the kata – all while enhancing physical fitness.

What are your thoughts about doing thousands of repetitions of one single technique in training, as in the old days? Is it a good training method?
Yes, without question. One needs to be reminded that the high repetitions approach is not about physical training – it is about mental training. The body is only as strong as one's mind. In the heat of competition, as one is experiencing repeated warm-up and cool-down, competing, waiting, dealing with fatigue and high stress, one gains a clear understanding to the questions, "did I train long enough and hard enough?"

How important is Dojo Kun to the art of Karate-do?
Dojo Kun is very important. Many differentiate Dojo Kun from ryu to ryu, but all are relevant to seeking the truth and as guidance for life's journey.

Karate Masters

What can karate offer to the individual in these troubled times we are living in?

Karate can be the catalyst to discovering a means for right thinking and right actions, a system for examining and maintaining ethics, honor, duty, and guidance for fulfilling one's responsibilities as a citizen of this world.

After so many years of training, what is it for you that is so appealing in this style of karate – and why?

The practice of karate is for me is an affirmation of my identity as a Japanese. For me, studying karate is studying my heritage.

How do you like to train yourself? Has this changed over the years?

My training has changed dramatically the last five years. I am still struggling to complete a solid 1-1/2 hour of intense karate training. Nothing too complicated – warm-ups, kihon, kumite, kata.

I had a near fatal car accident in April 2005 and I am still not fully recovered. As a result of the collision, I sustained a fractured left scapula, fractured left clavicle, nine fractured ribs (some with multiple fractures), five pelvic fractures, and hemo-pneumothorax. The first week in surgical intensive care I required emergent procedures to facilitate breathing, experienced atrial fibrillation resulting in emergency defibrillation, and severe gastric bleeding resulting in over two liters of blood loss. I was hospitalized for one month.

At the time of the accident I was heavy into karate training and running daily. I have no doubts that karate saved my life.

Westerners are generally physically bigger than Japanese; how do you think this has affected their karate?

In general, I think bigger, stronger athletes have a tendency to rely on their physical strength rather than technical skill in all sports. As a result I think the study of strategy and technique is de-emphasized. The current WKF competition rules reward physical prowess and the old ippon-shobu system rewarded strategy, fighting spirit, and technical skill. In the early years (60s and 70s), I think there was more a complementary mix of size and technical skill. Today, it is rare to see big and strong karate-ka with technical skills comparable to the likes of Val Mijailovic or Frank Smith.

How do you see your own karate as opposed to say ten or fifteen years ago?

I thought I was aging gracefully but ran into a little obstacle with my car accident. The accident most affected my ability to kick and I am no longer able to execute "jodan" (high) kicks with any degree of proficiency. My punching, striking, and blocking continue to get stronger. I have always trained with injuries and take pride in being able to take a good punch, but I have not engaged in jyu kumite since my accident so I do not know if this is still true. I was ordered by my doctors not to spar and cautioned not take any impact to my rib cage. I continue to study refereeing and hopefully I am maintaining a technical level that is still respected.

"The older I get, the more I know what I do not know."

Is your style of teaching the same as the traditional Japanese method, or do you have your own ideas?

I fundamentally believe in the benefits of traditional karate training so I continue to teach a very structured curriculum of warm-up, kihon, kumite, and kata. My wife Candice – who is a godan in karate and a sandan in naginata – has a Master's in Physical Therapy and she has been a valuable resource in refining and redefining many traditional karate practices. I have instituted more kihon training with a partner rather than practicing techniques against imaginary opponents.

What advice would you give to an instructor who is struggling with his or her own development?

Do not give up. Train every day and continue your study of karat-do. If you have young students, be honored that their parents have entrusted you with the welfare of their children. Recognize that not all of your students can be elite athletes but that you have the means to help all of them achieve their full potential. Be patient and compassionate with your students.

Finally, what advice would you like to give to all Karate practitioners and Martial Artists in general?

Train every day and share your knowledge. O

KATSUHIRO TSUYAMA

CHANGING LIVES

SENSEI TSUYAMA IS SYNONYMOUS WITH THE ART OF KARATE. ONE OF THE LEADING MEN IN THE "JAPAN KARATE-DO FEDERATION", HE HAS A RICH AND PROUD HERITAGE SPANNING OVER DECADES OF DEDICATED AND DISCIPLINED TRAINING. AS IMPRESSIVE AS HIS KARATE CREDENTIALS ARE, HOWEVER, WHAT SETS SENSEI TSUYAMA APART IS HIS UNCANNY ABILITY TO RELATE TO AND UNDERSTAND PEOPLE FROM ALL RACES, CULTURES AND BACKGROUNDS. HE BECAME ONE OF THE MOST SUCCESSFUL TRAINERS AND COACHES IN THE HISTORY OF SPORT KARATE, AND HE HAS COACHED AND TRAINED A LONG LIST OF INTERNATIONAL CHAMPIONS. FOR HIM, SPIRIT AND HEART ARE THE MOST IMPORTANT ATTRIBUTES IN KARATE TRAINING; "IN ORDER TO BE THE BEST," SENSEI TSUYAMA SAYS FIRMLY, "YOU MUST HAVE THE WARRIOR'S SPIRIT AND THE WARRIOR'S HEART."

Sensei Tsuyama, you are highly regarded teacher and coach in the world of Karate, is Shotokan your main style?
Yes, Shotokan is my main style and Karate is the art I dedicated my life to.

How do you remember yourself in the early days of your training?
Well, as a youngster you always try to show and do your best physically. The mental and spiritual aspect is not really inside of you yet but the hard Budo training will eventually make you realize that there is more to Karate than simply punching and kicking and winning competitions. I think tat my training was very natural from the very beginning. I knew what I was attracted to Karate and also what to expect of its training…obviously as a young man. My understanding of Karate evolved as I grew as human being and as my Karate matured too I saw other important elements that were not there when I started.

Training was very rigid and very hard. A lot of repetitions! Sensei you travel a lot around the world, what is the most important lesson that you have learn from teaching all over the globe?
I learned a lot from meeting people from all over the world and this developed my Karate style.

Karate Masters

"My understanding of Karate evolved as I grew as human being."

It made me realize that looking at the big picture not matter how big we think we are...we are very small. This changed my attitude and made me continue training and learn further from every single person I meet. People from different countries have different cultural backgrounds, different characters and different languages that affect how we see things but deep down we are all human. Karate makes no distinction between people and levels everybody up!

How good is the repetition training in the karateka's development?

I think that repetition training is the best way to make the body understand the proper way of delivering a technique. I'd like to differentiate between someone tat is young and someone that is in his 50s or 60s. When you are young you need to do hundreds of repetitions in each training session. Repeating a 'gyaku tsuki' twenty times in a class simply is not going to cut it in the early phases of training. You need to do 200, 300 or 1,000 reverse punches per training session. The same applies for the other basic punching techniques and the kicks. Don't waste you time with fancy things hat won't contribute to your progress in the later years of your Karate training.

How that changes when you get older?

When you get older I assume that you already have a solid technique and therefore doing 1,000 repetitions of the same technique in a training session doesn't have the same effect. Let me explain an important point; when you do 1,000 punches the idea is to force the body to learn the 'right way' without intellectualize the physical action. But the time you punch your 500 punch the body is naturally forced to save energy by itself and use the right mechanism to make the technique correct. By keep doing this kind of training the body leans by itself. That is the reason why you should do it when you are young and the joint can take that type of training. Once you know how to use the body properly...it is about quality and not necessarily quantity in the amount of repetitions.

Do you think participate in sport competitions is important?

Sport competition is a very important aspect of the development of every karateka. I understand that some people may think it is not, but today's world is different and the sportive aspect 'opens' the doors for a deeper understanding of other relevant values that are necessary in our society. The old times were about war and fighting for your life. Nowadays we can practice sport kumite and develop our skill in combat and at the same time to have a good sportive experience that will make us grow as human beings and karateka. It is important though that winning is not the reason why we do it. Winning is important of course but we should look at competition as a whole experience. Sport competition kumite is different than dojo kumite for many reasons.

Would you mind to elaborate?

When you spar in the dojo you know your opponents, you pretty much know their timing, their favorite techniques, their personalities, etc...but when you go to a competition and especially a national or international competition, you don't know the guy that your are going to fight. He is there with the same determination and passion to win that you have. He is not going to be 'nice' and take the win home. You don't have 5 or 6 minutes to figure out his timing, rhythm, technical tempo, etc...In a matter of 30 seconds or less you have to know 'who he is' and how you are going to defeat him. Therefore, sport competition allows you to develop the ability to decipher and read an opponent in a very short time. This is something that you simply don't get by sparring in the dojo. Here I am not talking about what kind of rules are being used in that competition. That's irrelevant now.

Does the rules affect how to approach a match?

Of course. If you are in a "Shobu Ippon" match is different that if it is a "Sanbon". Rules kind of determine how you are going to approach the match but this doesn't change the aspects I talked before. You still don't know your opponent, you don't know how he is going to play his cards and what kind of strategy he has prepared to deal with you. Your game plan is partially dictated by the rules. It is important to know how to use the rules for your own advantage as a competitor.

Do you feel that you still have more to learn?

Definitely. I look at Karate as an extension of life. In life you don't stop growing and learning new things. I believe that we always have something new to learn – I don't understand those who claim otherwise. I like to read new books and watch videos whenever I can to absorb more information. That helps me to improve my technical level and better understand how the different aspects and elements of the art and sport work together. I think it is very important to compete as much as possible because the art of Karate is evolving and there is always a new twist for an old technique. Competing gives you a sparring edge that is impossible to have otherwise.

Sensei, you are very strict about rank and titles in Martial Arts and specifically Karate. Why it bothers you when people claim a rank that doesn't match with their knowledge and skill?

They are a fraud for the rest of the people who really trained and dedicated their lives to Karate and Martial Arts. You have people who have trained very hard for decades to become who they are in Karate or any other style, then these other individuals are showing off their ranks and titles that they've got through the back door because or friendship or money. They should be embarrassed. But the one that should be embarrassed the most are those teachers whom gave that rank and title! They don't understand what Martial Arts and Karate training really means. The teachers are the ones to blame, the students, are just ignorant.

How do you achieve relaxation?

Number one is proper breathing. You need to keep your breathing pattern under control. The timing of the breath has to be steady and consistent under any circumstances. You also need to be confident of your technical ability. No confidence, no calmness. No calmness and you'll begin to gasp for air like crazy. In order to have confidence in your technique, you need to have proper training in the fundamentals so they become automatic reflexes. Only then can you be relaxed in a match.

What are the most important qualities of a successful competitor?

First and foremost, you have to be brave enough to expose yourself to the world. It is easy to talk about what you could do, but quite another thing to put it all on the line and step into that mat in front of everyone. You have to have a little bit of fearlessness and a lot of heart to make it through the tough moments. You have to be able to take your falls like a warrior and your wins like a champion. You have to have a well-rounded arsenal. You have to be courageous and intelligent with a sort of calmness of mind during hectic situations.

It's important to train hard, be healthy and do the right things. Mentally, it's important for your soul to choose between the spirit and the flesh. The flesh is immediate gratification such as having a good time. There's too much corruption in flesh. That is why the world is so dangerous. The spirit chooses wise things that are solid and stay forever. For some people, it's hard to stay on course, but as Karate practitioners we need to make sure we behave properly regardless if we win or we lose.

What are the actual qualities that make a good Coach?

I think that you have to be very patient with everyone. You have to know how to divide the competitors that you are coaching. Some guys you can't press hard, because they are just doing it for a hobby and for fun. Other guys train to be elite competitors and they are professional Karate teachers– so these guys you can push harder. But you can't treat everyone the same. I think the methodology you use to teach is very important. You have to stress the basics and always keep going back to the basics. The simple things are very hard to teach and to learn. You have to visualize every student. You also need to be able of adapting and changing to the change of rules and training methods.

"You have to be able to take your falls like a warrior and your wins like a champion."

So change is good?

People are afraid of changes but they're usually for the better. Intelligent people get used to change more quickly than others. It does upset them initially but they accept and embrace it.

Karate Masters

"People are afraid of changes but they're usually for the better. Intelligent people get used to change more quickly than others."

Do you think that the diet and nutrion plays an important part of the athlete?

Absolutely! I think that diet is very important, not just for a competition but for you entire life. You are what you eat. The way you eat is connected to your success. As a karateka you eat, you train, and then you rest. Everything is connected. If you train, train, train, and then afterwards go get unhealthy food and then sleep until 2 p.m. and then try to train again, you've never going to be at your full potential. You have to have the right diet. You have to mix the right amounts of protein, carbs, and fiber.

What is your approach when you coach elite competitors?

Over the years, I have learned that you can't change people that much from how they naturally are. You can't turn a leopard into a lion. What you have to do is to take what they do best, improve on it and find their weakest points. Then you can help them find alternatives so the weak point gets stronger. I can't tell you to fight the way I want or I would because you are not me and you are not like the rest of the competitors of the team. You have your own style so I have to take your characteristics and make you better. To do that, I don't need that much time, because I am not trying to reinvent the wheel; I am just trying to improve it. To be able to fight, you need to stay within your style of doing things. I won't try to change it; I'll just make the right adjustments. I have a lot of experience in Karate competition and people know that I talk from personal knowledge – not from something that I have just heard or read about.

"I think that repetition training is the best way to make the body understand the proper way of delivering a technique."

Finally, what do you think is your role now as a teacher in Karate?

I have to explain clearly the principles of techniques of the art in a way that people can understand. I enjoy training competitors and teaching people. It is important to develop instructors who can pass on the knowledge correctly. I see teaching and coaching as an art within an art. You have something inside you, which you know, and your goal is to get another person to know what you know and do their best. For me this is an art. O

VERN VADEN

UNCOMMON WISDOM

SENSEI VADEN BEGAN HIS SHOTOKAN STUDY IN THE EARLY 1960S UNDER SHIHAN TERUYUKI OKAZAKI IN PHILADELPHIA. SENSEI VADEN MOVED TO LOS ANGELES IN 1972 WHERE HE CONTINUED HIS TRAINING UNDER SENSEI HIDETAKA NISHIYAMA, AND FROM THAT YEAR THROUGH 1985, COMPETED EACH YEAR ON THE US NATIONAL TEAM IN NUMEROUS INTERNATIONAL CHAMPIONSHIPS. IN 1980, SENSEI VADEN OPENED HIS OWN KARATE ACADEMY. OVER HIS MANY YEARS OF TRAINING AND STUDY, SENSEI VADEN HAS TRAINED WITH MANY OF THE GREATEST SHOTOKAN MASTERS, SUCH AS ENOEDA, KISAKA, YAGUCHI, OISHI, SHIRAI, AND YAMAGUCHI. HE CURRENTLY RESIDES IN CALIFORNIA WHERE STILL SHARE HIS EXPERIENCE AND KNOWLEDGE WITH HIS STUDENTS.

How did you actually got to train under Sensei Nishiyama?

It was Sensei Teruyuki Okazaki, my first teacher, who recommend me in 1972 that I should contact Sensei Hidetaka Nishiyama to start training with him. Obviously, at that time, Sensei Nishiyama and Sensei Okazaki were very close and they actually had set up a lot of the JKA format in Japan. I can't think of any better teachers in the art of Shotokan. Sensei Nishiyama 'was' Karate. He was extremely methodical on how to train and how to do things. The basics were emphasized in every single training session. He used to say that I Karate 'everything always reverts to the basics'. And this is very important because without good basic technique, you kata can't be good and your kumite will suffer. I felt that his teaching ability and Karate quality was one of the best in the world so it didn't take me much to be at the Dojo at all times and follow Sensei Nishiyama for the rest of his life.

What are the points that you remember the most at Sensei Nishiyama's classes?

Sensei Nishiyama always emphasized the right application of body forces. This was because of the Karate idea of 'killing with one blow'. He taught us the importance of the proper body mechanics in every movement performed and how these apply to an efficient karate technique. The main prin-

Karate Masters

"Sensei Nishiyama always emphasized the right application of body forces. This was because of the Karate idea of 'killing with one blow'."

ciples were; timing, distance and finally technique...although you have to learn them in the reverse order. His fighting philosophy was that you don't have to win...but always to make sure you don't lose. This is a very important lesson in Budo. You don't have to fight to win...but fight to not lose.

Did he emphasize the aspect of self-defense?

Self-defense was something that was always present in all Sensei Nishiyama classes. Self-defense training is not about doing techniques for fighting but also how to develop a sense of 'safety' in your attitude and way of behaving. This is a very deep principle that people tend to miss these days. Self-defense is not about punching and kicking but about avoiding those circumstances that will lead to a physical altercation and when the situation arises, then to dissolve it with words and right attitude not with physical violence. This is what Sensei used to teach us when he linked Karate to self-defense.

Did he teach weapons in his classes?

Hidetaka Nishiyama never taught weapons as an art but in his teaching weapons were always present. He taught us how to defend against weapons but no how to attack with weapons in a Kobudo-style kind of way. His teachings were focused on empty hand style of Martial Arts and the study of weapons was always from a self-defense perspective. He never taught Kobudo or similar arts to us.

How did he approach the training of kata?

We had to complete learn and master 25 Shotokan kata under Sensei Nishiyama to be considered an advanced student. He was not into the accumulation of forms but into understand the kata principle behind the form. For him a kata was never a set of movements put together but a principle to be used in actual combat.

How do you remember him?

I remember the most what I always admired in him, his deep understanding of karate and the human body. And above all, his dedication to the art. I believe these qualities made him the legend he was.

What is the most important aspect of traditional training?

Traditional training is based on a constant repetition and work of the basic techniques, and there is a strong reason for that. This was the approach with all JKA instructors like Nishiyama and Okazaki Senseis. One of the things that I really enjoy of the Shotokan style is the 'directness' and "simplicity" of the technical aspects of the style. In the old JKA approach you tried to perfect the basics. These basic techniques have a sounds physiological base and what you try to do is to have the body to perform them at its very best. If you count the amount of basic "combative" defensive and attacking techniques including both hand and feet you will see that there are not that many. Put all the types of punches, elbows, knee, and kicking plus the blocking and parrying techniques and the amount is very small because the style was never designed to 'accumulate' more and more.

How important is the application of the kata movements?

All Shotokan kata have their respective 'bunkai' and applications for all the movements but I personally think that the way JKA Shotokan was designed by Sensei Nakayama, made of kata not a 'self-defense' tool per se, but a great training method for the art of Karate. Just think for a second that when the great legendary fighters at the JKA Headquarters were getting ready for a world championship they did a great amount of kata training! Why? When you spar or do kumite there are important points in the correct execution of your techniques; verticality, footwork, hip power, "zanchin", etc. All this elements are found in every kata. You can't simply do kata without these elements that are so important in kumite. Both kata and kumite are tied together.

What is your opinion of the competition aspect of Karate?

Competition and sport karate s not a bad thing. It teaches a lot of things if you approach it with the right frame of mind. On the contrary, if you think od karate only as a sport where to win trophies and medals, then you will miss the big picture of what the art can give you. Karate is about balance and you have to have a balanced approach to the sport and the art itself. Sport Karate allows you to develop your training and maintain a safe environment, but it is necessary to have the correct attitude in competition.

Do you consider Shotokan to be the best style?

I don't consider JKA karate to be the 'best' style or type of karate. That would be non-sense. Nakayama Sensei took the fundamentals and developed a very physical and strong style of karate. We can say that JKA Karate has 'its on way' of doing things. Other styles like Goju and Shito have a much stronger Okinawan influence and you can see that in the kata, kihon and ways of training. They are different than Shotokan as we know it. I think it is important to understand where these styles come from and how actually can be practiced by different individuals. For instance, if a 50 or 60 years old tries to do 'hardcore' JKA Shotokan, he is going to find out that it is simply not possible. That is the reason, I think, why some old JKA legendary instructors like Taiji Kase, T. Asai, etc…modified the base style and developed a 'softer' approach as they got older; their Karate was shaper but not rigid anymore, very flexible, and their actions like a whip. It makes sense to me. Don't forget that even Gichin Funakoshi was not doing JKA Shotokan as we know it…JKA Shotokan – as we know it know – it was developed after but his son Yoshitaka and Sensei Nakayama.

Nakayama Sensei was the first to do scientific research on Karate. His discoveries and knowledge allowed him to develop our Shotokan Karate into what it is today.

How important is the communication via words from a teacher to the students?

It is interesting because the greatest Karate instructors didn't really used a lot of words or tried to explain everything with words. Karate is a scientific art but it is learn through the body and not through words, otherwise anyone with a good memory would be a great karateka. The old masters knew that and they always based their instruction in the power on the student's body to learn the technique. I agree with explain things in detail but it is true that the intellect is the main obstacle for the body understand and learn Karate if we don't keep it under control. Western world students want to 'know' all the physical details and how the Newton's laws work in every movement but that won't develop their techniques. Some times is simply better 'shut up and do it'.

What is your opinion of "Ikken Hissatsu"?

This format allows the competitor to develop the old idea of "One punch, one kill" that in the spine of the art of Karate. You have to be able of scoring a perfect technique which represents finishing your opponent. This forces the competitor to have the right frame of mind and pushes him to develop a very correct technique or the point won't be scored.

What is the final goal of Karate training?

I think that karate today has lost the traditional idea of training with a strong spiritual awareness and a real appreciation of the values of Budo and life itself. Sensei Funakoshi always stressed the 'perfection of character' and I think this still should be our main goal in training.

Would you recommend training in different styles?

All Martial Arts in general are based in similar principles although the physical application of these principles may be different. It is important to look to other arts and try to see those principles that we use in karate because then we may have a chance to 'see' other ways of using the same concepts that we have in Karate or a different way of applying them.

How important is the relaxation of the body in Karate training?

Very important. In Karate seems natural to tense the body when we do the techniques but it is interesting to note that actually regardless of our age we should strive in relaxing the body. I don't think most of karatekas appreciate how important is the principle of relaxation not only for Karate but for life in general.

What would be your final advise for all Karate practitioners?

It is important to have a feeling of openness and understanding of one another not only in the Dojo but also outside in our daily life. Keep your focus on daily training and remember that Karate-Do is for your development as a human being. I still remember Sensei Okazaki telling us that our primary focus should be in being the best teacher possible for our students and to share truthfully with our disciples what we have learned. And that it is still true to me. And keep training not matter what age. Sensei Funakoshi used to say that Karate is like water...that water with a flame beneath it remains hot. Once the flame is extinguished the water cools...and your Karate is gone. O

ROBERT WEINBERG

INTEGRATING INTUITION

Sensei Weinberg is a direct student of the legendary Okinawan Karate master Eizo Shimabukuro. For many years, Richard Weinberg kept himself away from the limelight of magazines and interviews. His approach to training and teaching is based on quality more than quantity; "Real success in Martial Arts is based on the ability to perform a few things very, very well, rather than knowing a large range of items only a little," he says. An expert in the weaponry art, Sensei Weinberg recognizes the positive traditional side of training with weapons; "Kobudo allows the student to be in touch with another area of tradition, and provides a different kind of exercise and useful variety."

Can you give us a little background on your Karate-do training and experience? How long have you practiced? How did you get into the Shorin Ryu system of Karate-do?

I am a senior student of Grandmaster Eizo Shimabukuro of Okinawa, but leading up to my training with Shimabukuro Sensei I was extremely fortunate to meet many wonderful teachers.

I started my Martial Arts training at the Judo program of the American Buddhist Academy in New York City in October 1959. My first teacher was Rev. R. Nishi, followed by Sensei S. Kobayashi, N Higashi, and Y. Matsumora in New York. I also had contact with Rev. S. Kan, a true master Kendo instructor who was an inspiration, and others. In particular, I had a fortunate opportunity to study with Sogen Sakiyama Roshi in Rinzai Zen in 1972 while he was at the Satsuma Bushi Karate dojo in New York. I had some time before my first trip to Okinawa and Osho-san was generous to provide insights into Zen, karate and life. He is a truly remarkable individual.

I became involved with Shorin-ryu while I was at Wesleyan University from 1968–1972, beginning with Sensei Robert J. Inferrera, an intense and charismatic teacher who inspired me to travel to Okinawa and study full-

Karate Masters

"Karate provides a platform for improving one's spiritual self."

time after I graduated in from college 1972. Sensei Inferrera produced a large number of teachers and has had a major effect on karate, especially Shorin-ryu, in the United States. I am especially indebted to him.

I understand you studied in Okinawa; would you tell us about what you learned and from whom?

I travelled to Okinawa in the autumn of 1972 to become the student of Eizo Shimabukuro, the teacher of my U.S. instructor Robert J. Inferrera. I really did not know much about Osensei at that time, so I approached the trip with more than a little trepidation. Osensei and his family greeted me as if they had known me for years and quickly put me at ease. Back then, a karate master was considered almost a god, so the opportunity to travel there was a very religious experience.

I concentrated my time in Okinawa (about a year in 1972–73) with Shimabukuro Sensei, who provided all the knowledge I needed and could absorb, but I had the opportunity to see several other schools. I visited with my friend Zenko Heshiki from New York while he was with Nagamine Sensei in Naha, and with Sakiyama-Roshi.

Shimbukuro Sensei had (and still maintains) the following syllabus: kata from Tomari-te, via Chotoku Kyan; kata from Shuri-te, via Chosin Chibana; and from the Naha-te/Goju-ryu tradition via Chojun Miyagi. In addition, Shimabukuro Sensei taught four kobujutsu forms, influenced by Kyan and by the famous weapons master Shinken Taira. Sensei now also teaches his own wonderful kama form.

Osensei also taught a series of kumite techniques, including one step yakusoku kumite for Upper, Middle and Lower level defenses, "Breaking Kumite" (or Goshinjitsu), and escapes from holds. He expanded these latter two, which became his "Toei-ryu Torite Jujitsu," as he teaches them now.

Sensei also taught (and teaches) kumite for the traditional weapons, sai vs.

bo, kama vs. bo, tonfa vs. bo or sai, and so on. Kumite was about every third or fourth class, so the focus was clearly on form.

The most important lessons, however, were in Sensei's manner and purpose. He placed huge emphasis on the correct learning and practice of the forms (and this emphasis has not wavered in the nearly 40 years I have known him personally). The biggest part of classes were composed of detailed instructions on form, carefully breaking out the components including pattern, correction of techniques, breathing, timing or breakpoints (including the bunkai or combat application), focus or muscle control, use of the eyes, and kiai. There were lots of hands-on corrections and demonstrations of each of these components.

One of the most important aspects of his teaching struck me on the very first day of study with him in 1972. I was introduced to the class, and then Sensei provided a green belt to instruct me and check and correct my form. I was happy to be there and was thrilled to be receiving attention from anyone, so that was not an issue for me. However, I noticed the Grandmaster himself was working first with the beginner white belts.

Sensei offers us an opportunity to go back to the roots of karate and extract the real values, as we discussed earlier. When we understand our roots, we understand ourselves better. This is a benefit regardless of the type or style of martial art practiced.

Who is Eizo Shimabuku?

Eizo Shimabukuro is one of the few surviving direct students of the Meijin (Fist-saint) Chotoku Kyan. Osensei was with Chotoku Kyan for 1939–1942 as a young man. Shimabukuro Sensei has dedicated the rest of his life, more than 70 years, to practicing, teaching and preserving the forms and values he learned from Chotoku Kyan. Osensei has the forms Seisan, Nahanchin, Annanku, Wanshu, Gojushiho, and Chinto from Chotoku Kyan. He also studied after the war with the other most famous teachers of his time, including Miyagi Chojun, the founder of Goju-ryu, and with Choki Motobu while he was in Japan. Sensei keeps the forms Seiunchin and Sanchin from the Miyagi curriculum. Finally, he went to Chosin Chibana to obtain the proper form for the Shuri-te kata, including Passai Sho, Passai Dai, Kusanku Sho, Kusanku Dai and the five Pinan forms.

Sensei was the youngest of ten children. His father, a very tall man over six feet, was a bo master, and his eldest brother was Tatsuo Shimabukuro, also a student of Chotoku Kyan and the founder of Isshin-ryu. Sensei was the only other sibling to be involved in Martial Arts. Shimabukuro Sensei moved to Japan in 1941 and was drafted into the Japanese Navy. At the end of the war, he was assigned as a kamikaze boat pilot, but fortunately was called back at the last moment.

Sensei possesses extraordinary abilities of physical prowess, especially when I first knew him in the 1970s – amazingly strong and fast enough that you could not track his motion. As his students, we were all fortunate that he is also a man of tremendous patience and kindness.

But your question is "Who is this man?" Shimabukuro Sensei is his teaching. He has 100 percent belief in what he teaches and the principles involved. Further, he seems to have a belief in his students as well. After a while, each student feels a closeness with this great man that is simply unexpected. It is as if every student becomes a part of his family. Sensei wants to help each of his students succeed in karate and in life – whether that be military or civilian, Okinawan or American, man or woman.

Your Shorin Ryu incorporates unique theories and techniques. Can you talk about how it is applied, what worked and didn't work for you, how you choose when to use this system, etc.?

In a real sense, we use the system everyday in our daily lives, with the intensity we approach our obligations, with the decisions we make about events in our daily lives, how we go about our business or school work, with our relationships with our business associates, teachers, families, friends, and others.

However, in terms of the physical application of techniques in a self-defense situation, Sensei's long-standing principle is that you should not fight and that you should take whatever steps are needed to avoid a physical confrontation. However, if you do you fight, you must win. But "winning" should not mean unnecessary injury or pain to your opponent, as this will invariably reflect poorly on yourself and on your school. I have always been partial to the grappling and control aspects, from Shimabukuro Sensei's techniques as well as from my early experience in Judo and Jujitsu. I have used the Jujitsu techniques taught to my by Grandmaster to successfully defend against knife and empty-hand attacks in the past, so I know they work.

When you teach Karate, what are the benefits to the students?

In general, there are three main benefits. First, the benefit of self-defense, which not only helps protect the physical self but, far more importantly, protects the psyche and the ego. If someone's sense of his or her own worth and value is damaged by assault or bullying, that wound can last forever and influence a person's entire life, inhibiting him/her from many other potentials and possibilities. Of course, at the same time, if you defend yourself and so prevent that attack, then you have both prevented the pain and suffering to yourself and also prevented the would-be attacker from committing the offense, giving that person a better chance at redemption. Certainly, this is a mutual benefit.

By the way, for those people who believe that karate (or other unarmed techniques) are insufficient for "real-life" situations," I believe they probably have little real-life experience. You do not need to be a great champion in MMA to provide yourself with defense in most situations. A number of my students, men and women, have utilized our karate teaching to protect themselves in dire situations.

"Each system of martial art is a reflection of the culture in which it resides. Japanese culture is quite different from that in Okinawa."

Secondly, there is the benefit of improved health and fitness. Karate is excellent whole body exercise, which can be practiced at any age and for one's whole life. It provides an excellent introduction to fitness and to other subjects such as nutrition and alternative/complementary medicine. I have personally taught students from age 4 through 90-plus. Indeed, I believe there is particular use for karate to provide enjoyable and creative movement exercise to seniors and elders. Who says that the benefits of Martial Arts should be restricted to the young?

Finally, karate provides a platform for improving one's spiritual self. By setting personal goals, a student is able to develop a sense of self-worth and accomplishment and an attachment and admiration for the dojo and the system. I believe that what we do on a regular basis with our bodies has an effect on our mental and emotional selves, and that those changes we encourage in our bodies will have an effect on our minds and spirits as well.

Tell us a little about the principles and concepts of the Okinawan Shorin Ryu Karate-do.

Our Shorin-ryu is practiced in a natural manner, meaning that the breath

Karate Masters

"Bruce Lee's fantastic popularity changed it all, and had a huge effect not only on how the West saw karate Martial Arts."

and muscles are not forced. The breath is controlled, but relaxed. The muscles are kept relaxed except when needed to focus the body's energy. Strength comes from properly gripping the ground, pulling the heels together firmly, but not too hard, to support the stances. The stances are moderate to enable easy body motion at any time and in any direction.

Form is considered the key element. O' sensei spent hours reviewing the proper technique for each step of each kata, but there are several items that could be considered most important. These start with the wrist straight and the shoulder down when performing movements with the upper body. This allows energy to transfer effectively and unites the body with the extremities. It also prevents physical injuries, such as strained wrists and shoulders.

Next, keep the chin tucked and the neck aligned properly with the shoulders. This reduces the effective target for the enemy, sets the upper body in a good position to use its strengths, and corrects the body's posture to allow the internal organs to be in alignment. It also allows the eyes to effectively see and to influence the opponent with one's own strength and vigor.

The body is kept relaxed (not limp), except when it is to be used. The last foot or less of extension of techniques is the only time the muscles should be tight. It's amazing to me that so many karate-ka of many styles practice having strong focus, but that so few practice being relaxed. Stances also are kept firm, but not tight, except when actually using a punch or technique.

Why is it a "Do," as opposed to a "Jutsu"? Do they teach it as a "Do" in Okinawa?

Because it is the intention that karate practice affects and influences the whole life, it is a "Do." I cannot really comment on the methods of other schools, but Shimabukuro-Sensei definitely expects his students to bring the moral and ethical training of the dojo into the greater society.

What kata do you teach?

I teach the syllabus as presented by my teacher. There are 19 empty-handed forms. From Kyan Chotoku, we have the Tomari-te Seisan, three Nahanchin forms, Annanku, Wanshu, Gojushiho, and Chinto. Chinto was Shimabukuro Sensei's most famous and favorite forms, but in recent years, he has favored the Shuri-te Kusanku Sho.

From the Shuri-te group, we have the five Pinan forms, Passai Sho and Passai Dai, and Kusanku Sho and Kusanku Dai. Finally, we have a version of Seiunchin and Sanchin from Miyagi Sensei.

There also are five Kobudo forms. Toei no Sai, which some may know as Chatan Yara no Sai, is the creation of O'sensei. Tawada no Sai is from his contact with Shinken Taira, the great teacher and historian of Okinawa's traditional weapon methods. The Bo forms "Tokumine no Kun" and "Sakugawa no Kun" are from Kyan. The last in the series is Shimabukuro Sensei's Toei no Kama.

Why so many kata? What is the benefit of learning so many kata?

To be sure, the more traditional way was for a teacher to pick and choose from the system for the individual students. In pre-war instruction, it was unusual to learn more than a few forms. "One form - three years" was the general mode. Since the war, however, it is more common to learn many forms. In our system, a student will learn the full range of kata, as well as kumite techniques, on the way to Shodan. Then it becomes possible to concentrate on favorite forms or techniques, based on the student's available time and passion and abilities. Learning a wide range allows the student and teacher to pick intelligently the best areas in which to specialize.

What weaponry is taught in this system?

We have five weapon forms: Tawada no Sai and Toei no Sai, Tokumine no Kun and Sakugawa no Kun, and Toei no Kama. The "Toei" forms were developed by Shimabuku Sensei. I originally learned the Toei sai as "Chatan Yara no Sai," but now as Toei no Sai, perhaps to avoid confusion with another Okinawan sai form also named "Chatan Yara no Sai."

What is the benefit of learning weaponry?
Practicing weapon forms means that you are practicing against someone with a weapon. Clearly, this raises the mental and emotional stakes in the encounter to a higher level than when one is opposed by empty-handed methods alone.

What do you think Karate-ka and Martial Artists in general can gain through the study of this method? What do you think this means for U.S. Karate practitioners?
Sensei offers us an opportunity to go back to the roots of karate and extract the real values, as we discussed earlier. When we understand our roots, we understand ourselves better. This is a benefit regardless of the type or style of martial art practiced.

Would you go so far as to make a comparison of the effectiveness of Okinawan Karate-do with Japanese Karate-do?
Each system of martial art is a reflection of the culture in which it resides. Japanese culture is quite different from that in Okinawa, and so the Japanese adaptation of Okinawa's martial art is quite different from the original. I believe that Gichin Funakoshi's great genius lay in the way he was able to modify the Okinawan original to fit the Japanese culture. The same, of course, is true for the Okinawan adaptation of Chinese Martial Arts, which developed into karate.

Sensei, how would you sum up the changes in Karate-do that you've seen over the years?
There have been several major events. In the 50s and 60s, prior to Vietnam, Bruce Lee, and the popularization of Martial Arts in general, karate was a mystery to most people. Even Judo, more established and popular more years on the scene and already in the Olympics, was largely a mystery to the American public and shrouded in myth and fantasy. Our involvement in Vietnam was the first force to change that. With so many more service people in Okinawa and around Asia being exposed to Martial Arts, and particularly karate – America tends to be a pugilistic rather that a grappling society – America began to see and accept karate. Bruce Lee's fantastic popularity changed it all, and had a huge effect not only on how the West saw karate Martial Arts, but its vision of Asia and Asian people as well.

This popularity led to the popularity of competition and tournaments abounded, and provided a platform for Martial Arts teachers to make a living from their practice. Personally, I find karate tournaments clash directly with the root nature of karate as introduced from Okinawa. "Karate ni sente nashi," Funakoshi's great maxim, "There is no aggressive attack in karate." However, tournaments are nearly all aggressive attacking – that's how you get points and win. By falling into this trap, karate becomes boxing. Mind you, boxing is an excellent method of fighting, sport, and self-defense, but it comes from a different tradition than karate. Now karate has led to a new approach, commonly named Mixed Martial Arts

"My karate practice has become a means to measure and improve myself as a human being."

It is for the few traditionalists, like us, to maintain the old ways. Recently we have seen more movement in this direction, with several excellent books published that discuss the history and ethics of karate, and a volume of source materials translated and available for the first time. I hope this is a trend that will continue into the future, to assure that the real karate of Okinawa stays with us.

How long have you been practicing Karate and how many styles of Martial Arts have you trained in?

I began my Martial Arts training in 1959 studying Judo at the American Buddhist Academy in New York City, with Rev. R. Nishi, and later with Sensei Kobayashi, Higashi and Matsumura. I also have studied small amounts of Japanese Karate, Kendo, and Jujitsu, and I had a chance to wrestle in college. In particular, I had the opportunity to meet and know Rev. Shunshin T. Kan, the great Kendo Sensei in New York City, who was an inspiration to me and many others. I also was privileged to study Zen with Sogen Sakiyama, the famous Zen Monk and Goju-ryu Karate Master and student of Chojun Miyagi, who lived in New York for a period of time.

Karate Masters

"Forms ("kata") are the centerpiece of training and learning in traditional karate."

Although I sat with Sogen-Roshi only for a few months, the time I shared was life changing.

Of course, the Shorin-ryu Karate as taught to me by Grandmaster Eizo Shimabukuro has been my focus and passion for 40 years.

I believe that, as teachers, we are a conduit, bringing the past, our teachers, into the present, our students. I have been exceptionally fortunate to have wonderful teachers throughout my Martial Arts career, culminating with Shimabukuro.

What was your first impression of the art of Shorin Ryu and how did you get involved in training?

I became involved with Shorin-ryu karate while at Wesleyan University in Middletown, Connecticut. One of my friends was a student at the Middletown Karate Dojo and recommended that I try the classes there. As I had a lull in my Judo practice, I gave it a shot. The teacher there was Robert J. Inferrera, a dynamic and charismatic instructor, who had studied with Grandmaster Eizo Shimabukuro while stationed on Okinawa in the Marine Corps. I found Sensei Inferrera deeply involved in the classical approach to karate through the practice of form, as much or more so than his exceptional skill in kumite. He impressed with his direct approach to instruction, and by the quality of his senior students and his emphasis on form and basics. I also enjoyed the fact that I could do so much in solitary practice of forms. It was not long before I was hooked.

After finishing college in 1972, I traveled to Okinawa, with the encouragement of Sensei Inferrera, to meet and study with Grandmaster Eizo Shimabukuro. There was little information available about Okinawa at that time, except from a few Marine Corps "graduates" of the is and. Needless to say, I was more than a little apprehensive about meeting the Grandmaster. However, I found Osensei and his family both welcoming and kind, and immediately felt at home with him. I stayed about a year as a full-time karate trainee, usually with three classes of two or more hours each day, seven days per week. On Sundays, we usually had only two classes.

Grandmaster Shimabukuro is a wonderful and amazing teacher who changed the lives of his students in deep ways. In addition to his extraordinary technique and skill (in nearly 40 years, I have never known him to perform a kata poorly), dynamic strength and force of will, he is empathetic with people of a wide and diverse nature. He is truly a remarkable person.

The Grandmaster was extraordinarily generous and open with his teaching. One of the signal moments for me was when, on my first night in the dojo in Kin Village, he assigned a green belt (I do not recall his name) to correct my form. I believe this was a test of my attitude, to see if I would take offense, but I was just thrilled to be there at all. I noticed that Grandmaster himself was teaching, with focus and enthusiasm, the white belt beginners in his dojo. I did not expect that, and I have endeavored to emulate his concern that students get the best possible start to their training.

Over the years, I have come to realize how deeply the Grandmaster believes in this martial art and how devoted he is to preserving the tenets of his teacher, the Meijin Chotoku Kyan.

How does your daily life revolve around the Martial Arts?
My karate practice has become a means to measure and improve myself as a human being. Indeed, Grandmaster Shimabukuro has taught us that one of the purposes of karate training is to enable us to develop a strategy for the important things in life, such as family, work, ethics, and more. My karate training has given me a means to survive the hard parts of life and to evaluate my growth, not only in the dojo, but in every other aspect of myself as well.

In Karate, there are forms (kata) that comprise self-defense techniques. What do these really represent and how important are they?
Forms ("kata") are the centerpiece of training and learning in traditional karate Martial Arts. Forms comprise much more that self-defense techniques, of course. As Grandmaster Shimabukuro has taught me, there are

seven component to form: the pattern (i.e., the techniques and steps): the proper and detailed correction of those techniques; proper breathing; muscle control or focus (i.e., when and how to be tight and when to relax); the combinations or timing (the Japanese might call it the break-points) of the form, which includes the bunkai or combative applications; the use of the eyes; and finally the ki-ai or shout.

By learning and then practicing the forms in a coordinated manner with these seven components, we learn not just the root techniques but a structure by which to apply them; coordination to make them effective; speed, balance and the ability to surprise both our opponent and, sometimes, ourselves.

Even more, however, through the forms we practice an attitude. Grandmaster Shimabukuro and the whole tradition of Okinawan karate practice say that karate form begins and ends with respect (rei), and that karate begins and ends with defense. Our Dojo Kun, or precepts, also state "Through karate practice we learn to prevail without fighting..." By practicing the forms of karate wholeheartedly, we accustom ourselves, under the guidance of our teachers, to internalize this crucial message. Forms begin with a symbolic gesture showing that we would rather not fight but to find a better way to resolve our issues, such as the left hand covering the right hand in Seisan. However, we always maintain the strength of technique and purpose that allows us to defend ourselves in the first place.

Further, I believe, practicing combat through the form is a kind of serious make-believe, similar in many ways to the actions of police recruits when they learn to use firearms, or to EMTs when then learn CPR by using a dummy, or the use of a flight simulator by trainee pilots. The "serious make-believe" of the forms in Karate, teaches the means and also the attitude needed for defense. Just as your body becomes stronger through the physical exercise, your mind and spirit can grow if you stretch them during the form.

Further, I believe that kata provides a means for a student to channel aggressive feelings in a way that not only eliminates harm to others, but also chastens the practitioner from using violence to start with. By acting out a fight repeatedly we curb the need to act out physically. This, perhaps, provides the close connection that these Martial Arts seem to have with Buddhism and other religious and ethical beliefs.

What are the most important points in your teaching methods?

My teaching centers around the correct practice of Karate kata. We emphasize learning the seven components of the form, and coordinating

"My teaching centers around the correct practice of karate kata."

them as a single unit. From the very beginning, I try to encourage students to pay careful attention to key points of techniques, such as keeping the wrists straight and the shoulders down, while at the same time reminding them that this "serious make believe" is not a dance or a gymnastic exercise, but rather representative of a combat situation in which they are at jeopardy.

Do you think there still are "pure" styles of Shorin Ryu Karate?

In my view, karate history is more like a sandstorm than a bullet. It is convoluted and sometimes confused, and difficult or impossible to draw a direct path from the 17th century to the present time, although the major waypoints of such masters as Kusanku, Sakugawa, Sokon "Bushi" Matsumora, Kosaku "Tomari" Matsumura, Ankoh Itosu, Chotoku Kyan, and others certainly mark the path. Many of the most important figures studied with several other great practitioners over the course of their lifetimes, so it is difficult to determine who exactly learned what from where. It is therefore difficult at best to determine what "pure" might mean in terms of this martial art.

Karate Masters

My teacher studied with Chotoku Kyan, whom he still refers to as "Sensei," early in his life, as well as with such iconic martial artists as Chojun Miyagi, Choki Motobu, Chosin Chibana, Zenryo Shimabuku, and the famous Kobudo expert Shinken Taira. Karate is an oral tradition (very little was ever written down in pre-war Okinawa) and much was lost during World War II.

Having said all that, and having had the opportunity to visit with or observe many of famous karate sensei of Okinawa since 1972, I am satisfied that the Shorin-ryu as taught by my teacher is the best choice for me. It is the karate of Chotoku Kyan coupled with that of Ankoh Itosu (via Chosin Chibana), and nuanced by my teachers contact with other famous masters and his own life experience. It works for me.

What is your personal opinion of modern fighting events such as the UFC and Mixed Martial Arts fights?

MMA and UFC have certainly broadened the competitive field, and these "fights" have come a long way since their beginning. This remarkable sport brings together many aspects of combat and is both fascinating and instructive to see what techniques and approaches these incredible athletes use. We can certainly learn from their experience. However, the essential techniques and methods used in MMA are present in our karate. Striking and grappling/holding are integral to our method as well.

Karate nowadays is referred to as a sport... would you agree with this definition, or is a martial art?

Karate is a martial art that influences all aspects of the life of its practitioners. In my opinion, Karate works poorly as a sport, because the basic philosophical foundations, often expressed in the expression "Karate ni sente nashi," which I translate as "Karate has no aggressive attack." This is in direct opposition to the method of competition, in which aggressive attack is the way to gain points and win. This is in no way to criticize the sportsmen and women who participate in karate competitions throughout the world. There are thousands upon thousands of talented athletes of all ages and genders who have dedicated themselves to competition, improved themselves, found personal growth and done well. However, I question, not their skill or ability or enthusiasm, but whether what they do should be called "Karate." I feel it is more aligned to boxing, also a great practice and art, but an activity that is more in line with aggressive competition.

Consider this. Okinawa, the birthplace of what we now call Karate, was for hundreds of years a small but independent country that survived a political tug of war between two giant powers, China and Japan. Okinawa could only survive do this through a philosophy of conciliation and courtesy, and could never have succeeded so long through military means. I believe the philosophy of their Martial Arts reflects that history closely, and is demonstrated in the actions of the forms we practice and expressed in the many stories about karate masters who would rather lose that take on an unnecessary fight which might injure of kill people with karate techniques.

How do you see mental and spiritual training applied to Martial Arts in general and to Karate specifically?

In our approach to Karate, we believe spiritual growth comes from consistent practice. After all, my teacher's dojo name, and mine as well, is "Ren Do Kan," indicating that the way ("Do") is attained through practice ("Ren"). By setting goals in practice, with the help and challenge of an effective teacher, a student earns and accepts greater respect and learns to offer respect to others. By challenging oneself through effective forms practice, one learns to deal with the concepts of winning and losing, life and death, increasing the spiritual awareness of these issues.

One of my students actually told me, shortly before he died from an insidious cancer, that Karate had not only helped him to grow and love his life, but also to die.

Do you feel that you still have further to go in your studies?

I have practiced Martial Arts more than 50 years altogether. I think I have a good start.

What do you think the future will bring to the art of Karate?

Although Karate has become more involved in the sport aspect, I believe that we are witnessing a trend back toward the classical approach. Many valuable and well-researched books have come out speaking about the use and application of form as a means of learning. In addition, as my generation of "baby-boomers" ages, many are putting down their competitive gear and picking up the serious, but non-competitive aspects. I think this is a wonderful trend that will help to assure that karate art continue.

Do you think the Olympic recognition helped Karate or not?

I believe an Olympic presence will make Karate more popular, which is good for everyone involved, but will also put more emphasis on the sport aspect.

Karate Masters

"Karate is a martial art that influences all aspects of the life of its practitioners."

What are the most important qualities for a student to become proficient in karate?

Humility, patience, and determination. First, it is hard to learn when your head is filled with preconceived ideas of what it is you are trying to accomplish. A student needs to be open to the ideas of the teacher. When I first went to Okinawa, I had ideas about what a Karate dojo should be like, but my experience with Grandmaster Shimabukuro there quickly opened my mind. Progress in karate comes slowly, and real success takes staying power. It is said that one should learn slowly, like an ox, walking 1,000 miles. Of course, if you become frustrated by injury, changes to your life, or other distractions, you are sure to fail. Real progress takes determination, and the moral value of that determination increases with our progress.

Kihon, Kata and Kumite, what is the proper ratio in training?

When I teach, I usually devote about half of class time to exercise, basics, and various kinds of partner drills, which increase the social contact between students. Of the remaining time, I spend about three of every four hours practicing form, the rest on kumite. I need to add that I rarely teach free sparring (jiyu kumite), as I believe this decreases the effect of studying form and technique dramatically.

When teaching the art of karate, what is the most important element – self-defense or sport?

I see karate as an art centered around self-defense. For me, I really do not see karate as a sport, although it is practiced that way, successfully and enjoyably, by millions.

The famous Karate Master Ankoh Itosu asks us, in his ten precepts, to decide if our martial art is for our health or to assist us in our duty. Perhaps this is the more important question. Are we doing it to benefit ourselves and

"In our approach to Karate, we believe spiritual growth comes from consistent practice."

lead a longer, safer and healthier life, or to allow us to make needed sacrifices for our family, and our country?

Any advice for the readers and karate practitioners?

Take the time to find a worthy teacher who actually knows something worth learning, and then commit the time and effort to learn that system. Success in Karate does not happen overnight. In the words of my great teacher, Eizo Shimabukuro, "Karate is a journey of practice ..." Learn to enjoy the journey and your karate practice will bring a lifetime of fulfillment for you, your family and your nation. O

Karate's Finest Masters Teach

KARATE MASTERS Vol.1 (Revised Edition)
By Jose M. Fraguas

Through conversations with many historical figures such as Osamu Ozawa, Teruo Hayashi, Kenzo Mabuni, Masatoshi Nakayama, and numerous current world-class masters such as Hirokazu Kanazawa, Fumio Demura, Takayuki Mikami, Teruyuki Okazaki, Morio Higaonna, Hidetaka Nishiyama, James Yabe, Tak Kubota, Bill Dometrich, Dan Ivan, and Stan Schmidt, the many threads of karate learning, lore, and legend are woven together to present an integrated and complete view of the empty-handed art of fighting, philosophy, and self-defense. Containing information that has not appeared anywhere else, the interviews contain intriguing thoughts, fascinating personal details, hidden history, and revealing philosophies.

#110 – 7 x 10 – 350 pages
ISBN: 978-1-933901-22-0

KARATE MASTERS Vol. 2
By Jose M. Fraguas

The second volume of the series offers a new repertoire of historical figures, such as Mas Oyama, Kyoshi Yamazaki. Masahiko Tanaka, Eihachi Ota, Yukiyoshi Marutani, Randall Hassell, Keinosuke Enoeda, Richard Kim, Shinpo Matayoshi, Tsutomu Ohshima, Yoshiaki Ajari, Goshi Yamaguchi, and other world-recognized professional martial artists. In this volume, new interviews with the world's top karate masters have been gathered to present an integrated and complete view of the empty-handed art of fighting, philosophy, and self-defense.

111 – 7 x 10 – 350 pages
ISBN: 978-1-933901-20-9

TO ORDER VISIT: www.empirebooks.com

Budo Greatest Lessons

KARATE MASTERS Vol.3
By Jose M. Fraguas

Including twenty-three exclusive interviews with legendary masters, such as Gogen "The Cat" Yamaguchi, Teruo Chinen, Edmond Otis, Akio Minakami, Jiro Ohtsuka, Shojiro Koyama, Ryusho Sakagami, Katsutaka Tanaka, Anthony Mirakian, Tetsuhiko Asai, Mikio Yahara, and other karate giants, this volume contains intriguing thoughts, fascinating personal details, hidden histories, and inspiring philosophies, as each master reveals his true love for the art and a deep understanding of every facet associated with the practice and spirit of the Japanese art of Karate-do as a way of life. This invaluable reference book is a "must have" addition to your personal library.
112 – 7 x 10 – 350 pages
ISBN: 978-1-933901-04-6

KARATE MASTERS Vol.4
By Jose M. Fraguas

After the acclaimed success of the first three volumes of Karate Masters, the author proudly presents "Karate Masters 4", with a new repertoire of historical figures, such as Yutaka Yaguchi, Hiroyasu Fujishima, Takeshi Uchiage, Kenneth Funakoshi, Kunio Murayama, Shoji Nishimura, Hiroshi Okazaki, Gene Tibon, Les Safar, Koss Yokota, Richard Amos, Taku Nakasaka, and other world-recognized Karate masters like George E. Mattson, Joe Carbonara, Tony Annesi, etc... In this fourth volume, new interviews with the world's top Karate masters have been gathered to present an integrated and complete view of the empty-handed art of fighting, philosophy, and self-defense. Containing information that has not appeared anywhere else, the interviews contain intriguing thoughts, fascinating personal details, hidden history, and revealing philosophies as each master reveals his true love for the art and a deep understanding of every facet associated with the practice and spirit of the Japanese art of Karate-do as a way of life. It's a detailed reference work, and a "must have" addition to your personal library.
#133 – 7 x 10 – 370 pages
ISBN: 978-1-933901-49-7

TO ORDER VISIT: www.empirebooks.com

Karate Masters

www.ingramcontent.com/pod-product-compliance
Lightning Source LLC
Chambersburg PA
CBHW081344080526
44588CB00016B/2372